Summary of Contents

HTML5 & CSS3 FOR THE REAL WORLD

BY **ALEXIS GOLDSTEIN**
LOUIS LAZARIS
ESTELLE WEYL

HTML5 & CSS3 for the Real World

by Alexis Goldstein, Louis Lazaris, and Estelle Weyl

Copyright © 2015 SitePoint Pty. Ltd.

Product Manager: Simon Mackie   **English Editor**: Kelly Steele

Technical Editor: Aurelio De Rosa   **Cover Designer**: Alex Walker

Printing History:

    First Edition: May 2011

    Second Edition: March 2015

Published by SitePoint Pty. Ltd.

48 Cambridge Street Collingwood
VIC Australia 3066
Web: www.sitepoint.com
Email: business@sitepoint.com

ISBN 978-0-9874674-8-5 (print)

ISBN 978-0-9874674-9-2 (ebook)
Printed and bound in the United States of America

About Alexis Goldstein

Alexis Goldstein first taught herself HTML while a high school student in the mid-1990s, and went on to get her degree in Computer Science from Columbia University. She runs her own software development and training company, aut faciam LLC. Before striking out on her own, Alexis spent seven years in technology on Wall Street, where she worked in both the cash equity and equity derivative spaces at three major firms, and learned to love daily code reviews. She taught dozens of classes to hundreds of students as a teacher and co-organizer of Girl Develop It, a group that conducts low-cost programming classes for women. You can find Alexis at her website, http://alexisgo.com/.

About Louis Lazaris

Louis Lazaris is a freelance web designer and front-end developer based in Toronto, Canada who has been involved in the web design industry since 2000, when table layouts and one-pixel GIFs dominated the industry. In recent years he has transitioned to embrace web standards while endeavoring to promote best practices that help both developers and their clients reach practical goals for their projects. Louis is Managing Editor for SitePoint's HTML/CSS content, blogs about front-end code on his website Impressive Webs (http://www.impressivewebs.com/), and curates Web Tools Weekly (http://webtoolsweekly.com/), a weekly newsletter focused on tools for front-end developers.

About Estelle Weyl

Estelle Weyl is a front-end engineer from San Francisco who has been developing standards-based accessible websites since 1999. Estelle began playing with CSS3 when the iPhone was released in 2007, and after four years of web application development for mobile WebKit, she knows (almost) every CSS3 quirk on WebKit, and has vast experience implementing components of HTML5. She writes two popular technical blogs with tutorials and detailed grids of CSS3 and HTML5 browser support (http://www.standardista.com/). Estelle's passion is teaching web development, where you'll find her speaking on CSS3, HTML5, JavaScript, and mobile web development at conferences around the USA (and, she hopes, the world).

About the Technical Editor

Aurelio De Rosa is a (full-stack) web and app developer with more than 5 years' experience programming for the web using HTML, CSS, Sass, JavaScript, and PHP. He's an expert on JavaScript and HTML5 APIs, but his interests include web security, accessibility, performance, and SEO. He's also a regular writer for several networks, speaker, and author of the books *jQuery in Action, third edition* and *Instant jQuery Selectors.*

About SitePoint

SitePoint specializes in publishing fun, practical, and easy-to-understand content for web professionals. Visit http://www.sitepoint.com/ to access our blogs, books, newsletters, articles, and community forums. You'll find a stack of information on JavaScript, PHP, Ruby, mobile development, design, and more.

To my mother, who always encourages and believes in me.

And to my father, who taught me so much about living up to my full potential. I miss you every day.

To Cakes, the most brilliant person I know. Thank you for everything you do for me. I'm so grateful for each and every day with you.

—Alexis

To Melanie, the best cook in the world.

And to my parents, for funding the original course that got me into this unique industry.

—Louis

To Amie, for putting up with me, and to Spazzo and Puppers, for snuggling with me as I worked away.

—Estelle

Table of Contents

Chapter 5   HTML5 Video and Audio 99

Chapter 8   CSS3 Transforms and Transitions

Chapter 9   Embedded Fonts and Multicolumn Layouts

Chapter 12   Canvas, SVG, and Drag and Drop

Preface

Welcome to *HTML5 & CSS3 for the Real World*. We're glad you've decided to join us on this journey of discovering some of the latest and the greatest in front-end website building technology.

If you've picked up a copy of this book, it's likely that you've dabbled to some degree in HTML and CSS. You might even be a bit of a seasoned pro in certain areas of markup, styling, or scripting, and now want to extend those skills further by dipping into the features and technologies associated with HTML5 and CSS3.

Learning a new task can be difficult. You may have limited time to invest in poring over the official documentation and specifications for these web-based languages. You also might be turned off by some of the overly technical books that work well as references but provide little in the way of real-world, practical examples.

To that end, our goal with this book is to help you learn through hands-on, practical instruction that will assist you to tackle the real-world problems you face in building websites today—with a specific focus on HTML5 and CSS3.

But this is more than just a step-by-step tutorial. Along the way, we'll provide plenty of theory and technical information to help fill in any gaps in your understanding—the whys and hows of these new technologies—while doing our best not to overwhelm you with the sheer volume of cool new stuff. So let's get started!

Who Should Read This Book

This book is aimed at web designers and front-end developers who want to learn about the latest generation of browser-based technologies. You should already have at least intermediate knowledge of HTML and CSS, as we won't be spending any time covering the basics of markup and styles. Instead, we'll focus on teaching you what new powers are available to you in the form of HTML5 and CSS3.

The final two chapters of this book cover some of the new JavaScript APIs that have come to be associated with HTML5. These chapters, of course, require some basic familiarity with JavaScript—but they're not critical to the rest of the book. If you're unfamiliar with JavaScript, there's no harm in skipping over them for now, returning later when you're better acquainted with it.

Conventions Used

You'll notice that we've used certain typographic and layout styles throughout the book to signify different types of information. Look out for the following items:

Code Samples

Code in this book will be displayed using a fixed-width font, like so:

```
<h1>A Perfect Summer's Day</h1>
<p>It was a lovely day for a walk in the park. The birds
were singing and the kids were all back at school.</p>
```

If the code is to be found in the book's code archive, the name of the file will appear at the top of the program listing, like this:

example.css

```
.footer {
  background-color: #CCC;
  border-top: 1px solid #333;
}
```

If only part of the file is displayed, this is indicated by the word *excerpt*:

example.css (excerpt)

```
  border-top: 1px solid #333;
```

If additional code is to be inserted into an existing example, the new code will be displayed in bold:

```
function animate() {
  new_variable = "Hello";
}
```

Where existing code is required for context, rather than repeat all the code, a vertical ellipsis will be displayed:

```
function animate() {
  ⋮
  return new_variable;
}
```

Some lines of code are intended to be entered on one line, but we've had to wrap them because of page constraints. A ➥ indicates a line break that exists for formatting purposes only, and should be ignored:

```
URL.open("http://www.sitepoint.com/blogs/2015/05/28/user-style-she
➥ets-come-of-age/");
```

Tips, Notes, and Warnings

Hey, You!

Tips will give you helpful little pointers.

Ahem, Excuse Me ...

Notes are useful asides that are related—but not critical—to the topic at hand. Think of them as extra tidbits of information.

Make Sure You Always ...

... pay attention to these important points.

Watch Out!

Warnings will highlight any gotchas that are likely to trip you up along the way.

Supplementary Materials

http://www.learnable.com/books/htmlcss2/

The book's website, which contains links, updates, resources, and more.

https://github.com/spbooks/htmlcss2/

The downloadable code archive for this book.

http://community.sitepoint.com/

SitePoint's forums, for help on any tricky web problems.

books@sitepoint.com

Our email address, should you need to contact us for support, to report a problem, or for any other reason.

Acknowledgments

We'd like to offer special thanks to the following members of the SitePoint and Learnable community who made valuable contributions to this edition of the book:

Martin Ansdell-Smith, Ilya Bodrov, Jacob Christiansen, Ethan Glass, Gerard Konars, Dityo Nurasto, Thom Parkin, Guilherme Pereira, Jason Rogers, Bernard Savonet, and Julian Tancredi.

Alexis Goldstein

Thank you to Simon Mackie and Aurelio DeRosa. Simon, you always kept us on track and helped to successfully wrangle three co-authors, no small feat. And Aurelio, your incredible attention to detail, impressive technical expertise and catching of errors has made this book so much better than it would have been without your immense contributions. Thank you to my co-authors, Louis and Estelle, who never failed to impress me with their deep knowledge, vast experience, and uncanny ability to find bugs in the latest browsers. A special thank you to Estelle for the encouragement, for which I am deeply grateful.

Louis Lazaris

Thank you to my wife for putting up with my odd work hours while I took part in this great project. Thanks to my talented co-authors, Estelle and Alexis, for gracing me with the privilege of having my name alongside theirs, and, of course, to our expert reviewer Aurelio De Rosa for always challenging me with his great technical insight. And special thanks to the talented staff at SitePoint for their super-professional handling of this project and everything that goes along with such an endeavor.

Estelle Weyl

Thank you to the entire open source community. With the option to "view source," I have learned from every developer who opted for markup rather than plugins. I would especially like to thank Jen Mei Wu and Sandi Watkins, who helped point me in the right direction when I began my career. Thank you to Dave Gregory and Laurie Voss who have always been there to help me find the words when they escaped me. Thank you to Stephanie Sullivan for brainstorming over code into the wee hours of the morning. And thank you to my developer friends at Opera, Mozilla, and Google for creating awesome browsers, providing us with the opportunity to not just play with HTML5 and CSS, but also to write this book.

Want to Take Your Learning Further?

Thanks for buying this book—we appreciate your support. Do you want to continue learning? You can now gain unlimited access to courses and ALL SitePoint books at Learnable for one low price. Enroll now and start learning today! Join Learnable and you'll stay ahead of the newest technology trends: http://www.learnable.com.

Chapter **1**

Introducing HTML5 and CSS3

This chapter gives a basic overview of how the web development industry has evolved and why HTML5 and CSS3 are so important to modern websites and web apps. It will show how using these technologies will be invaluable to your career as a web professional.

Of course, if you'd prefer to just get into the meat of the project that we'll be building, and start learning how to use all the new bells and whistles that HTML5 and CSS3 bring to the table, you can always skip ahead to Chapter 2 and come back later.

What is HTML5?

What we understand today as HTML5 has had a relatively turbulent history. You probably already know that HTML is the predominant markup language used to describe content, or data, on the World Wide Web (another lesser-used markup language is XML). HTML5 is the latest iteration of the HTML5 language and includes new features, improvements to existing features, and JavaScript APIs.

That said, HTML5 is not a reformulation of previous versions of the language—it includes all valid elements from both HTML4 and XHTML 1.0. Furthermore, it's been designed with some principles in mind to ensure it works on just about every platform, is compatible with older browsers, and handles errors gracefully. A summary of the design principles that guided the creation of HTML5 can be found on the W3C's HTML Design Principles page.[1]

First and foremost, HTML5 includes redefinitions of existing markup elements in addition to new elements that allow web designers to be more expressive in describing the content of their pages. Why litter your page with `div` elements when you can use `article`, `section`, `header`, `footer`, and so on?

The term "HTML5" has also been used to refer to a number of other new technologies and APIs. Some of these include drawing with the `canvas` element, offline storage, the new `video` and `audio` elements, drag-and-drop functionality, Microdata, and embedded fonts. In this book, we'll be covering a number of those technologies, and more.

Application Programming Interface

API stands for Application Programming Interface. Think of an API in the same way you think of a graphical user interface or GUI—except that instead of being an interface for humans, it's an interface for your code. An API provides your code with a set of "buttons" (predefined methods) that it can press to elicit the desired behavior from the system, software library, or browser.

API-based commands are a way of abstracting the more complex workings that are done in the background (or sometimes by third-party software). Some of the HTML5-related APIs will be introduced and discussed in later sections of this book.

Overall, you shouldn't be intimidated if you've had little experience with JavaScript or other APIs. While it would certainly be beneficial to have some experience with JavaScript or other languages, it isn't mandatory. Whatever the case, we'll walk you through the scripting parts of our book gradually, ensuring that you're not left scratching your head!

At the time of writing, it's been a good 5-plus years since HTML5 has had wide use in terms of the semantic elements and the various APIs. So it's no longer correct to categorize HTML5 as a "new" set of technologies—but it is still maturing and there

---

[1] http://www.w3.org/TR/html-design-principles/

are ongoing issues that continue to be addressed (such as bugs in browsers, and inconsistent support·across browsers and platforms).

It should also be noted that some technologies were never part of HTML5 (such as CSS3 and WOFF), yet have at times been lumped in under the same label. This has instigated the use of broad, all-encompassing expressions such as "HTML5 and related technologies." In the interest of brevity—and also at the risk of inciting heated arguments—we'll generally refer to these technologies collectively as "HTML5."

How did we get here?

The web development industry has evolved significantly in a relatively short time period. In the late 1990s, a website that included images and an eye-catching design was considered top of the line in terms of web content and presentation.

Today, the landscape is quite different. Simple performance-driven, Ajax-based websites (usually differentiated as "web apps") that rely on client-side scripting for critical functionality are becoming more and more common. Websites today often resemble standalone software applications, and an increasing number of developers are viewing them as such.

Along the way, web markup has evolved. HTML4 eventually gave way to XHTML, which is really just HTML4 with strict XML-style syntax. HTML5 has taken over as the most-used version of markup, and we now rarely, if ever, see new projects built with HTML4 or XHTML.

HTML5 originally began as two different specifications: Web Forms 2.0[2] and Web Apps 1.0.[3] Both were a result of the changed web landscape and the need for faster and more efficient maintainable web applications. Forms and app-like functionality are at the heart of web apps, so this was the natural direction for the HTML5 spec to take. Eventually, the two specs were merged to form what we now call HTML5.

For a short time, there was discussion about the production of XHTML 2.0,[4] but that project has long since been abandoned to allow focus on the much more practical HTML5.

---

[2] http://www.w3.org/TR/web-forms-2/
[3] https://whatwg.org/specs/web-apps/2005-09-01/
[4] http://www.w3.org/TR/xhtml2/

Would the real HTML5 please stand up?

Because the HTML5 specification is being developed by two different bodies (the WHATWG and the W3C), there are two versions of the spec. The W3C (or World Wide Web Consortium) you're probably familiar with: it's the organization that maintains the original HTML and CSS specifications, as well as a host of other web-related standards such as SVG (Scalable Vector Graphics) and WCAG (Web Content Accessibility Guidelines).

The WHATWG (aka the Web Hypertext Application Technology Working Group), on the other hand, was formed by a group of people from Apple, Mozilla, and Opera after a 2004 W3C meeting left them disheartened. They felt that the W3C was ignoring the needs of browser makers and users by focusing on XHTML 2.0, instead of working on a backwards-compatible HTML standard. So they went off on their own and developed the Web Apps and Web Forms specifications that we've discussed, which were then merged into a spec they called HTML5. On seeing this, the W3C eventually gave in and created its own HTML5 specification based on the WHAT-WG's spec.

This can seem a little confusing. Yes, there are some politics behind the scenes that we, as designers and developers, have no control over. But should it worry us that there are two versions of the spec? In short, no.

The WHATWG's version of the specification can be found at http://www.whatwg.org/html/, and in January 2011 was renamed "HTML" (dropping the "5"). It's now called a "living standard,"[5] meaning that it will be in constant development and will no longer be referred to using incrementing version numbers.

The WHATWG version contains information covering HTML-only features, including what's new in HTML5. Additionally, there are separate specifications being developed by WHATWG that cover the related technologies. These specifications include Microdata, Canvas 2D Context, Web Workers, Web Storage, and others.

---

[5] http://blog.whatwg.org/html-is-the-new-html5

The W3C's version of the spec can be found at ht-tp://www.w3.org/html/wg/drafts/html/master/, and the separate specifications for the other technologies can be accessed through http://dev.w3.org/html5/.[6]

So what's the difference between the W3C spec and that of WHATWG? Besides the name ("Living Standard" versus "HTML5.1"), the WHATWG version is a little more informal and experimental (and, some might argue, more forward-thinking). But in most places they're identical, so either one can be used as a basis for studying new HTML5 elements and related technologies.[7]

Why should I care about HTML5?

As mentioned, at the core of HTML5 are a number of new semantic elements, as well as several related technologies and APIs. These additions and changes to the language have been introduced with the goal of allowing developers to build web pages that are easier to code, use, and access.

These new semantic elements, along with other standards such as WAI-ARIA and Microdata (which we cover in Appendix B and Appendix C respectively), help to make our documents more accessible to both humans and machines—resulting in benefits for both accessibility and search engine optimization.

The semantic elements, in particular, have been designed with the dynamic Web in mind, with a particular focus on making pages more accessible and modular. We'll go into more detail on this in later chapters.

Finally, the APIs associated with HTML5 help improve on a number of techniques that web developers have been using for years. Many common tasks are now simplified, putting more power in developers' hands. Furthermore, the introduction of HTML5 audio and video means that there will be less dependence on third-party software and plugins when publishing rich media content on the Web.

---

[6] Technically, the W3C's version has now been upgraded to a new version: "HTML5.1" [http://www.w3.org/TR/html51/]. For simplicity we'll continue to refer to both versions as "HTML5". In addition, the W3C's website has a wiki page dedicated to something called "HTML.next [http://www.w3.org/wiki/HTML/next]", which discusses some far-future features of HTML that we won't cover in this book.

[7] There's a document published by the W3C [http://www.w3.org/wiki/HTML/W3C-WHATWG-Differences] that details many of the differences between the two specs, but most of the differences aren't very relevant or useful.

Overall, there are good reasons to start looking into HTML5's new features and APIs, and we'll discuss more of those reasons as we go through this book.

What is CSS3?

Another separate—but no less important—part of creating web pages is Cascading Style Sheets (CSS). As you probably know, CSS is a style language that describes how HTML markup is presented to the user. CSS3 is the latest version of the CSS specification.

CSS3 contains just about everything that's included in CSS2.1, the previous version of the spec. It also adds new features to help developers solve a number of presentation-related problems without resorting to scripting plugins or extra images.

New features in CSS3 include support for additional selectors, drop shadows, rounded corners, updated layout features, animation, transparency, and much more.

CSS3 is distinct from HTML5. In this publication, we'll be using the term CSS3 to refer to the current level of the CSS specification, with a particular focus on what's been added since CSS2.1. Thus, CSS3 is separate from HTML5 and its related APIs.

One final point should be made here regarding CSS and the current "version 3" label. Although this does seem to imply that there will one day be a "CSS4," Tab Atkins, a member of the CSS Working Group, has noted that there are no plans for it.[8] Instead, as he explains, the specification has been divided into separate modules, each with its own version number. So you might see something like "CSS Color Module Level 4"[9]—but that does not refer to "CSS4." No matter what level an individual module is at, it will still technically be under the umbrella of "CSS3," or better yet, simply "CSS." For the purposes of this book, we'll still refer to it as "CSS3," but just understand that this is likely to be the last version number for the language as a whole.

---

[8] http://www.xanthir.com/b4Ko0
[9] http://dev.w3.org/csswg/css-color/

Why should I care about CSS3?

Later in this book, we'll look in greater detail at many of the new features in CSS. In the meantime, we'll give you a taste of why CSS3's new techniques are so exciting to web designers.

Some design techniques find their way into almost every project. Drop shadows, gradients, and rounded corners are three good examples. We see them everywhere. When used appropriately, and in harmony with a site's overall theme and purpose, these enhancements can make a design flourish. Perhaps you're thinking: we've been creating these design elements using CSS for years now. But have we?

In the past, in order to create gradients, shadows, and rounded corners, web designers have had to resort to a number of tricky techniques. Sometimes extra HTML elements were required. In cases where the HTML is kept fairly clean, scripting hacks were required. In the case of gradients, the use of extra images was inevitable. We put up with these workarounds, because there was no other way of accomplishing those designs. CSS3 allows you to include these and other design elements in a forward-thinking manner that leads to so many benefits: cleaner markup, maintainable code, fewer extraneous images, and faster-loading pages.

A Short History on Vendor Prefixes

Ever since experimental features in CSS3 have begun to be introduced, developers have had to use prefixes in their CSS to target those features in various browsers. Browsers add vendor prefixes to features that might still be experimental in the specification (that is, they're not very far along in the standards process).[10] For example, at one time it was common to see something like this for a simple CSS transition:

```
a {
    color: #3381d6;
    -webkit-transition: color 0.4s ease;
    -moz-transition: color 0.4s ease;
```

---

[10] For more info, see: http://www.sitepoint.com/web-foundations/vendor-specific-properties/

```
    -o-transition: color 0.4s ease;
    transition: color 0.4s ease;
}
```

This would seem counterproductive to what was just mentioned, namely that CSS3 makes the code cleaner and easier to maintain. Fortunately, many prefixes are no longer needed. Additionally, we highly recommend that developers use a tool that will add prefixing automatically to your CSS.

One such tool is called Autoprefixer.[11] Autoprefixer can be included as part of your Grunt[12] workflow to post-process your CSS. With this, you need to include only the standard version of any CSS feature, and Autoprefixer will look through the Can I use... database[13] to determine if any vendor prefixes are needed. It will then build your CSS automatically, with all necessary prefixes. You also have the option to manually process your CSS using an online tool such as pleeease.[14] Whatever the case, in many places in this book we will include vendor prefixes, however be sure to use an online resource for up-to-date information on which features still require prefixes.

What do we mean by "the Real World"?

In the real world, we create web applications and we update them, fine-tune them, test them for potential performance problems, and continually tweak their design, layout, and content.

In other words, in the real world, we don't write code that we have no intention of revisiting. We write code using the most reliable, maintainable, and effective methods available, with every intention of returning to work on that code again to make any necessary improvements or alterations. This is evident not only in websites and web apps that we build and maintain as personal projects, but also in those we create and maintain for our clients.

We need to continually search out new and better ways to write our code. HTML5 and CSS3 are a big step in that direction.

---

[11] https://github.com/postcss/autoprefixer

[12] http://gruntjs.com/

[13] http://caniuse.com/

[14] http://pleeease.io/play/

The Current Browser Market

Although HTML5 is still in development, presenting significant changes in the way content is marked up, it's worth noting that those changes won't cause older browsers to choke, nor result in layout problems or page errors.

What this means is that you could take any old project containing valid HTML4 or XHTML markup, change the doctype to HTML5 (which we'll cover in Chapter 2), and the page will appear in the browser the same as it did before. The changes and additions in HTML5 have been implemented into the language in such a way as to ensure backwards-compatibility with older browsers—even older versions of Internet Explorer! Of course, this is no guarantee that the new features will work, it simply means they won't break your pages or cause any visible problems.

Even with regards to the more complex new features (for example, the APIs), developers have come up with various solutions to provide the equivalent experience to non-supporting browsers, all while embracing the exciting new possibilities offered by HTML5 and CSS3. Sometimes this is as simple as providing fallback content, such as a Flash video player to browsers without native video support. At other times, though, it's been necessary to use scripting to mimic support for new features.

These "gap-filling" techniques are referred to as **polyfills**. Relying on scripts to emulate native features isn't always the best approach when building high-performance web apps, but it's a necessary growing pain as we evolve to include new enhancements and features, such as the ones we'll be discussing in this book. Fortunately, as of writing, older browsers such as Internet Explorer 6 through 9 that fail to support many of the new features in HTML5 and CSS3, are used by less than 10% of web visitors today.[15] More and more people are using what has been termed evergreen browsers;[16] that is, browsers that automatically update. This means that new features will be functional to a larger audience, and eventually to all, as older browser shares wane.

---

[15] http://gs.statcounter.com/#browser_version-ww-monthly-201502-201502-bar

[16] http://tomdale.net/2013/05/evergreen-browsers/

In this book we may occasionally recommend fallback options or polyfills to plug the gaps in browser incompatibilities; we'll also try to do our best in warning you of potential drawbacks and pitfalls associated with using these options.

Of course, it's worth noting that sometimes no fallbacks or polyfills are required at all; for example, when using CSS3 to create rounded corners on boxes in your design, there's often no harm in users of really old browsers seeing square boxes instead. The functionality of the site has no degradation, and those users will be none the wiser about what they're missing.

As we progress through the lessons and introduce new subjects, if you plan on using one of these in a project we strongly recommend that you consult a browser-support reference such as the aforementioned Can I use...[17] That way, you'll know how and whether to provide fallbacks or polyfills. Where necessary, we'll occasionally discuss ways you can ensure that non-supporting browsers have an acceptable experience, but the good news is that it's becoming less and less of an issue as time goes on.

The Growing Mobile Market

Another compelling reason to start learning and using HTML5 and CSS3 today is the exploding mobile market. According to one source, in 2009 less than 1% of all web usage was on mobile devices and tablets.[18] By the middle of 2014, that number had risen to more than 35%![19] That's an astounding growth rate in a little more than five years. So what does this mean for those learning HTML5 and CSS3?

HTML5, CSS3, and related cutting-edge technologies are very well supported in many mobile web browsers. For example, mobile Safari on iOS devices such as the iPhone and iPad, Opera Mobile, Android Browser, and UC Browser all provide strong levels of HTML5 and CSS3 support. New features and technologies supported by some of those browsers include CSS3 animations, CSS flexbox, the Canvas API, Web Storage, SVG, Offline Web Apps, and more.

In fact, some of the new technologies we'll be introducing in this book have been specifically designed with mobile devices in mind. Technologies such as Offline Web Apps and Web Storage have been designed, in part, because of the growing

---

[17] http://caniuse.com/

[18] http://gs.statcounter.com/#desktop+mobile+tablet-comparison-ww-monthly-200901-200901-bar

[19] http://gs.statcounter.com/#desktop+mobile+tablet-comparison-ww-monthly-201408-201408-bar

number of people accessing web pages with mobile devices. Such devices can often have limitations with online data usage, and thus benefit greatly from the ability to access web applications offline.

We'll be touching on those subjects in Chapter 11, as well as others throughout the course of the book, providing the tools you'll need to create web pages for a variety of devices and platforms.

On to the Real Stuff

It's unrealistic to push ahead into new technologies and expect to author pages and apps for only one level of browser. In the real world, and in a world where we desire HTML5 and CSS3 to make further inroads, we need to be prepared to develop pages that work across a varied landscape. That landscape includes modern browsers, any remaining older versions of Internet Explorer, and an exploding market of mobile devices.

Yes, in some ways, supplying a different set of instructions for different user agents resembles the early days of the Web with its messy browser sniffing and code forking. But this time around, the new code is much more future-proof: when older browsers fall out of general use, all you need to do is remove any fallbacks and polyfills, leaving only the code base that's aimed at modern browsers.

HTML5 and CSS3 are the leading technologies that have ushered in a much more exciting world of web page authoring. Because all modern browsers provide excellent levels of support for a number of HTML5 and CSS3 features, creating powerful and simple-to-maintain future-proof web pages is easier than ever before.

So, enough about the "why," let's start digging into the "how"!

Markup, HTML5 Style

Now that we've given you a bit of a history primer, along with some compelling reasons to learn HTML5 and start using it in your projects today, it's time to introduce you to the sample site that we'll be progressively building in this book.

After we briefly cover what we'll be building, we'll discuss some HTML5 syntax basics, along with some suggestions for best-practice coding. We'll follow that with some important info on cross-browser compatibility, and the basics of page structure in HTML5. Lastly, we'll introduce some specific HTML5 elements and see how they'll fit into our layout.

So let's get into it!

Introducing *The HTML5 Herald*

For the purpose of this book, we've put together a sample website project that we'll be building from scratch. The website is already built—you can check it out now at thehtml5herald.com.[1] It's an old-time newspaper-style website called *The HTML5 Herald*. The home page of the site contains some media in the form of video, images,

---

[1] http://thehtml5herald.com/

articles, and advertisements. There's also another page comprising a registration form.

Go ahead and view the source, and try some of the functionality if you like. As we proceed through the book, we'll be working through the code that went into making the site. We'll avoid discussing every detail of the CSS involved, as most of it should already be familiar to you—float layouts, absolute and relative positioning, basic font styling, and the like. We'll primarily focus on the new HTML5 elements, along with the APIs, plus all the new CSS3 techniques being used to add styles and interactivity to various elements.

Figure 2.1 shows a bit of what the finished product looks like.

Figure 2.1. The front page of *The HTML5 Herald*

While we build the site, we'll do our best to explain the new HTML5 elements, APIs, and CSS3 features, and aim to recommend some best practices. Of course, some of these technologies are still new and in development, so we'll try not to be too dogmatic about what you can and can't do.

A Basic HTML5 Template

As you learn HTML5 and add new techniques to your toolbox, you're likely to want to build yourself a boilerplate, from which you can begin all your HTML5-based projects. We encourage this, and you may also consider using one of the many online sources that provide a basic HTML5 starting point for you.[2]

In this project, however, we want to build our code from scratch and explain each piece as we go along. Of course, it would be impossible for even the most fantastical and unwieldy sample site we could dream up to include *every* new element or technique, so we'll also explain many new features that don't fit into the project. This way, you'll be familiar with a wide set of options when deciding how to build your HTML5 and CSS3 websites and applications, enabling you to use this book as a quick reference for a number of features and techniques.

Let's start simple, with a bare-bones HTML5 page:

```
<!DOCTYPE html>
<html lang="en">
  <head>
    <meta charset="utf-8">

    <title>The HTML5 Herald</title>
    <meta name="description" content="The HTML5 Herald">
    <meta name="author" content="SitePoint">

    <link rel="stylesheet" href="css/styles.css">

    <!--[if lt IE 9]>
      <script src="js/html5shim.js"></script>
    <![endif]-->

  </head>
  <body>

    <script src="js/scripts.js"></script>
```

---

[2] A few you might want to look into can be found at html5boilerplate.com [https://html5boilerplate.com/] and https://github.com/murtaugh/HTML5-Reset.

```
    </body>
</html>
```

With that basic template in place, let's now examine some of the significant parts of the markup and how these might differ from how HTML was written prior to HTML5.

The Doctype

First, we have the Document Type Declaration, or **doctype**. This is simply a way to tell the browser—or any other parser—what type of document it's looking at. In the case of HTML files, it means the specific version and flavor of HTML. The doctype should always be the first item at the top of any HTML file. Many years ago, the doctype declaration was an ugly and hard-to-remember mess. For XHTML 1.0 Strict:

```
<!DOCTYPE html PUBLIC "-//W3C//DTD XHTML 1.0 Strict//EN" "http://www
➡.w3.org/TR/xhtml1/DTD/xhtml1-strict.dtd">
```

And for HTML4 Transitional:

```
<!DOCTYPE HTML PUBLIC "-//W3C//DTD HTML 4.01 Transitional//EN" "http
➡://www.w3.org/TR/html4/loose.dtd">
```

Although that long string of text at the top of our documents hasn't really hurt us (other than forcing our sites' viewers to download a few extra bytes), HTML5 has done away with that indecipherable eyesore. Now all you need is this:

```
<!DOCTYPE html>
```

Simple, and to the point. The doctype can be written in uppercase, lowercase, or mixed case. You'll notice that the "5" is conspicuously missing from the declaration. Although the current iteration of web markup is known as "HTML5," it really is just an evolution of previous HTML standards—and future specifications will simply be a development of what we have today.

Because browsers are usually required to support all existing content on the Web, there's no reliance on the doctype to tell them which features should be supported in a given document. In other words, the doctype alone is not going to make your pages HTML5-compliant. It's really up to the browser to do this. In fact, you can use one of those two older doctypes with new HTML5 elements on the page and the page will render the same as it would if you used the new doctype.

The html Element

Next up in any HTML document is the html element, which has not changed significantly with HTML5. In our example, we've included the lang attribute with a value of en, which specifies that the document is in English. In XHTML-based markup, you were required to include an xmlns attribute. In HTML5, this is no longer needed, and even the lang attribute is unnecessary for the document to validate or function correctly.

So here's what we have so far, including the closing html tag:

```
<!DOCTYPE html>
<html lang="en">

</html>
```

The head Element

The next part of our page is the head section. The first line inside the head is the one that defines the character encoding for the document. This is another element that's been simplified since XHTML and HTML4, and is an optional feature, but recommended. In the past, you may have written it like this:

```
<meta http-equiv="Content-Type" content="text/html; charset=utf-8">
```

HTML5 improves on this by reducing the character-encoding meta tag to the bare minimum:

```
<meta charset="utf-8">
```

In nearly all cases, utf-8 is the value you'll be using in your documents. A full explanation of character encoding is beyond the scope of this book, and it probably won't be that interesting to you, either. Nonetheless, if you want to delve a little deeper, you can read up on the topic on W3C[3] or WHATWG.[4]

 Encoding Declaration

To ensure that all browsers read the character encoding correctly, the entire character-encoding declaration must be included somewhere within the first 512 characters of your document. It should also appear before any content-based elements (such as the `title` element that follows it in our example site).

There's much more we could write about this subject, but we want to keep you awake—so we'll spare you those details! For now, we're content to accept this simplified declaration and move on to the next part of our document:

```html
<title>The HTML5 Herald</title>
<meta name="description" content="The HTML5 Herald">
<meta name="author" content="SitePoint">

<link rel="stylesheet" href="css/styles.css">
```

In these lines, HTML5 barely differs from previous syntaxes. The page title (the only mandatory element inside the `head`) is declared the same as it always was, and the meta tags we've included are merely optional examples to indicate where these would be placed; you could put as many valid `meta` elements[5] here as you like.

The key part of this chunk of markup is the stylesheet, which is included using the customary `link` element. There are no required attributes for `link` other than `href` and `rel`. The `type` attribute (which was common in older versions of HTML) is not necessary, nor was it ever needed to indicate the content type of the stylesheet.

Leveling the Playing Field

The next element in our markup requires a bit of background information before it can be introduced. HTML5 includes a number of new elements, such as `article` and `section`, which we'll be covering later on. You might think this would be a major problem for older browser support for unrecognized elements, but you'd be

---

[3] http://www.w3.org/html/wg/drafts/html/master/infrastructure.html#encoding-terminology

[4] https://html.spec.whatwg.org/multipage/infrastructure.html#encoding-terminology

[5] https://html.spec.whatwg.org/multipage/semantics.html#the-meta-element

wrong. This is because the majority of browsers don't actually care what tags you use. If you had an HTML document with a `recipe` tag (or even a `ziggy` tag) in it, and your CSS attached some styles to that element, nearly every browser would proceed as if this were totally normal, applying your styling without complaint.

Of course, such a hypothetical document would fail to validate and may have accessibility problems, but it *would* render correctly in *almost* all browsers—the exception being old versions of Internet Explorer (IE). Prior to version 9, IE prevented unrecognized elements from receiving styling. These mystery elements were seen by the rendering engine as "unknown elements," so you were unable to change the way they looked or behaved. This includes not only our imagined elements, but also any elements that had yet to be defined at the time those browser versions were developed. That means (you guessed it) the new HTML5 elements.

The good news is, at the time of writing, most people still using a version of IE are using version 9 or higher, and very few are on version 9, so this is not a big problem for most developers anymore; however, if a big chunk of your audience is still using IE8 or earlier, you'll have to take action to ensure your designs don't fall apart.

Fortunately, there's a solution: a very simple piece of JavaScript originally developed by John Resig.[6] Inspired by an idea by Sjoerd Visscher, it can make the new HTML5 elements styleable in older versions of IE.

We've included this so-called "HTML5 shiv"[7] in our markup as a script tag surrounded by conditional comments. Conditional comments are a proprietary feature implemented in Internet Explorer in version 9 and earlier. They provide you with the ability to target specific versions of that browser with scripts or styles.[8] The following conditional comment is telling the browser that the enclosed markup should only appear to users viewing the page with Internet Explorer prior to version 9:

---

[6] http://ejohn.org/blog/html5-shiv/

[7] You might be more familiar with its alternative name: the HTML5 shim. Whilst there are identical code snippets out there that go by both names, we'll be referring to all instances as the HTML5 shiv, its original name.

[8] For more information see the SitePoint Reference
[http://www.sitepoint.com/web-foundations/internet-explorer-conditional-comments/].

```
<!--[if lt IE 9]>
  <script src="js/html5shim.js"></script>
<![endif]-->
```

It should be noted that if you're using a JavaScript library that deals with HTML5 features or the new APIs, it's possible that it will already have the HTML5-enabling script present; in this case, you could remove reference to the script. One example of this would be Modernizr,[9] a JavaScript library that detects modern HTML and CSS features. Modernizr gives you the option to include code that enables the HTML5 elements in older versions of IE, so the shiv would be redundant. We take a closer look at Modernizr in Appendix A.

 Not Everyone Can Benefit from the HTML5 Shiv

Of course, there's still a group of users unable to benefit from the HTML5 shiv: those who have for one reason or another disabled JavaScript and are using IE8 or lower. As web designers, we're constantly told that the content of our sites should be fully accessible to all users, even those without JavaScript. But it's not as bad as it seems. A number of studies have shown that the number of users who have JavaScript disabled is low enough to be of little concern, especially when you factor in how few of those will be using IE8 or lower.

In a study published in October, 2013, the UK Government Digital Service determined that users browsing government web services in the UK with JavaScript disabled or unavailable was 1.1%.[10] In another study conducted on the Yahoo Developer Network[11] (published in October 2010), users with JavaScript disabled amounted to around 1% of total traffic worldwide.

The Rest Is History

Looking at the rest of our starting template, we have the usual body element along with its closing tag and the closing html tag. We also have a reference to a JavaScript file inside a script element.

---

[9] http://www.modernizr.com/

[10] https://gds.blog.gov.uk/2013/10/21/how-many-people-are-missing-out-on-javascript-enhancement/

[11] https://developer.yahoo.com/blogs/ydn/many-users-javascript-disabled-14121.html

Much like the `link` tag discussed earlier, the `script` tag does not require that you declare a `type` attribute. If you ever wrote XHTML, you might remember your `script` tags looking like this:

```
<script src="js/scripts.js" type="text/javascript"></script>
```

Since JavaScript is, for all practical purposes, the only real scripting language used on the Web, and since all browsers will assume that you're using JavaScript even when you don't explicitly declare that fact, the `type` attribute is unnecessary in HTML5 documents:

```
<script src="js/scripts.js"></script>
```

We've put the `script` element at the bottom of our page to conform to best practices for embedding JavaScript. This has to do with the page-loading speed; when a browser encounters a script, it will pause downloading and rendering the rest of the page while it parses the script. This results in the page appearing to load much more slowly when large scripts are included at the top of the page before any content. It's why most scripts should be placed at the very bottom of the page, so that they'll only be parsed after the rest of the page has loaded.

In some cases, however, (such as with the HTML5 shiv) the script may *need* to be placed in the head of your document, because you want it to take effect before the browser starts rendering the page.

HTML5 FAQ

After this quick introduction to HTML5 markup, you probably have a bunch of questions swirling in your head. Here are some answers to a few of the likely ones.

Why do these changes still work in older browsers?

To understand why this isn't a problem, we can compare HTML5 to some of the new features added in CSS3, which we'll be discussing in later chapters.

In CSS, when a new feature is added (for example, the `border-radius` property that adds rounded corners to elements), that feature also has to be added to browsers' rendering engines, so older browsers will fail to recognize it. If a user is viewing the page on a browser with no support for `border-radius`, the rounded corners will appear square. This happens because square corners are the default and the browser will ignore the `border-radius` declaration. Other CSS3 features behave similarly, causing the experience to be degraded to some degree.

Many developers expect that HTML5 will work in a similar way. While this might be true for some of the advanced features and APIs we'll be considering later in the book, it's not the case with the changes we've covered so far; that is, the simpler syntax, fewer superfluous attributes, and the new doctype.

HTML5's syntax was more or less defined after a careful study of what older browsers can and can't handle. For example, the 15 characters that comprise the doctype declaration in HTML5 are the minimum characters required to make every browser display a page in standards mode.

Likewise, while XHTML required a lengthier character-encoding declaration and an extra attribute on the `html` element for the purpose of validation, browsers never actually required them in order to display a page correctly. Again, the behavior of older browsers was carefully examined, and it was determined that the character encoding could be simplified and the `xmlns` attribute removed—and browsers would still see the page the same way.

Unlike changes to CSS3 and JavaScript, where additions are only supported when browser makers actually implement them, there's no need to wait for new browser versions to be released before using HTML5's markup syntax. And when it comes to using the new semantic elements, a small snippet of JavaScript is all that's required to bring any really old browsers into line.

 Standards Mode versus Quirks Mode

When standards-based web design was in its infancy, browser makers were faced with a problem: supporting emerging standards would, in many cases, break backwards compatibility with existing web pages that were designed to older, nonstandard browser implementations. Browser makers needed a signal indicating that a given page was meant to be rendered according to the standards. They found such a signal in the doctype: new standards-compliant pages included a correctly formatted doctype, while older nonstandard pages generally didn't. Using the doctype as a signal, browsers could switch between standards mode (in which they try to follow standards to the letter in the way they render elements) and quirks mode (where they attempt to mimic the "quirky" rendering capabilities of older browsers to ensure that the page renders how it was intended).

It's safe to say that in the current development landscape, nearly every web page has a proper doctype, and thus will render in standards mode; it's therefore unlikely that you'll ever have to deal with a page rendered in quirks mode. Of course, if a user is viewing a web page using a very old browser (such as IE4), the page will be rendered using that browser's rendering mode. This is what quirks mode mimics, and it will do so regardless of the doctype being used.

Although the XHTML and older HTML doctypes include information about the exact version of the specification they refer to, browsers have never actually made use of that information. As long as a seemingly correct doctype is present, they'll render the page in standards mode. Consequently, HTML5's doctype has been stripped down to the bare minimum required to trigger standards mode in any browser. Further information, along with a chart that outlines what will cause different browsers to render in quirks mode, can be found on Wikipedia.[12] You can also read a good overview of standards and quirks mode on SitePoint's CSS reference.[13]

Shouldn't all tags be closed?

In XHTML, all elements were required to be closed—either with a corresponding closing tag (such as `html`) or in the case of void elements, a forward slash at the end of the tag. Void elements are elements that *can't* contain child elements (such as `input`, `img`, or `link`).

You can still use that style of syntax in HTML5—and you might prefer it for consistency and maintainability reasons—but adding a trailing slash on void elements is no longer required for validation. Continuing with the theme of "cutting the fat," HTML5 allows you to omit the trailing slash from such elements, arguably leaving your markup cleaner and less cluttered.

It's worth noting that in HTML5, most elements that *can* contain nested elements—but simply happen to be empty—still need to be paired with a corresponding closing tag. There are exceptions to this rule (such as `p` tags and `li` tags), but it's simpler to assume that it's universal.

---

[12] http://en.wikipedia.org/wiki/Quirks_mode/
[13] http://reference.sitepoint.com/css/doctypesniffing/

What about other XHTML-based syntax customs?

While we're on the subject, omitting closing slashes is just one aspect of HTML5-based syntax that differs from XHTML. In fact, syntax style issues are completely ignored by the HTML5 validator, which will only throw errors for code mistakes that threaten to disrupt your document in some way.

What this means is that through the eyes of the validator, the following five lines of markup are identical:

```
<link rel="stylesheet" href="css/styles.css" />
<link rel="stylesheet" href="css/styles.css">
<LINK REL="stylesheet" HREF="css/styles.css">
<Link Rel="stylesheet" Href="css/styles.css">
<link rel=stylesheet href=css/styles.css>
```

In HTML5, you can use lowercase, uppercase, or mixed-case tag names or attributes, as well as quoted or unquoted attribute values (as long as those values don't contain spaces or other reserved characters), and it will all validate just fine.

In XHTML, all attributes were required to have values, even if those values were redundant. For example, in XHTML you'd often see markup like this:

```
<input type="text" disabled="disabled" />
```

In HTML5, attributes that are either "on" or "off" (called Boolean attributes) can simply be specified with no value. So, the aforementioned `input` element can be written as follows:

```
<input type="text" disabled>
```

Hence, HTML5 has very loose requirements for validation, at least as far as syntax is concerned. Does this mean you should just go nuts and use whatever syntax you want on any given element? No, we certainly don't recommend that.

We encourage developers to choose a syntax style and stick to it—especially if you are working in a team environment where code maintenance and readability are crucial. We also recommend (though this is optional) that you choose a minimalist coding style while staying consistent.

Here are some guidelines for you to consider using:

- Use lowercase for all elements and attributes as you would in XHTML.

- Despite some elements not requiring closing tags, we recommend that all elements containing content be closed (as in `<p>Text</p>`).

- Although you can leave attribute values unquoted, it's highly likely that you'll have attributes that require quotes (for example, when declaring multiple classes separated by spaces, or when appending a query string value to a URL). As a result, we suggest that you always use quotes for the sake of consistency.

- Omit the trailing slash from void elements (such as `meta` or `input`).

- Avoid providing redundant values for Boolean attributes (for instance, use `<input type="checkbox" checked>` rather than `<input type="checkbox" checked="checked">`).

Again, these recommendations are by no means universally accepted; however, we believe that they're reasonable syntax suggestions for achieving clean, easy-to-read maintainable markup.

If you do run amok with your code style, including too much that's unnecessary, you're just adding extra bytes for no reason. You're also potentially making your code harder to maintain, especially if you work with other developers on the same code base.

Defining the Page's Structure

Now that we've broken down the basics of our template, let's start adding some meat to the bones and give our page some structure.

Later in the book, we're going to specifically deal with adding CSS3 features and other HTML5 goodness; for now, we'll consider what elements we want to use in building our site's overall layout. We'll be covering a lot in this section and throughout the coming chapters about semantics. When we use the term "semantics," we're referring to the way a given HTML element describes the meaning of its content.

If you look back at the screenshot of *The HTML5 Herald* (or view the site online), you'll see that it's divided up as follows:

- header section with a logo and title
- navigation bar
- body content divided into three columns
- articles and ad blocks within the columns
- footer containing some author and copyright information

Before we decide which elements are appropriate for these different parts of our page, let's consider some of our options. First of all, we'll introduce you to some of the new HTML5 semantic elements that could be used to help divide our page and add more meaning to our document's structure.

The header Element

Naturally, the first element we'll look at is the header element. The spec describes it succinctly as "a group of introductory or navigational aids."[14]

Contrary to what you might normally assume, you can include a new header element to introduce each section of your content. It's not just reserved for the page header (which you might normally mark up with `<div id="header">`). When we use the word "section" here, we're not limiting ourselves to the actual section element described in the next part; technically, we're referring to what HTML5 calls "sectioning content." This means any chunk of content that might need its own header, even if that means there are multiple such chunks on a single page.

A header element can be used to include introductory content or navigational aids that are specific to any single section of a page, or apply to the entire page, or both.

While a header element will frequently be placed at the top of a page or section, its definition is independent from its position. Your site's layout might call for the title of an article or blog post to be off to the left, right, or even below the content; regardless of which, you can still use header to describe this content.

---

[14] https://html.spec.whatwg.org/multipage/semantics.html#the-header-element

The `section` Element

The next element you should become familiar with is HTML5's `section` element. The spec defines `section` as follows:[15]

> The `section` element represents a generic section of a document or application. A section, in this context, is a thematic grouping of content, typically with a heading.

It further explains that a `section` shouldn't be used as a generic container that exists for styling or scripting purposes only. If you're unable to use `section` as a generic container—for example, in order to achieve your desired CSS layout—then what should you use? Our old friend, the `div` element, which is semantically meaningless.

Going back to the definition from the spec, the `section` element's content should be "thematic," so it would be incorrect to use it in a generic way to wrap unrelated pieces of content.

Some examples of acceptable uses for `section` elements include:

- individual sections of a tabbed interface

- segments of an "About" page; for example, a company's "About" page might include sections on the company's history, its mission statement, and its team

- different parts of a lengthy "terms of service" page

- various sections of an online news site; for example, articles could be grouped into sections covering sports, world affairs, and economic news

Using `section` Correctly

Every time new semantic markup is made available to web designers, there will be debate over what constitutes correct use of these elements, what the spec's intention was, and so on. You may remember discussions about the appropriate use of the `dl` element in previous HTML specifications. Unsurprisingly, HTML5 has not been immune to this phenomenon, particularly when it comes to the `section` element. Even Bruce Lawson, a well-respected authority on HTML5, has admitted

---

[15] https://html.spec.whatwg.org/multipage/semantics.html#the-section-element

to using `section` incorrectly in the past. For a bit of clarity, it's well worth reading Bruce's post explaining his error.[16]

In short:

- `section` is *generic*, so if a more specific semantic element is appropriate (such as `article`, `aside`, or `nav`), use that instead.

- `section` *has semantic meaning*; it implies that the content it contains is related in some way. If you're unable to succinctly describe all the content you're trying to put in a `section` using just a few words, it's likely you need a semantically neutral container instead: the humble `div`.

That said, as is always the case with semantics, it's open to interpretation in some instances. If you feel you can make a case for why you're using a given element rather than another, go for it. In the unlikely event that anyone ever calls you on it, the resulting discussion can be both entertaining and enriching for everyone involved, and might even contribute to the wider community's understanding of the specification.

Keep in mind, also, that you're permitted to nest `section` elements inside existing `section` elements, if it's appropriate. For example, for an online news website, the World News section might be further subdivided into a section for each major global region.

The `article` Element

The `article` element is similar to the `section` element, but there are some notable differences. Here's the definition according to the spec:[17]

> The article element represents a complete, or self-contained, composition in a document, page, application, or site and that is, in principle, independently distributable or reusable, e.g. in syndication.

The key terms in that definition are *self-contained composition* and *independently distributable*. Whereas a `section` can contain any content that can be grouped thematically, an `article` must be a single piece of content that can stand on its

---

[16] http://html5doctor.com/the-section-element/

[17] https://html.spec.whatwg.org/multipage/semantics.html#the-article-element

own. This distinction can be hard to wrap your head around, so when in doubt, try the test of syndication: if a piece of content can be republished on another site without being modified, or if it can be pushed out as an update via RSS, or on social media sites such as Twitter or Facebook, it has the makings of an `article`.

Ultimately, it's up to you to decide what constitutes an article, but here are some suggestions in line with recommendations in the spec:

- a forum post
- a magazine or newspaper article
- a blog entry
- a user-submitted comment on a blog entry or article

Finally, just like `section` elements, `article` elements can be nested inside other `article` elements. You can also nest a `section` inside an `article`, and vice versa. It all depends on the content you're marking up.

The nav Element

It's safe to assume that the `nav` element will appear in virtually every project. `nav` represents exactly what it implies: a group of navigation links. Although the most common use for `nav` will be for wrapping an unordered list of links, there are other options. For example, you could wrap the `nav` element around a paragraph of text that contained the major navigation links for a page or section of a page.

In either case, the `nav` element should be reserved for navigation that is of primary importance. So, it's recommended that you avoid using `nav` for a brief list of links in a footer, for example.

 Skip Navigation Links

A design pattern you may have seen implemented on many sites is the "skip navigation" link. The idea is to allow users of screen readers to quickly skip past your site's main navigation if they've already heard it—after all, there's no point listening to a large site's entire navigation menu every time you click through to a new page! The `nav` element has the potential to eliminate this need; if a screen reader sees a `nav` element, it could allow its users to skip over the navigation without requiring an additional link. The specification states: "User agents (such as screen readers) that are targeted at users who can benefit from navigation information being omitted in the initial rendering, or who can benefit from navigation information being immediately available, can use this element as a way to determine what content on the page to initially skip or provide on request (or both)."

Although not all assistive devices recognize nav as of this writing, by building to the standards now you ensure that as screen readers improve, your page will become more accessible over time.

 User Agents

You'll encounter the term "user agent" a lot when browsing through specifications. Really, it's just a fancy term for a browser—a software "agent" that a user employs to access the content of a page. The reason the specs don't simply say "browser" is that user agents can include screen readers or any other technological means to read a web page.

You can use nav more than once on a given page. If you have a primary navigation bar for the site, this would call for a nav element. Additionally, if you had a secondary set of links pointing to different parts of the current page (using in-page anchors or "local" links), this too could be wrapped in a nav element.

As with section, there's been some debate over what constitutes acceptable use of nav and why it isn't recommended in some circumstances (such as in a footer). Some developers believe this element is appropriate for pagination or breadcrumb links, or for a search form that constitutes a primary means of navigating a site (as is the case on Google).

This decision will ultimately be up to you, the developer. Ian Hickson, the primary editor of WHATWG's HTML5 specification, responded to the question directly: "use [it] whenever you would have used class=nav".[18]

---

[18] See http://html5doctor.com/nav-element/#comment-213.
[http://html5doctor.com/nav-element/#comment-213]

The `aside` Element

This element represents a part of the page that's "tangentially related to the content around the `aside` element, and which could be considered separate from that content."[19]

The `aside` element could be used to wrap a portion of content that is tangential to:

- a specific standalone piece of content (such as an `article` or `section`).

- an entire page or document, as is customarily done when adding a sidebar to a page or website.

The `aside` element should never be used to wrap sections of the page that are part of the primary content; in other words, `aside` is not meant to be parenthetical. The `aside` content could stand on its own, but it should still be part of a larger whole.

Some possible uses for `aside` include a sidebar, a secondary list of links, or a block of advertising. It should also be noted that the `aside` element (as in the case of `header`) is not defined by its position on the page. It could be on the side, or it could be elsewhere. It's the content itself, and its relation to other elements, that defines it.

The `footer` Element

The final element we'll discuss in this chapter is the `footer` element. As with `header`, you can have multiple `footer` elements on a single page, and you should use `footer` instead of something generic such as `<div id="footer">`.

A footer element, according to the spec, represents a footer for the section of content that is its nearest ancestor. The section of content could be the entire document, or it could be a `section`, `article`, or `aside` element.

Often a `footer` will contain copyright information, lists of related links, author information, and similar information that you normally think of as coming at the end of a block of content; however, much like `aside` and `header`, a footer element is not defined in terms of its position on the page, so it does not have to appear at the end

---

[19] https://html.spec.whatwg.org/multipage/semantics.html#the-aside-element

of a section, or at the bottom of a page. Most likely it will, but this is not required. For example, information about the author of a blog post might be displayed above the post instead of below it, and will still be considered footer information.

How did we get here?

If you're wondering a little bit about the path to HTML5 and how we ended up with the tags that we did, you might want to check out Luke Stevens' book called *The Truth about HTML5*.[20] Currently in its 2nd edition, Luke's book is somewhat controversial. In addition to covering many of the HTML5 technologies such as video and canvas, he also goes in-depth in his coverage of the history of HTML5, explaining some of the semantic and accessibility problems inherent in the new elements and providing some recommendations on how to handle these issues.

Structuring *The HTML5 Herald*

Now that we've covered the basics of page structure and the elements in HTML5 that will assist in this area, it's time to start building the parts of our page that will hold the content.

Let's start from the top, with a `header` element. It makes sense to include the logo and title of *The Herald* in here, as well as the tagline. We can also add a `nav` element for the site navigation.

After the `header`, the main content of our site is divided into three columns. While you might be tempted to use `section` elements for these, stop and think about the content. If each column contained a separate "section" of information (such as a sports section and an entertainment section), that would make sense. As it is, though, the separation into columns is really only a visual arrangement, so we'll use a plain old `div` for each column.

Inside those `div`s, we have newspaper articles; these, of course, are perfect candidates for the `article` element.

The column on the far right, though, contains three ads in addition to an article. We'll use an `aside` element to wrap the ads, with each ad placed inside an `article` element. This may seem odd, but look back at the description of `article`: "a self-

---

[20] http://www.truthabouthtml5.com/

contained composition [...] that is, in principle, independently distributable or re-usable." An ad fits the bill almost perfectly, as it's usually intended to be reproduced across a number of websites without modification.

Next up, we'll add another `article` element for the final article that appears below the ads. That final article will be *excluded* from the `aside` element that holds the three ads. To belong in the `aside`, the `article` needs to be tangentially related to the page's content. This isn't the case: this article is part of the page's main content, so it would be wrong to include it in the `aside`.

Now the third column consists of two elements: an `aside` and an `article`, stacked one on top of the other. To help hold them together and make them easier to style, we'll wrap them in a `div`. We're not using a `section`, or any other semantic markup, because that would imply that the `article` and the `aside` were somehow topically related. They're not—it's just a feature of our design that they happen to be in the same column together.

The New `main` Element

At this point, it's probably a good time to introduce another major structural element that's been introduced in HTML5: the `main` element. This element was not originally part of the HTML5 spec, but has been added since the first edition of this book was published.

Unfortunately, defining the `main` element and how it can be used is a little tricky. But let's start with where the element originated. In some HTML documents, developers were wrapping their primary content in a generic element, like this:

```
<body>
  <header>
    ...
  </header>

  <div id="main">
    ...
  </div>

  <footer>
```

```
    ...
  </footer>
</body>
```

Notice the generic `div` element used here as a sibling to the `header` and `footer` elements. Notice also the ID attribute with a value of `"main"`. In addition to this, many developers were adding an ARIA `role` to this element:

```
<div id="main" role="main">
  ...
</div>
```

We'll avoid going into the details of ARIA here—that's covered in Appendix B —but basically, the new `main` element is meant to replace this practice.

The W3C spec defines `main` as follows:[21] "The `main` element represents the main content of the body of a document or application. The main content area consists of content that is directly related to or expands upon the central topic of a document or central functionality of an application."

The WHATWG spec defines it similarly; however, the two specs have very different definitions beyond that. The WHATWG spec says[22]:

> "There is no restriction as to the number of `main` elements in a document. Indeed, there are many cases where it would make sense to have multiple `main` elements. For example, a page with multiple `article` elements might need to indicate the dominant contents of each such element."

But uncharacteristically, in complete contradiction to that, the W3C spec says:

> "Authors must not include more than one `main` element in a document. Authors must not include the `main` element as a descendant of an `article`, `aside`, `footer`, `header`, or `nav` element."

In addition, the W3C spec adds the recommendation to use the `role="main"` attribute on the `main` element until the `main` element is fully recognized by user agents.

---

[21] http://www.w3.org/html/wg/drafts/html/master/grouping-content.html#the-main-element

[22] https://html.spec.whatwg.org/multipage/semantics.html#the-main-element

Having that knowledge, we're going to adopt the W3C's recommendation, and use only a single `main` element on our page, using an ARIA role as a fallback.

Going back to our *Herald* markup, this is how it will look after we've added the `main` element inside the `body` tag:

```
<body>
  <header>
    ...
  </header>
  <main role="main">

  </main>
  <footer>
    ...
  </footer>
  <script src="js/scripts.js"></script>
</body>
```

As you can see, the `main` element exists outside the `header` and `footer`. Inside the `main` is where we'll put the three columns we discussed, which make up the layout and primary content for *The HTML5 Herald*.

Continuing to Structure *The Herald*

The last part of our layout we'll consider here is the footer, which you can see in *The Herald* screenshot in its traditional location—at the bottom of the page. Because the footer contains a few different chunks of content, each of which forms a self-contained and topically related unit, we've split these out into `section` elements inside the footer. The author information will form one `section`, with each author sitting in their own nested `section`. Then there's another `section` for the copyright and additional information.

Let's add the new elements to our page so that we can see where our document stands:

```
<body>
  <header>
    <nav></nav>
  </header>
```

```
<main role="main">
  <div class="primary">
    <article></article>
  </div>

  <div class="secondary">
    <article></article>
  </div>

  <div class="tertiary">
    <aside>
      <article></article>
    </aside>

    <article>
    </article>

  </div>
</main><!-- main -->

<footer>
  <section id="authors">
    <section></section>
  </section>
  <section id="copyright">
  </section>
</footer>

<script src="js/scripts.js"></script>
</body>
```

Figure 2.2 shows a screenshot that displays our page with some labels indicating the major structural elements we've used.

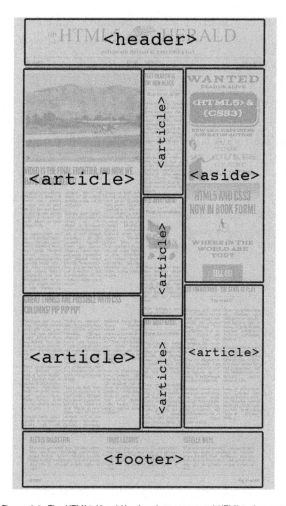

Figure 2.2. *The HTML5 Herald* broken into structural HTML5 elements

We now have a structure that can serve as a solid basis for the content of our website.

What if I use the wrong element?

Although it can be confusing at times to remember which elements to use in which situations, we encourage you to avoid stressing or spending too much time making decisions on semantics. While it is good to be consistent, there are few repercussions from using the wrong elements. If your pages are accessible, that's what is important. Of course, there are cases where the correct semantic element will be beneficial to accessibility, so we encourage you to research this and make sure your choice of element won't cause your pages to become inaccessible. A good place to start might be HTML5 Accessibility[23] or The Accessibility Project.[24]

Wrapping Things Up

That's it for this chapter. We've learned some of the basics of content structure in HTML5, and we've started to build our sample project using the knowledge we've gained.

In the next chapter, we'll have a more in-depth look at HTML5 content, and continue to add semantics to our page when we deal with some of the other elements available in HTML5.

---

[23] http://www.html5accessibility.com/
[24] http://a11yproject.com/

Chapter 3

More HTML5 Semantics

Our sample site is coming along nicely. We've given it some basic structure, along the way learning more about marking up content using HTML5's new elements.

In this chapter, we'll discuss even more new elements, along with some changes and improvements to familiar elements. We'll also add some headings and basic text to our project, and we'll discuss the potential impact of HTML5 on accessibility.

Before we dive into that, though, let's take a step back and examine a few new—and a little tricky—concepts that HTML5 brings to the table.

A New Perspective on Content Types

For layout and styling purposes, developers have become accustomed to thinking of elements in an HTML page as belonging to one of two categories: block and inline. Although elements are still rendered as either block or inline by browsers, the HTML5 spec takes the categorization of content a step further. The specification now defines a set of more granular content models. These are broad definitions about the kind of content that should be found inside a given element. Most of the time they'll have little impact on the way you write your markup, but it's worth having a passing familiarity with them, so let's have a quick look:

- **Metadata content**: This category is what it sounds like—data that's not present on the page itself, but affects the page's presentation or includes other information *about* the page. This includes elements such as `title`, `link`, `meta`, and `style`.

- **Flow content**: This includes just about every element that's used in the body of an HTML document, including elements such as `header`, `footer`, and even `p`. The only elements *excluded* are those that have no effect on the document's flow: `script`, `link`, and `meta` elements in the page's `head`, for example.

- **Sectioning content**: This is the most interesting—and for our purposes, most relevant—type of content in HTML5. In the last chapter, we often found ourselves using the generic term "section" to refer to a block of content that could contain a heading, footer, or aside. In fact, what we were actually referring to was sectioning content. In HTML5, this includes `article`, `aside`, `nav`, and `section`. Shortly, we'll talk in more detail about sectioning content and how it can affect the way you write your markup.

- **Heading content**: This type of content defines the header of a given section, and includes the various levels of heading (`h1`, `h2`, and so on).

- **Phrasing content**: This category is roughly the equivalent to what you're used to thinking of as *inline* content; it includes elements such as `em`, `strong`, `cite`, and the like.

- **Embedded content**: This one's fairly straightforward, and includes elements that are, well, *embedded* into a page, such as `img`, `object`, `embed`, `video`, and `canvas`.

- **Interactive content**: This category includes any content with which users can interact. It consists mainly of form elements, as well as links and other elements that are interactive only when certain attributes are present. Two examples include the `audio` element when the `controls` attribute is present, and the `input` element with a `type` attribute set to anything but `"hidden"`.

As you might gather from reading the list, some elements can belong to more than one category. There are also some elements that fail to fit into *any* category (for example, the `head` and `html` elements). Don't worry if any of this seems confusing.

The truth is, as a developer, you won't need to think about these categories in order to decide which element to use in which circumstance. More than anything, they're simply a way to encapsulate the different kinds of HTML tags available.

The Document Outline

In the previous edition of this book, we described in detail a new feature called the "document outline." The purpose of this feature is to allow browsers to create page hierarchy by means of sectioning content elements instead of headings (h1 through to h6) as is done now; however, the spec gives the following warning regarding the document outline:

> "There are currently no known implementations of the outline algorithm in graphical browsers or assistive technology user agents, although the algorithm is implemented in other software such as conformance checkers. Therefore the outline algorithm cannot be relied upon to convey document structure to users. Authors are advised to use heading rank (h1-h6) to convey document structure."

If you'd like to research the document outline algorithm on your own, you can visit the W3C's website.[1] But because there is no practical use for the outline algorithm as of this writing, we'll avoid delving into it here.

No More hgroup

Now that we have a solid handle on HTML5's content types and document outlines, it's time to dive back into *The HTML5 Herald* and add some headings to our newspaper's articles.

For brevity, we'll deal with each part individually. Let's add a title and subtitle to our header, just above the navigation:

```
<header>
  <hgroup>
    <h1>The HTML5 Herald</h1>
    <h2>Produced With That Good Ol' Timey HTML5 &amp; CSS3</h2>
  </hgroup>
```

---

[1] http://www.w3.org/html/wg/drafts/html/master/sections.html#outlines

```
    <nav>
    ⋮
    </nav>

</header>
```

But wait! This is the wrong markup. In fact, this is the markup we used for our title and tagline in the previous edition of this book. But things have changed.

You'll notice we introduced three elements into our markup: the title of the website, which is marked up with the customary h1 element; a tagline immediately below the primary page title, marked up with h2; and a new element that wraps our title and tagline, the hgroup element.

The hgroup element was originally introduced in HTML5 to help prevent problems occurring in the document outline. Unfortunately, although some people liked the element, browser makers and screen readers stopped short of implementing it in any beneficial way, so it has been officially dropped from the W3C's version of the HTML5 specification.

Oddly, the WHATWG's version of the specification still includes hgroup[2], so you might still consider using it if you wish. In our case, we're going to favor the W3C's take on this element and refrain from using it to group our headings like we did in the previous code snippet. Instead, we'll do this:

```
<h1>HTML5 Herald
  <span class="tagline">Produced With That Good Ol' Timey HTML5
↪&amp; CSS3</span>
</h1>
```

That's how the W3C recommends you group headings and subheadings or taglines now, with the absence of hgroup. The goal here is to ensure that the structure you use doesn't mess in a detrimental way with the document outline.

---

[2] https://developers.whatwg.org/sections.html#the-hgroup-element

More New Elements

In addition to the structural elements we saw in Chapter 2 and the now defunct hgroup, HTML5 includes a number of other semantic elements. Let's examine some of the more useful ones.

The `figure` and `figcaption` Elements

The `figure` and `figcaption` elements are another pair of new HTML5 elements that contribute to the improved semantics in HTML5. The `figure` element is explained in the spec[3] as follows:

> The `figure` element can [...] be used to annotate illustrations, diagrams, photos, code listings, etc. [...] A `figure` element's contents are part of the surrounding flow.

Think of charts, graphs, images to accompany text, or example code. All those types of content might be good places to use `figure` and potentially `figcaption`.

The `figcaption element` is simply a way to mark up a caption for a piece of content that appears inside of a `figure`.

In order to use the `figure` element, the content being placed inside it must have some relation to the main content in which the figure appears. If you can completely remove it from a document, and the document's content can still be fully understood, you probably shouldn't be using `figure`; you might, however, need to use `aside` or an alternative.

Let's look at how we'd mark up a `figure` inside an `article`:

```
<article>
  <h1>Accessible Web Apps</h1>

  <p>Lorem ipsum dolor … </p>

  <p>As you can see in <a href="#fig1">Figure 1</a>,

  <figure id="fig1">
    <figcaption>Screen Reader Support for WAI-ARIA</figcaption>
```

---

[3] http://www.w3.org/TR/2011/WD-html5-author-20110809/the-figure-element.html

```
    <img src="figure1.png" alt="JAWS: Landmarks 1/1, Forms 4/5 … ">
  </figure>

  <p>Lorem ipsum dolor … </p>
</article>
```

Using `figcaption` is fairly straightforward. It has to be inside a `figure` element and it can be placed either before or after the `figcaption` content. In the example here, we've placed it before the image.

The mark Element

The `mark` element "represents a run of text in one document marked or highlighted for reference purposes, due to its relevance in another context." Admittedly, there are very few uses we can think of for the `mark` element. The most common is in the context of a search, where the keywords that were searched for are highlighted in the results.

The spec also mentions using `mark` to draw attention to text inside a quote. In any case, you want to use it to indicate "a part of the document that has been highlighted due to its likely relevance to the user's current activity".

Avoid confusing `mark` with `em` or `strong`; those elements add contextual importance, whereas mark separates the targeted content based on a user's current browsing or search activity.

To use the search example, if a user has arrived at an article on your site from a Google search for the word "HTML5," you might highlight words in the article using the `mark` element like this:

```
<h1>Yes, You Can Use <mark>HTML5</mark> Today!</h1>
```

The `mark` element can be added to the document either using server-side code, or on the client side with JavaScript after the page has loaded. Search content, for example, can be derived from a URL using `search.php?query=html5`, for example. In that case, your server-side code might grab the content of the variable in the query string, and then use `mark` tags to indicate where the word is found on the page.

The progress and meter Elements

Two new elements added in HTML5 allow for marking up of data that's being measured or gauged in some way. The difference between them is fairly subtle: progress is used to describe the current status of a changing process that's headed for completion, regardless of whether the completion state is defined. The traditional progress bar indicating download progress is a perfect example of this.

The meter element, meanwhile, represents an element whose range is known, meaning it has definite minimum and maximum values. The spec gives the examples of disk usage, or a fraction of a voting population—both of which have a definite maximum value. Therefore, it's likely you would avoid using meter to indicate an age, height, or weight—all of which normally have unknown maximum values.

Let's look in more detail at progress. The progress element can have a max attribute to indicate the point at which the task will be complete, and a value attribute to indicate the task's status. Both of these attributes are optional. Here's an example:

```
<h1>Your Task is in Progress</h1>
<p>Status: <progress max="100" value="0"><span>0</span>% </progress>
➡</p>
```

This element would best be used with JavaScript to dynamically change the value of the percentage as the task progresses. You'll notice that the code includes span tags, isolating the number value; this facilitates targeting the number directly from your script when you need to update it.

The meter element has six associated attributes. In addition to max and value, it also allows use of min, high, low, and optimum.

The min and max attributes reference the lower and upper boundaries of the range, while value indicates the current specified measurement. The high and low attributes indicate thresholds for what is considered "high" or "low" in the context. For example, your grade on a test can range from 0% (min) to 100% (max), but anything below 60% is considered low and anything above 85% is considered high. The optimum attribute refers to the ideal value. In the case of a test score, the value of optimum would be 100.

Here's an example of meter, using the premise of disk usage:

```
<p>Total current disk usage: <meter value="130" min="0" max="320"
➥low="10" high="300" title="gigabytes">63 GB</meter></p>
```

In Figure 3.1, you can see how the meter element looks by default in Chrome and Firefox.

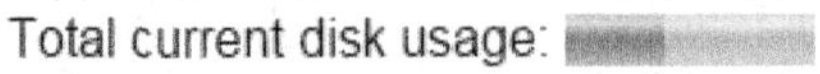

Total current disk usage: ▓▓▓▓▓▓

Figure 3.1. The meter element in Chrome and Firefox

For better accessibility, when using either progress or meter, you're encouraged to include the value as text content inside the element. So if you're using JavaScript to adjust the current state of the value attribute, you should change the text content to match.

The time Element

Dates and times are invaluable components of web pages. Search engines are able to filter results based on time, and in some cases, a specific search result can receive more or less weight by a search algorithm depending on when it was first published.

The time element has been specifically designed to deal with the problem of humans reading dates and times differently from machines. Take the following example:

```
<p>We'll be getting together for our next developer conference on 12
➥ October of this year.</p>
```

While humans reading this paragraph would likely understand when the event will take place, it would be less clear to a machine attempting to parse the information.

Here's the same paragraph with the time element introduced:

```
<p>We'll be getting together for our next developer conference on
➥<time datetime="2015-10-12">12 October of this year</time>.</p>
```

The time element also allows you to express dates and times in whichever format you like while retaining an unambiguous representation of the date and time behind the scenes, in the datetime attribute. This value could then be converted into a localized or preferred form using JavaScript, or by the browser itself (although no browsers at the time of writing support this behavior).

In earlier versions of the spec, the `time` element allowed use of the `pubdate` attribute. This was a Boolean attribute, indicating that the content within the closest ancestor `article` element was published on the specified date. If there was no `article` element, the `pubdate` attribute would apply to the entire document. But this attribute has been removed from the spec, even though it did seem to be useful. In his in-depth article on the `time` element,[4] Aurelio De Rosa provides an alternative for the now dropped `pubdate` attribute, if you want to look at another method for achieving this.

The `time` element has some associated rules and guidelines:

- You should not use `time` to encode unspecified dates or times (for example, "during the ice age" or "last winter"; this is because the `time` element does not allow for ranges).

- The date represented cannot be "BC" or "BCE" (before the common era); it must be a date on the Gregorian Calendar.

- If the `time` element lacks a valid `datetime` attribute, the element's text content (whatever appears between the opening and closing `time` tags) needs to be a valid `datetime` value.

Here's a chunk of HTML that includes many of the different ways to write a `datetime` value according to the spec:

```
<!-- month -->
<time>2015-11</time>

<!-- date -->
<time>2015-11-12</time>

<!-- yearless date -->
<time>11-12</time>

<!-- time -->
<time>14:54:39</time>
```

---

[4] http://www.sitepoint.com/html5-time-element-guide/

```
<!-- floating date and time -->
<time>2015-11-12T14:54:39</time>

<!-- time-zone offset -->
<time>-0800</time>

<!-- global date and time -->
<time>2015-11-12T06:54:39.929-0800</time>

<!-- week -->
<time>2015-W46</time>

<!-- duration -->
<time>4h 18m 3s</time>
```

The uses for the time element are endless: calendar events, publication dates (for blog posts, videos, press releases, and so forth), historic dates, transaction records, article or content updates, and much more.

Changes to Existing Features

While new elements and APIs have been the primary focus of HTML5, this latest iteration of web markup has also brought with it changes to existing elements. For the most part, any changes made have been done with backwards-compatibility in mind, to ensure that the markup of existing content is still usable.

We've already considered some of the changes (the doctype declaration, character encoding, and content types, for example). Let's look at other significant changes introduced in the HTML5 spec.

The Word "Deprecated" is Deprecated

In previous versions of HTML and XHTML, elements that were no longer recommended for use (and so removed from the spec), were considered "deprecated." In HTML5, there is no longer any such thing as a deprecated element; the term now used is "obsolete."

Obsolete elements fall into two basic categories: "conforming" obsolete features and "non-conforming" obsolete features. Conforming features will provide warnings in the validator, but will still be supported by browsers. So you are permitted to use them but their use is best avoided.

Non-conforming features, on the other hand, are considered fully obsolete and should not be used. They will produce errors in the validator.

The W3C has a description of these features, with examples.[5]

Block Elements Inside Links

Although most browsers handled this situation well in the past, it was never actually valid to place a block-level element (such as a `div`) inside an a element. Instead, to produce valid HTML, you'd have to use multiple a elements and style the group to appear as a single block.

In HTML5, you're now permitted to wrap almost anything in an a element without having to worry about validation errors. The only block content you're unable to wrap with an a element are other interactive elements such as form elements, buttons, and other a elements.

Bold Text

A few changes have been made in the way that bold text is semantically defined in HTML5. There are essentially two ways to make text bold in most browsers: by using the b element, or the `strong` element.

Although the b element was never deprecated, before HTML5 it was discouraged in favor of `strong`. The b element previously was a way of saying "make this text appear in boldface." Since HTML is supposed to be all about the meaning of the content, leaving the presentation to CSS, this was unsatisfactory.

According to the spec[6], in HTML5, the b element has been redefined to represent a section of text "to which attention is being drawn for utilitarian purposes without conveying any extra importance and with no implication of an alternate voice or mood." Examples given are key words in a document abstract, product names in a review, actionable words in interactive text-driven software, or an article lede.

---

[5] http://www.w3.org/html/wg/drafts/html/master/obsolete.html
[6] http://dev.w3.org/html5/spec-preview/the-b-element.html

The `strong` element, meanwhile, still conveys more or less the same meaning. In HTML5, it represents "strong importance, seriousness, or urgency for its contents." Interestingly, the HTML5 spec allows for nesting of `strong` elements. So, if an entire sentence consisted of an important warning, but certain words were of even greater significance, the sentence could be wrapped in one `strong` element, and each important word could be wrapped in its own nested `strong`.

Italicized Text

Along with modifications to the `b` and `strong` elements, changes have been made in the way the `i` element is defined in HTML5.

Previously, the `i` element was used to simply render italicized text. As with `b`, this definition was unsatisfactory. In HTML5, the definition has been updated to "a span of text in an alternate voice or mood, or otherwise offset from the normal prose in a manner indicating a different quality of text." So the appearance of the text has nothing to do with the semantic meaning, although it may very well still be italic—that's up to you.

An example of content that can be offset using `i` tags might be an idiomatic phrase from another language, such as *reductio ad absurdum*, a latin phrase meaning "reduction to the point of absurdity." Other examples could be text representing a dream sequence in a piece of fiction, or the scientific name of a species in a journal article.

The `em` element is unchanged, but its definition has been expanded to clarify its use. It still refers to text that's emphasized, as would be the case colloquially. For example, the following two phrases have the exact same wording, but their meanings change because of the different use of `em`:

```
<p>Harry's Grill is the best <em>burger</em> joint in town.</p>
<p>Harry's Grill <em>is</em> the best burger joint in town.</p>
```

In the first sentence, because the word "burger" is emphasized, the meaning of the sentence focuses on the type of "joint" being discussed. In the second sentence, the emphasis is on the word "is," thus moving the sentence focus to the question of whether Harry's Grill really is the best of all burger joints in town.

Neither i nor em should be used to mark up a publication title; instead, you should use cite.

Of all the four elements discussed here (b, i, em, and strong), the only one that gives contextual importance to its content is the strong element.

Big and Small Text

The big element was previously used to represent text displayed in a large font. The big element is now a non-conforming obsolete feature and should not be used. The small element, however, is still valid but has a different meaning.

Previously, small was intended to describe "text in a small font." In HTML5, it represents "side comments such as small print." Some examples where small might be used include information in footer text, fine print, and terms and conditions. The small element should only be used for short runs of text. So you wouldn't use small to mark up the body of an entire "terms of use" page.

Although the presentational implications of small have been removed from the definition, text inside small tags will more than likely still appear in a smaller font than the rest of the document.

For example, the footer of *The HTML5 Herald* includes a copyright notice. Since this is essentially legal fine print, it's perfect for the small element:

```
<small>&copy; SitePoint Pty. Ltd.</small>
```

A cite for Sore Eyes

The cite element was initially redefined in HTML5 accompanied by some controversy. In HTML4, the cite element represented "a citation or a reference to other sources." Within the scope of that definition, the spec permitted a person's name to be marked up with cite (in the case of a quotation attributed to an individual, for example).

The earlier versions of the HTML5 spec forbade the use of cite for a person's name, seemingly going against the principle of backwards compatibility. Now the spec has gone back to a more similar definition to the original one, defining cite as "a reference to a creative work. It must include the title of the work or the name of the author (person, people, or organization) or a URL reference, or a reference in abbreviated form."

Here's an example, taken from the spec:

```
<p>In the words of <cite>Charles Bukowski</cite> -
<q>An intellectual says a simple thing in a hard way. An artist says
➥a hard thing in a simple way.</q></p>
```

Description (not Definition) Lists

The existing dl (definition list) element, along with its associated dt (term) and dd (description) children, has been redefined in the HTML5 spec. Previously, in addition to terms and definitions, the spec allowed the dl element to mark up dialogue, but the spec now prohibits this.

In HTML5, these lists are no longer called "definition lists"; they're now the more generic-sounding "description lists" or "association lists." They should be used to mark up any kind of name-value pairs, including terms and definitions, metadata topics and values, and questions and answers.

Here's an example using CSS terms and their definitions:

```
<dl>
  <dt>Selector:</dt>
  <dd>The element(s) targeted.</dd>
  <dt>Property:</dt>
  <dd>The feature used to add styling to the targeted element,
➥defined before a colon.</dd>
  <dt>Value:</dt>
  <dd>The value given to the specified property, declared after the
➥colon.</dd>
</dl>
```

Other New Elements and Features

We've introduced you to and expounded on some of the more practical new elements and features. In this section, let's touch on lesser-known elements, attributes, and features that have been added to the HTML5 spec.

The **details** Element

This new element helps mark up a part of the document that's hidden, but can be expanded to reveal additional information. The aim of the element is to provide native support for a feature common on the Web—a collapsible box that has a title, and more info or functionality hidden away.

Normally this kind of widget is created using a combination of HTML and JavaScript. The inclusion of it in HTML5 removes the scripting requirements and simplifies its implementation for web authors, thus contributing to decreased page load times.

Here's how it might look when marked up:

```
<details>
  <summary>Some Magazines of Note</summary>
  <ul>
    <li><cite>Bird Watcher's Digest</cite></li>
    <li><cite>Rower's Weekly</cite></li>
    <li><cite>Fishing Monthly</cite></li>
  </ul>
</details>
```

In the example, the contents of the summary element will appear to the user, but the rest of the content will be hidden. Upon clicking summary, the hidden content appears.

If details lacks a defined summary, the browser will define a default summary (for example, "Details"). If you want the hidden content to be visible by default, you can use the Boolean open attribute on the details element.

The summary element can be used only as a child of details, and it must be the first child if used.

As of this writing, details lacks complete browser support (IE and Firefox don't support it), but it's improving. To fill the gaps, a couple of JavaScript-based polyfills are available, including a jQuery version by Mathias Bynens[7] and a vanilla JavaScript version by Maksim Chemerisuk.[8]

---

[7] http://mathiasbynens.be/notes/html5-details-jquery
[8] https://github.com/chemerisuk/better-details-polyfill

Customized Ordered Lists

Ordered lists, marked up using the ol element, are quite common in web pages. HTML5 introduces a new Boolean attribute called reversed so that when present, it reverses the numbers on the list items, allowing you to display lists in descending order. Additionally, HTML5 has brought back the start attribute, deprecated in HTML4. The start attribute lets you specify with which number your list should begin.

Support is good for both reversed and start. As of this writing, Internet Explorer is the only browser without support for reverse-ordered lists. If you want a polyfill, you can use a script by one of the book's authors.[9]

Scoped Styles

In HTML5, the style element, used for embedding styles directly in your pages (as opposed to referencing a linked stylesheet), allows use of a Boolean attribute called scoped. Take the following code example:

```
<h1>Page Title</h1>
<article>
  <style scoped>
    h1 {
      color: blue;
    }
  </style>
  <h1>Article Title</h1>
  <p>Article content.</p>
</article>
```

Because the scoped attribute is present, the styles declared inside the style element will apply only to the parent element and its children (if cascading rules permit), instead of the entire document. This allows specific sections inside documents (such as the article element in this example) to be easily portable along with their associated styles.

This is certainly a handy new feature, but it's likely going to take some time for it to be implemented in all browsers. The only browser that currently supports scoped

---

[9] https://github.com/impressivewebs/HTML5-Reverse-Ordered-Lists

styles is Firefox. Chrome previously supported it, but it was removed due to "high code complexity.[10]" And at the time of writing, the IE team has no immediate plans to add this feature.[11]

The `async` Attribute for Scripts

The `script` element now allows the use of the `async` attribute, which is similar to the existing `defer` attribute. Using `defer` specifies that the browser should wait until the page's markup is parsed before loading the script. The new `async` attribute allows you to specify that a script should load asynchronously. This means it should load as soon as it's available, without causing other elements on the page to delay while it loads. Both `defer` and `async` are Boolean attributes.

These attributes must only be used when the `script` element defines an external file. For legacy browsers, you can include both `async` and `defer` to ensure that one or the other is used, if necessary. In practice, both attributes will have the effect of not pausing the browser's rendering of the page while scripts are downloaded; however, `async` can often be more advantageous, as it will load the script in the background while other rendering tasks are taking place, and execute the script as soon as it's available.

The `async` attribute is particularly useful if the script you're loading has no other dependencies, and if it benefits the user experience for the script to be loaded as soon as possible, rather than after the page loads. It should also be noted, however, that if you have a page that loads multiple scripts, the `defer` attribute ensures that they're loaded in the order in which they appear, while there's no guaranteeing the order with `async`.

The `picture` element

One of the most recent additions to the HTML5 spec is the `picture` element, which is intended to help with responsive web design, specifically responsive images. `picture` lets you define multiple image sources. This allows users on mobile browsers to download a low-res version of the image, while offering a larger version for tablets and desktops.

---

[10] https://www.chromestatus.com/features/5374137958662144

[11] https://status.modern.ie/scopedstyles

The `picture` element has its accompanying `source` elements (which are also used for `video` and `audio` elements, as described in Chapter 5), in addition to some new attributes such as `srcset` and `sizes`. These two attributes can be used on `picture`, `img`, and `source`.

For a good discussion of the way these new features are used in responsive image implementations, see this excellent article by Eric Portis on *A List Apart*.[12]

Other Notables

Here are some further new HTML5 features you'll want to look at using, each with varying levels of browser support:

- The `dialog` element, which represents "a part of an application that a user interacts with to perform a task; for example, a dialog box, inspector, or window."

- The `download` attribute for a elements, used to indicate that the targeted resource should be downloaded rather than navigated to (useful for PDFs, for example).

- The `sandbox` and `seamless` attributes for `iframe` elements. `sandbox` lets you run an external page with restrictions and the `seamless` attribute integrates the `iframe` content more closely with the parent document, adopting its styles more seamlessly.

- The `menu` element and its `menuitem` child elements, which allow you to create a list of interactive commands. For example, you can mark up an **Edit** menu with options for **Copy**, **Cut**, and **Paste**, adding scripting functionality as needed.

- The `address` element, which lets you mark up contact information applying to the nearest `article` or `body` element.

There are other new elements not discussed here, simply because of lack of space. Be sure to check out the specs from time to time to see if anything new has been added or changed.[13]

---

[12] http://alistapart.com/article/responsive-images-in-practice
[13] http://www.w3.org/html/wg/drafts/html/master/

The Future of Markup — Web Components?

In the last year or so a new specification called "Web Components", initiated by engineers working on Google's Chrome browser, has gained a lot of traction in the industry with already some significant browser support. In brief, Web Components are divided into four main sections, summarized briefly here.

Custom Elements   Custom elements[14] allow developers to define their own DOM elements with a custom API. These elements and their associated scripts and styling are meant to be easily portable and reusable as encapsulated components.

Shadow DOM   Shadow DOM[15] allows you to define a sort of hidden sub-tree of DOM nodes that exists in its own namespace, inside a custom element. This encapsulates the sub-tree to prevent naming collisions, allowing the entire node tree to be portable along with the custom element.

HTML Imports   The HTML Imports[16] feature is a way to include and reuse HTML documents inside of other HTML documents, similar to how you might use "include" files in PHP. Imports are included by means of HTML's `<link>` tag, which is commonly used to embed external CSS.

HTML Templates   Finally, there's the new template tag[17]. This new element is part of an answer to a popular trend in front-end development called client-side templating. The template element itself does nothing, but it's used in conjunction with some scripting to allow predefined document fragments to be inserted into the document whenever they're needed.

Many expect that Web Components — in particular, Custom Elements — are the future of web markup and scripting. But time will tell. Web Components go pretty

---

[14] http://w3c.github.io/webcomponents/spec/custom/

[15] http://w3c.github.io/webcomponents/spec/shadow/

[16] http://w3c.github.io/webcomponents/spec/imports/

[17] http://www.w3.org/html/wg/drafts/html/master/#the-template-element

deep; we could probably write an entire book on the topic! If you want to read more, check out the spec links referenced above or the sources listed below:

- WebComponents.org[18]

- Polymer[19] (A Custom Elements polyfill)

- An Introduction to Web Components and Polymer[20] by Pankaj Parashar

- Intro to Shadow DOM[21] by Agraj Mangal

- HTML's New Template Tag[22] by Eric Bidelman

- An Introduction to HTML Imports[23] by Armando Roggio

Validating HTML5 Documents

In Chapter 2, we introduced you to a number of syntax changes in HTML5, and touched on some issues related to validation. Let's expand upon those concepts a little more so that you can better understand how validating pages has changed.

The HTML5 validator is no longer concerned with code style. You can use uppercase or lowercase, omit quotes from attributes, exclude optional closing tags, and be as inconsistent as you like, and your page will still be valid.

So, you ask, what *does* count as an error for the HTML5 validator? It will alert you to the incorrect use of elements, elements included where they shouldn't be, missing required attributes, incorrect attribute values, and the like. In short, the validator will let you know if your markup conflicts with the specification, so it's still a valuable tool when developing your pages.

To give you a good idea of how HTML5 differs from the overly strict XHTML, let's go through some specifics. This way, you can understand what is considered valid in HTML5:

---

[18] http://webcomponents.org/

[19] https://www.polymer-project.org/

[20] http://www.sitepoint.com/introduction-to-web-components-and-polymer-tutorial/

[21] http://code.tutsplus.com/tutorials/intro-to-shadow-dom--net-34966

[22] http://www.html5rocks.com/en/tutorials/webcomponents/template/

[23] http://www.sitepoint.com/introduction-html-imports-tutorial/

- Some elements that were required in XHTML-based syntax are no longer required for a document to pass HTML5 validation; examples include the html and body elements. This happens because even if you exclude them, the browser will automatically include them in the document for you.

- Void elements (that is, elements without a corresponding closing tag or without any content) aren't required to be closed using a closing slash; examples include meta and br.

- Elements and attributes can be in uppercase, lowercase, or mixed case.

- Quotes are unnecessary around attribute values. The exceptions are when multiple space-delimited values are used, or a URL appears as a value and contains a query string with an equals (=) character in it.

- Some attributes that were required in XHTML-based syntax are no longer required in HTML5. Examples include the type attribute for script elements, and the xmlns attribute for the html element.

- Some elements that were deprecated and thus invalid in XHTML are now valid; one example is the embed element.

- Stray text that doesn't appear inside any element but is placed directly inside the body element would invalidate an XHTML document; this is not the case in HTML5.

- Some elements that had to be closed in XHTML can be left open without causing validation errors in HTML5; examples include p, li, and dt.

- The form element isn't required to have an action attribute.

- Form elements, such as input, can be placed as direct children of the form element; in XHTML, another element (such as fieldset or div) was required to wrap form elements.

- textarea elements are not required to have rows and cols attributes.

- The target attribute for links was previously deprecated in XHTML. It's now valid in HTML5.

- As discussed earlier in this chapter, block-level elements can be placed inside link (a) elements.

- The ampersand character (&) doesn't need to be encoded as & if it appears as text on the page.

That's a fairly comprehensive, though hardly exhaustive, list of differences between XHTML strict and HTML5 validation. Some are style choices, so you're encouraged to choose a style and be consistent. We outlined some preferred style choices in the previous chapter, and you're welcome to incorporate those suggestions in your own HTML5 projects.

Stricter Validation Tools

If you want to validate your markup's syntax style using stricter guidelines, there are tools available that can help you. One such tool is Philip Walton's HTML Inspector.[24] To use it, you can include the script in your pages during the development phase, then open your browser's JavaScript console in the developer tools and run the command `HTMLInspector.inspect()`. This will display a number of warnings and recommendations right inside the console on how to improve your markup. HTML Inspector also lets you change the configuration to customize the tool to your own needs.

Summary

By now, we've gotten our heads around just about all the new semantic and syntactic changes in HTML5. Some of this information may be a little hard to digest straight away, but don't worry! The best way to become familiar with HTML5 is to use it—start with your next project. Try using some of the structural elements we covered in the last chapter, or some of the text-level semantics we saw in this chapter. If you're unsure about how an element is meant to be used, go back and read the section about it, or better yet, read the specification itself. While the language is certainly drier than the text in this book (at least, we hope it is!), the specs can provide a more complete picture of how a given element is intended to be used. Remember that the HTML5 specification is still in development, so some of what we've covered is still subject to change in the new HTML5.1 version (or in the HTML5 "living

---

[24] https://github.com/philipwalton/html-inspector

standard," if you go by the WHATWG's definition). The specifications will always contain the most up-to-date information.

In the next chapter, we'll look at a crucial segment of new functionality introduced in HTML5: forms and form-related features.

HTML5 Forms

We've coded most of the page, and you now know almost all of what there is to know about new HTML5 elements and their semantics. But before we start work on the *look* of the site—which we do in Chapter 6—we'll take a quick detour away from *The HTML5 Herald*'s front page to look at the sign-up page. This will illustrate what HTML5 has to offer in terms of web forms.

HTML5 web forms have introduced new form elements, input types, attributes, native validation, and other form features. Many of these features we've been using in our interfaces for years: form validation, combo boxes, placeholder text, and the like. The difference is that before we had to resort to JavaScript to create these behaviors; now they're available directly in the browser. All you need to do is include attributes in your markup to make them available.

HTML5 not only makes marking up forms easier on the developer, it's also better for the user. With client-side validation being handled natively by the browser, there will be greater consistency across different sites, and many pages will load faster without all that redundant JavaScript.

Let's dive in!

Dependable Tools in Our Toolbox

Forms are often the last thing developers include in their pages—many developers find forms just plain boring. The good news is HTML5 injects a little bit more joy into coding forms. By the end of this chapter, we hope you'll look forward to employing form elements as appropriate in your markup.

Let's start off our sign-up form with plain old-fashioned HTML:

```
<form id="register" method="post">
  <header>
    <h1>Sign Me Up!</h1>
    <p>I would like to receive your fine publication.</p>
  </header>

  <ul>
    <li>
      <label for="register-name">My name is:</label>
      <input type="text" id="register-name" name="name">
    </li>
    <li>
      <label for="address">My email address is:</label>
      <input type="text" id="address" name="address">
    </li>
    <li>
      <label for="url">My website is located at:</label>
      <input type="text" id="url" name="url">
    </li>
    <li>
      <label for="password">I would like my password to be:</label>
      <p>(at least 6 characters, no spaces)</p>
      <input type="password" id="password" name="password">
    </li>
    <li>
      <label for="rating">On a scale of 1 to 10, my knowledge of
➥HTML5 is:</label>
      <input type="text" name="rating" id="rating">
    </li>
    <li>
      <label for="startdate">Please start my subscription on:
➥</label>
      <input type="text" id="startdate" name="startdate">
    </li>
    <li>
```

```
      <label for="quantity">I would like to receive <input
➥type="text" name="quantity" id="quantity"> copies of <cite>
➥The HTML5 Herald</cite>.</label>
    </li>
    <li>
      <label for="upsell">Also sign me up for <cite>The CSS3
➥Chronicle</cite></label>
      <input type="checkbox" id="upsell" name="upsell" value="CSS
➥Chronicle">
    </li>
    <li>
      <input type="submit" id="register-submit" value="Send Post
➥Haste">
    </li>
  </ul>
</form>
```

This sample registration form uses form elements that have been available since the earliest versions of HTML. This form provides clues to users about what type of data is expected in each field via the label and p elements, so even your users on Netscape 4.7 and IE5 (kidding!) can understand the form. It works, but it can certainly be improved upon.

In this chapter we're going to enhance this form to include HTML5 form features. HTML5 provides new input types specific to email addresses, URLs, numbers, dates, and more. In addition to these, HTML5 introduces attributes that can be used with both new and existing input types. These allow you to provide placeholder text, mark fields as required, and declare what type of data is acceptable—all without JavaScript.

We'll cover all the newly added input types later in the chapter. Before we do that, let's look at the new form attributes HTML5 provides.

HTML5 Form Attributes

For years, developers have written (or copied and pasted) snippets of JavaScript to validate the information users entered into form fields: what elements are required, what type of data is accepted, and so on. HTML5 provides us with several attributes that allow us to dictate what is an acceptable value and inform the user of errors, all without the use of any JavaScript.

Browsers that support these HTML5 attributes will compare data entered by the user against the attribute values, such as regular expression patterns provided by the developer (you). They check to see if all required fields are indeed filled out, enable multiple values if allowed, and so on. Even better, including these attributes won't harm older browsers; they simply ignore the attributes they're unable to understand. In fact, you can use these attributes and their values to power your scripting fallbacks instead of hardcoding validation patterns into your JavaScript code or adding superfluous classes to your markup. We'll look at how this is done later; for now, let's go through some of the new attributes.

The `required` Attribute

The Boolean `required` attribute tells the browser to only submit the form if the field in question is filled out. Obviously, this means that the field can't be left empty, but it also means that, depending on other attributes or the field's type, only certain types of values will be accepted. Later in the chapter, we'll be covering different ways of letting browsers know what kind of data is expected in a form.

If a required field is empty the form will fail to submit. Opera, Firefox, Internet Explorer 10+, and Chrome provide the user with error messages; for example, "Please fill out this field" or "You have to specify a value" if left empty.

Time to Focus

Time for a quick refresher: a form element is focused either when users click on the field with their mouse, tap into the field with their finger on a touch device, tab to it with their keyboard, or click or touches the label associated with that form element. For input elements, typing with the keyboard will enter data into that element.

In JavaScript `focus` event terminology, the `focus` event will fire on a form element when it receives focus, and the `blur` event will fire when it *loses* focus.

In CSS, the `:focus` pseudo-class can be used to style elements that currently have focus.

The `required` attribute is valid on any input type except `button`, `submit`, `image`, `range`, `color`, and `hidden`, all of which generally have a default value so the attribute would be redundant. As with other Boolean attributes we've seen so far, the syntax is either simply `required`, or `required="required"` if you're using XHTML syntax.

Let's add the `required` attribute to our sign-up form. We'll make the name, email address, password, and subscription start date fields required:

```
<ul>
  <li>
    <label for="register-name">My name is:</label>
    <input type="text" id="register-name" name="name" required aria-
➥required="true">
  </li>
  <li>
    <label for="email">My email address is:</label>
    <input type="text" id="email" name="email" required aria-
➥required="true">
  </li>
  <li>
    <label for="url">My website is located at:</label>
    <input type="text" id="url" name="url">
  </li>
  <li>
    <label for="password">I would like my password to be:</label>
    <p>(at least 6 characters, no spaces)</p>
    <input type="password" id="password" name="password" required
➥aria-required="true">
  </li>
  <li>
    <label for="rating">On a scale of 1 to 10, my knowledge of
➥HTML5 is:</label>
    <input type="text" name="rating" type="range">
  </li>
  <li>
    <label for="startdate">Please start my subscription on:
➥</label>
    <input type="text" id="startdate" name="startdate" required aria
➥-required="true">
  </li>
  <li>
    <label for="quantity">I would like to receive <input
➥type="text" name="quantity" id="quantity"> copies of <cite>
➥The HTML5 Herald</cite></label>
  </li>
  <li>
    <label for="upsell">Also sign me up for <cite>The CSS3
➥Chronicle</cite></label>
    <input type="checkbox" id="upsell" name="upsell"
➥value="CSS Chronicle">
```

```
   </li>
   <li>
     <input type="submit" id="register-submit" value="Send Post
➥Haste">
   </li>
</ul>
```

 Improving Accessibility

You can include the WAI-ARIA attribute `aria-required="true"` for improved accessibility; however, as most browsers and screen readers now natively support the `required` attribute, this will soon by unnecessary. See Appendix B for a brief introduction to WAI-ARIA.

Figure 4.1, Figure 4.2, and Figure 4.3 show the behavior of the `required` attribute when you attempt to submit the form.

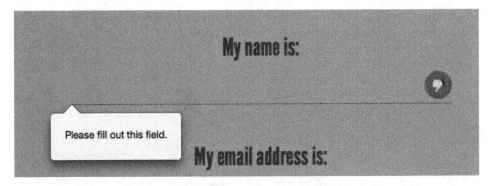

Figure 4.1. The required field validation message in Firefox

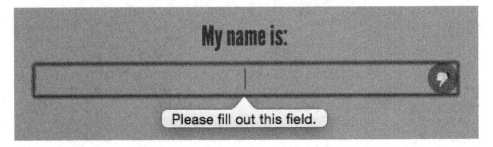

Figure 4.2. How it looks in Opera ...

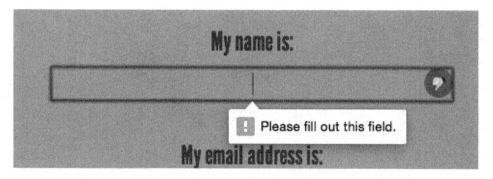

Figure 4.3. ... and in Google Chrome

Styling Required Form Fields

You can style required form elements with the :required pseudo-class, and optional form elements with the :optional pseudo-class (or use the negation pseudo-class :not(:required)). You can also style valid and invalid fields with the :valid and :invalid pseudo-classes respectively. With these pseudo-classes and a little CSS magic, you provide visual cues to sighted users indicating which fields are required, and give feedback for successful data entry:

```
input {
  background-position: 0% 50%;
  background-repeat: no-repeat;
  padding-left: 15px;
}
input:required {
  background-image: url('../images/required.png');
}
input:focus:invalid {
  background-image: url('../images/invalid.png');
}
input:focus:valid {
  background-image: url('../images/valid.png');
}
```

We're adding a background image (an asterisk) to required form fields. We can't include generated content on an input as they're replaced or empty elements, so we use a background image instead. We've also added separate background images to valid and invalid fields. The change is only apparent when the form element has focus, to keep the form from looking too cluttered.

Firefox Applies Styles to Invalid Elements

Note that Firefox applies its own styles to invalid elements (a red shadow), as shown in Figure 4.1 earlier. You may want to remove the native drop shadow with the following CSS:

```
:invalid { box-shadow: none; }
```

Targeted Styles for Older Browsers

Older browsers such as IE8 and IE9 don't support the `:required` pseudo-class, but you can still provide targeted styles using the attribute selector:

```
input:required,
input[required] {
  background-image: url('../images/required.png');
}
```

You can also use this attribute as a hook for form validation in browsers without support for HTML5 form validation. Your JavaScript code can check for the presence of the `required` attribute on value-less inputs, and not submit the form if any are found.

The `placeholder` Attribute

The `placeholder` attribute allows a short hint to be displayed inside the form element—space permitting—telling the user what type of data should be entered in that field. The placeholder text disappears when the field gains focus and the user enters at least one character, and reappears when the value is null. Developers have provided similar functionality with JavaScript for years—adding a temporary value, then clearing the value on focus—but in HTML5 the placeholder attribute allows it to happen natively with no JavaScript required, and stays present until a value is entered.

For *The HTML5 Herald*'s sign-up form, we'll put a `placeholder` on the website URL and start date fields:

```
<li>
  <label for="url">My website is located at:</label>
  <input type="text" id="url" name="url"
➡ placeholder="e.g. http://example.com">
</li>
⋮
<li>
  <label for="startdate">Please start my subscription on:</label>
  <input type="text" id="startdate" name="startdate" required
➡aria-required="true" >
</li>
```

In Internet Explorer, because the `placeholder` attribute only received support in IE10, and because the placeholder text disappears once the user enters data, you shouldn't rely on it as the only way to inform users of requirements. If your hint exceeds the size of the field, describe the requirements in the input's title attribute, in the label or in text next to the input element. Some developers suggest adding "e.g." as part of the placeholder text to make it evident that it's placeholder text and not actually prefilled data.

All browsers starting with Safari 4, Chrome 10, Opera 11.1, Firefox 4, Android 2.3, and Internet Explorer 10 support the `placeholder` attribute, though the original implementation of `placeholder` removed the placeholder text on focus rather than on data entry.

Polyfilling Support with JavaScript

Like everything else in this chapter, it won't hurt to include the `placeholder` attribute even when dealing with older browsers that lack support.

As with the `required` attribute, you can make use of the `placeholder` attribute and its value to make older versions of Internet Explorer behave as if they supported it—all by using a little JavaScript polyfill magic.

Here's how you'd go about it: first, use JavaScript to determine which browsers are without support. Then, in those browsers, use a function that creates a faux placeholder. The function needs to determine which form fields contain the `placeholder` attribute, then temporarily grab that attribute's content and replace empty value attributes with that text.

Then you need to set up two event handlers: one to clear the field's value on focus, and another to replace the `placeholder` value on blur if the form control's value is still an empty string. If you do use this trick, make sure that the value of your placeholder attribute isn't one that users might actually enter, or alternatively use the "e.g." precursor to indicate that the placeholder is an example and not a valid value. Additionally, remember to clear the faux placeholder when the form is submitted. Otherwise, you'll have lots of "(XXX) XXX-XXXX" submissions!

Let's look at a sample JavaScript snippet to progressively enhance our form elements using the `placeholder` attribute.

Here's our placeholder polyfill:

```
<script>
  // check if supported
  if(!Modernizr.input.placeholder) {
  // get all the form controls with the placeholder attribute
  var fcToCheck = document.querySelectorAll("*[placeholder]"),
      frmsToCheck = document.querySelectorAll('form'),
      i, count;

  // loop through form controls with placeholder attribute,
  // copy placeholder value into value, clearing on focus and
  // resetting, if empty, on blur
  for(var i = 0, count = fcToCheck.length; i < count; i++) {
    if(fcToCheck[i].value == "") {
      fcToCheck[i].value = fcToCheck[i].getAttribute("placeholder");
      fcToCheck[i].classList.add('placeholder');
      fcToCheck[i].addEventListener('focus', function() {
          if (this.value==this.getAttribute("placeholder")) {
            this.value = '';
            this.classList.remove('placeholder');
          }
      });
      fcToCheck[i].addEventListener('blur', function() {
        if (this.value == '') {
            this.value = this.getAttribute("placeholder");
            this.classList.add('placeholder');
        }
      });
    }
  }
}
```

```
  for(i = 0, count = frmsToCheck.length; i < count; i++) {

    frmsToCheck[i].addEventListener('submit', function(e) {
      var i, count, plcHld;

    // first do all the checking for required
    // element and form validation.
    // Only remove placeholders before final submission
      plcHld = this.querySelectorAll('[placeholder]');
      for(i = 0, count = plcHld.length; i < count; i++){
        //if the placeholder still equals the value
        if(plcHld[i].value == plcHld[i].getAttribute(
➥'placeholder')){
          // don't submit if required
          if(plcHld[i].hasAttribute('required')) {
            // create error messaging
            plcHld[i].classList.add('error');
            e.preventDefault();
          } else {
            // if not required, clear value before submitting.
            plcHld[i].value = '';
          }
        } else {
          // remove legacy error messaging
          plcHld[i].classList.remove('error');
        }
      }
    });
  }
</script>
```

The first point to note about this script is that we're using the Modernizr[1] JavaScript library to detect support for the placeholder attribute. There's more information about Modernizr in Appendix A, but for now it's enough to understand that it provides you with a whole raft of true or false properties for the presence of given HTML5 and CSS3 features in the browser. In this case, the property we're using is fairly self-explanatory. Modernizr.input.placeholder will be true if the browser supports placeholder, and false if it doesn't.

If we've determined that placeholder support is absent, we grab all the elements on the page with a placeholder attribute. For each of them, we check that the value

---

[1] http://www.modernizr.com/

isn't empty, then replace that value with the value of the `placeholder` attribute. In the process, we add the `placeholder` class to the element, so you can lighten the color of the font in your CSS or otherwise make it look more like a native placeholder. When the user focuses on the input with the faux placeholder, the script clears the value and removes the class. When the user removes focus, the script checks to see if there is a value. If not, we add the placeholder text and class back in.

Before submitting the form, we need to check if any form controls have a value that matches their `placeholder` attribute. In this scenario, we could have also checked to see whether any required input still has the `placeholder` class when the form is submitted. If a form control is required, we add error messaging and prevent the form from submitting. If the form control isn't required, we clear the placeholder values that are still in place before submitting, only clearing those if no required elements have prevented form submission.

Before adding a reset button to your form, determine whether your users will ever want to throw away all of their work. If the answer is yes and you include a reset button, note that if the user clicks on the reset button, our faux placeholders will disappear but the `placeholder` class will remain, as we are using the value in our polyfill.

This is a great example of an HTML5 polyfill: we use JavaScript to provide support only for those browsers without native support, and we do it by leveraging the HTML5 elements and attributes already in place, rather than resorting to additional classes or hard-coded values in our JavaScript.

While the `placeholder` attribute may not be the most important one to polyfill, it's a good example of how we can simplify form validation scripts while polyfilling support for all the new attributes, all while maintaining separation between the content and presentation layers.

The `pattern` Attribute

The `pattern` attribute enables you to provide a regular expression that the user's input must match in order to be considered valid. For any input where the user can enter free-form text, you can limit what syntax is acceptable with the `pattern` attribute.

The regular expression language used in patterns is the same Perl-based regular expression syntax as JavaScript, except that the pattern attribute must match the entire value, not just a subset. When including a pattern, you should always indicate to users what is the expected (and required) pattern.

The global `title` attribute has special significance when used in conjunction with the `pattern` attribute. Since browsers currently show the value of the `title` attribute on hover such as a tooltip, include pattern instructions that are more detailed than placeholder text, and which form a coherent statement. That `title` attribute will also be displayed with the browser's default error message in browsers that support native form validation with error messaging, which we'll cover later in this chapter.

Regular Expressions

Regular expressions are a feature of most programming languages that allow developers to specify patterns of characters and check to see if a given string matches the pattern. Regular expressions are famously indecipherable to the uninitiated. For instance, one possible regular expression to check if a string is formatted as a hexidecimal color value is this: `#[A-Fa-f0-9]{6}`.

A full tutorial on the syntax of regular expressions is beyond the scope of this book, but there are plenty of great resources,[2] tutorials,[3] and cheat sheets[4] available online if you'd like to learn. Alternatively, you can search the Web or ask around on forums for a pattern that will serve your purpose.

For a basic example, let's add a `pattern` attribute to the password field in our form. We want to enforce the requirement that the password be at least six characters long with no spaces:

```
<li>
  <label for="password">I would like my password to be:</label>
  <p>(at least 6 characters, no spaces)</p>
```

---

[2] http://shop.oreilly.com/product/9780596528126.do
[3] http://qntm.org/files/re/re.html
[4] http://www.cheatography.com/davechild/cheat-sheets/regular-expressions/

```
    <input type="password" id="password" name="password" required
title="(at least 6 characters, no spaces)" pattern="\S{6,}">
</li>
```

\S refers to "any nonwhitespace character," and {6,} means "at least six times." If you wanted to stipulate the maximum amount of characters, the syntax for between six and ten characters, for example, would be \S{6,10}.

As with the `required` attribute, the `pattern` attribute will prevent the form from being submitted if there is no match for the pattern, and will provide an error message.

If your pattern is not a valid regular expression, it will be ignored for the purposes of validation.

The `pattern` attribute has been supported to some extent in all browsers since Firefox 4, Safari 5, Chrome 10, Opera 11, IE10, and Android 2.3. By "some extent," we mean that while all browsers now support the `pattern` attribute, some—notably Safari and Android through 4.4—allow invalid data to be sent on form submission.

Additionally, similar to the `placeholder` and `required` attributes, you can use the value of this attribute to provide the basis for your JavaScript validation code for nonsupporting browsers.

The `disabled` Attribute

The Boolean `disabled` attribute has been around longer than HTML5 but has been expanded on, to a degree. It can be used with any form control except the new `output` element, and, unlike previous versions of HTML, HTML5 allows you to set the `disabled` attribute on a fieldset and have it apply to all the form elements contained in that fieldset.

Generally, form elements with the `disabled` attribute have the content grayed out by default in the browser. Browsers will prohibit the user from focusing on a form control that has the `disabled` attribute set. This attribute is often used to disable the submit button until all fields are correctly filled out.

You can employ the `:disabled` pseudo-class in your CSS to style disabled form controls, and use either `:enabled` or `:not(:disabled)` pseudo-classes to target form controls that aren't disabled.

Form controls with the `disabled` attribute aren't submitted along with the form so their values will be inaccessible to your form processing code on the server side. If you want a form value that users are unable to edit but can still see and submit, use the `readonly` attribute.

The `readonly` Attribute

The `readonly` attribute is similar to the `disabled` attribute: it makes it impossible for the user to edit the form field. Unlike `disabled`, however, the field *can* receive focus and its value is submitted with the form.

In a comments form, we may want to include the URL of the current page or the title of the article that is being commented on, letting the user know that we're collecting this data without allowing them to change it:

```
<label for="about">Article Title</label>
<input type="text" name="about" id="about" readonly
➥value="http://www.thehtml5herald.com/register.html">
```

The `multiple` Attribute

The `multiple` attribute, if present, indicates that multiple values can be entered in a form control. While it was available in previous versions of HTML, it only applied to the `select` element. In HTML5, it can be added to `file`, `email`, and `range` input types as well. If present, the user can select more than one file, include several comma-separated email addresses, or have a range with two sliders.

While `multiple` file input is supported in all browsers since mobile Safari 7 and IE10, the `multiple` attribute on range input is yet to be supported anywhere at the time of writing.

 Spaces or commas?

You may notice that the iOS touch keyboard for email inputs includes a space. Of course, spaces aren't permitted in email addresses, but browsers allow you to separate multiple emails with spaces along with the required comma. Originally the spaces were disallowed in some browsers, but adding spaces after the comma separator has been included in the specification.

The `form` Attribute

Not to be confused with the `form` element, the `form` *attribute* in HTML5 allows you to associate `form` elements with forms in which they're not nested. It means that you can now associate a fieldset or form control with any other form in the document. This solves the age-old issue of forms not being nestable. While you're still unable to nest forms, you can associate "nested" form controls with a form that's not an ancestor.

The `form` attribute takes as its value the ID of the form element with which the fieldset or control should be associated.

If the attribute is omitted, the control will only be submitted with the form in which it's nested. If you include the `form` attribute and remove it, make sure to use `el.removeAttribute('form')` and not `el.setAttribute('form', '')`. If the `form` attribute is included but the value is either empty or points to an invalid form ID, the form control will be disassociated from all forms on the page and will not be submitted with any form, including any ancestral form in which it may be nested.

This attribute is supported in all browsers, starting with Android 4 and IE 11.

The `autocomplete` Attribute

The `autocomplete` attribute specifies whether the form, or a form control, should have autocomplete functionality. For most form fields, this will be a drop-down that appears when the user begins typing. For password fields, it's the ability to save the password in the browser. Support for this attribute has been present in browsers for years, though it was never in the specification until HTML5.

If the `autocomplete` attribute is omitted from the form control or the form, the default value is on. You may have noticed this the last time you filled out a form. In order to disable autocomplete on a form control (or form), use `autocomplete="off"`. This is a good idea for sensitive information, such as a credit card number, or data that will never need to be reused, such as a CAPTCHA.

Autocompletion is also controlled by the browser, ignoring developer-set preferences. While the default value is on, the browser must have it enabled for it to work at all; however, setting the autocomplete attribute to off overrides the browser's on preference for the relevant form control.

The datalist Element and the list Attribute

Datalists are currently supported in all browsers except Safari, starting with IE10 and Android 4.4.3. In the default form, they fulfill a common requirement: a text field with a set of predefined autocomplete options. Unlike the select element, users can enter whatever value they like, but they'll be presented with a set of suggested options.

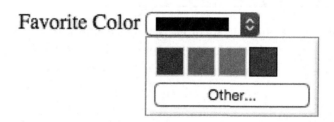

Figure 4.4. The datalist element in action in Firefox

For some input types, like text and date input types, a drop-down list of options is presented as users type into the field, as shown in Figure 4.4. For the range input type, the browser will display little tick marks along the slider rule indicating where suggested options are found. For the color input type, users are presented with swatches of color suggestions, with the option to switch to the device's default color picker if they prefer to pick a different color.

The datalist element, much like select, is a list of options, with each one placed in an option element. You then associate the datalist with an input using the list attribute on the input. The list attribute takes as its value the id attribute of the datalist you want to associate with the input. One datalist can be associated with several input fields.

Here's what this would look like in practice:

```
<label for="favcolor">Favorite Color</label>
<input type="color" list="colors" id="favcolor" name="favcolor">

<datalist id="colors">
  <option value="#0000FF" label="blue">
  <option value="#008000" label="green">
  <option value="#ff0000" label="red">
  <option value="#663399" label="RebeccaPurple">
</datalist>
```

[5]Here, the user will be presented with a selection of four color swatches, with the choice to see the full color picker if they prefer a different color.

The `autofocus` Attribute

The Boolean `autofocus` attribute specifies that a form control should be focused as soon as the page loads. Only one form element can have autofocus in a given page. For a better user experience and for accessibility reasons, it is best *not* to use this attribute.

The input elements support many more attributes, with some being type-specific. The attributes include `alt`, `src`, `height`, and `width` for the image input type, and `step`, `min`, and `max` for numeric input types, including dates and range. `dirname` helps tell the server the form control's directionality. `formaction`, `formenctype`, `formmethod`, `formnovalidate`, and `formtarget` provide methods to override the form's attributes. `inputmode` helps indicate to the browser what keypad to show when the device is capable of displaying dynamic keypads. `minlength` and `maxlength` dictate the length of allowable input. `checked`, `name`, `size`, `type`, and `value` should already be familiar to you, though `:checked` and `:default` pseudo-classes may be new. We'll cover some of these with their relevant input types next.

Input Types

You're probably already familiar with the `input` element's `type` attribute. This is the attribute that determines what kind of form input will be presented to the user. If it is omitted—or in the case of new input types and older browsers, not understood—it still works; the input will default to `type="text"`. This is the key that

---

[5] The named color "rebeccapurple" #663399, is a tribute to Eric Meyer's daughter, who passed away in 2014. It is a mark of support from all the web community to Eric Meyer.

makes HTML5 forms usable today even if you're still supporting older browsers. If you use a new input type, such as `email` or `search`, older browsers will simply present users with a standard text field.

Our sign-up form currently uses four of the ten input types you're familiar with: `checkbox`, `text`, `password`, and `submit`. Here's the full list of types that were available before HTML5:

- button

- checkbox

- file

- hidden

- image

- password

- radio

- reset

- submit

- text

The HTML5 specification[6] gave us nine more input types that provide for more data-specific UI elements and native data validation:

- search

- email

- url

- tel

- date

---

[6] http://www.w3.org/TR/html5/forms.html

- `time`

- `number`

- `range`

- `color`

HTML5.1 and the WHATWG HTML Living Standard includes four additional date input types, three of which are well supported in modern browsers:

- `datetime-local`

- `month`

- `week`

- `datetime` (not supported in any browser)

Let's look at each of these new types in detail, and see how we can put them to use.

Search

The `search` input type (`type="search"`) provides a search field—a one-line text input control for entering one or more search terms. The spec states:

> The difference between the text state and the search state is primarily stylistic: on platforms where search fields are distinguished from regular text fields, the search state might result in an appearance consistent with the platform's search fields rather than appearing like a regular text field.

Many browsers style `search` inputs in a manner consistent with the browser or the operating system's search boxes. Currently, Chrome, Safari, Opera, and IE have added the ability to clear the input with the click of a mouse by providing an × icon once text is entered into the field, as shown in Figure 4.5. The date/time input types are also clearable in Chrome and Opera, and IE11 includes an × icon to clear most input types now, including inputs of type text.

search: my search query

Figure 4.5. The search input type is styled to resemble the operating system's search fields

On Apple devices, the search field has rounded corners by default in Chrome, Safari, and Opera, matching the devices' search field appearance. On touch pads with dynamic keyboards, the "go" button appears as a search icon or the word "search," depending on the device. If you include the non-standard `results` attribute, Chrome and Opera will display a magnifying/looking glass icon within the form field.

While you can still use `type="text"` for search fields, the new search type is a visual cue as to where the user needs to go to search the site, and provides an interface to which the user is accustomed. *The HTML5 Herald* has no search field, but here's an example of how you'd use it:

```
<form id="search" method="get">
  <label for="s">Search</label>
  <input type="search" id="s" name="s">
  <input type="submit" value="Search">
</form>
```

Since `search`, like all the new input types, appears as a regular text box in nonsupporting browsers, there's no reason not to use it when appropriate.

Email Addresses

The `email` type (`type="email"`) is, not surprisingly, used for specifying one or more email addresses. It supports the Boolean `multiple` attribute, allowing for multiple comma-separated (with optional space) email addresses.

Let's change our form to use `type="email"` for the registrant's email address:

```
<label for="email">My email address is</label>
<input type="email" id="email" name="email">
```

If you change the input type from `text` to `email`, as we've done here, you'll notice no visible change in the user interface; the input still looks like a plain text field. However, there are differences behind the scenes.

The change becomes apparent if you're using a touchpad device. When you focus on the email field, most touchpad devices—such as the iPad or Android phone running Chromium—will all display a keyboard optimized for email entry, including the @ symbol, period, and space buttons, but no comma, as shown in Figure 4.6.

Figure 4.6. The `email` input type provides a custom keyboard on iOS devices

Firefox, Chrome, Opera, and Internet Explorer 10 also provide error messaging for invalid `email` inputs: if you try to submit a form with content unrecognizable as one or more email addresses, the browser will tell you what's wrong. The default error messages are shown in Figure 4.7.

Figure 4.7. Error messages for incorrectly formatted email addresses on Opera (left) and Firefox (right)

 Custom Validation Messages

Dislike the default error messages the browsers provide? Set your own with `.setCustomValidity(errorMsg)`. `setCustomValidity` takes as its only parameter the error message you want to provide. If you set a custom validation message, once that value becomes valid you must set the validation message to an empty string (a falsy value) to enable form submission:

```
function setErrorMessages(formControl) {
  var validityState_object = formControl.validity;
  if (validityState_object.valueMissing) {
      formControl.setCustomValidity('Please set an age
➥(required)');
  } else if (validityState_object.rangeUnderflow) {
      formControl.setCustomValidity('You\'re too young');
  } else if (validityState_object.rangeOverflow) {
      formControl.setCustomValidity('You\'re too old');
  } else if (validityState_object.stepMismatch) {
      formControl.setCustomValidity('Counting half
➥birthdays?');
  } else {
      //if valid, must set falsy value or will always error
      formControl.setCustomValidity('');
  }
}
```

Unfortunately, while you can change the *content* of the message, you're stuck with its appearance, at least for now.

URLs

The url input (`type="url"`) is used for specifying a web address. Much like email, it will appear as a normal text field. On many touch screens, the onscreen keyboard displayed will be optimized for web address entry, with a forward slash (/) and a ".com" shortcut key.

Let's update our registration form to use the url input type:

```
<label for="url">My website is located at:</label>
<input type="url" id="url" name="url">
```

Validation of URLs

All modern browsers starting with Internet Explorer 10 support the url input type, reporting the input as invalid if the value doesn't begin with a protocol. Only the general protocol format of a URL is validated, so, for example, q://example.xyz will be considered valid, even though q:// isn't a real protocol and .xyz isn't a real top-level domain. If you want the value entered to conform to a more specific format, provide information in your label (or in a placeholder) to let your users know, and use the `pattern` attribute to ensure that it's correct, as previously described.

Telephone Numbers

For telephone numbers, use the `tel` input type (`type="tel"`). Unlike the `url` and `email` types, the `tel` type doesn't enforce a particular syntax or pattern. Letters and numbers—indeed, any characters other than new lines or carriage returns—are valid. There's a good reason for this: all over the world, countries have valid phone numbers of various lengths and punctuation, so it would be impossible to specify a single format as standard. For example, in the USA, +1(415)555-1212 is just as well understood as 415.555.1212, but companies may also use letters in their phone number, such as (800)CALL-NOW.

You can encourage a particular format by including a placeholder with the correct syntax, or a comment after the input with an example. Additionally, you can stipulate a format by using the `pattern` attribute. Include a title with the `pattern` attribute to provide for a tooltip and to improve the UX of the native validation error message. You can also use the `setCustomValidity` method to provide more informative client-side validation.

In using the `tel` input type, dynamic touch pads will usually display the telephone keyboard, including the asterisk and pound key. You can use `tel` for more than just phone numbers. For example, it is likely to be the best keypad for social security number form entry.

Numbers

The `number` type (`type="number"`) provides an input for entering a number. Usually, this is a spinner box, where you can either enter a number, or click on the up/down arrows in a native browser spinner UI to select a number.

Let's change our quantity field to use the `number` input type:

```
<label for="quantity">I would like to receive <input type="number"
➥min="1" name="quantity" id="quantity"> copies of <cite>The HTML5
➥ Herald</cite></label>
```

Figure 4.8 shows what this looks like in Opera.

I would like to receive   **3**   copies of *The HTML5 Herald.*

Figure 4.8. The number input seen in Opera

On many touchscreen devices, focusing on a number input type will bring up a number touch pad (rather than a full keyboard).

The number input has min, max, and step attributes to specify the minimum, maximum, and incremental values allowed. If the step is omitted it defaults to 1. If you would like to allow float values, you must specify a float step, such as 0.1 or the keyword any to allow for any value. Note that some browsers will minimize the width of the number form field for restricted numbers. For example, min="0" max="10" step="1" doesn't need to be as wide as step="any", where the user could enter the full value of Pi.

 Use number with Caution

There will be times when you may think you want to use number, when in reality another input type is more appropriate. For example, it might seem to make sense that a street address should be a number. But think about it: would you want to click the spinner box all the way up to 34154? More importantly, many street numbers have non-numeric portions: think 24½ or 36B, neither of which work with the number input type.

Additionally, account numbers may be a mixture of letters and numbers, or have dashes. If you know the pattern of your number, use the pattern attribute. Just remember not to use number if the range is extensive or the number could contain non-numeric characters and the field is required. If the field is optional, you might want to use number anyway, or tel in order to prompt the number or telephone keyboard as the default on touchscreen devices.

Ranges

The range input type (type="range") displays a slider control. As with the number type, it allows the min, max, and step attributes. The difference between number and range, according to the spec, is that the exact value of the number is unimportant with range. It's ideal for inputs where you want an imprecise number; for example, a customer satisfaction survey asking clients to rate aspects of the service they received.

Let's change our registration form to use the `range` input type. We'll create a field asking users to rate their knowledge of HTML5 on a scale of 1 to 10:

```
<label for="rating">On a scale of 1 to 10, my knowledge of HTML5
➥is:</label>
<input name="rating" type="range" min="1" max="10" step="1">
```

Figure 4.9 shows what this input type looks like in Safari. In this case the `step` attribute is not required, as it defaults to 1. A negative value for `step` will break the range by making the thumb immovable in Firefox.

Figure 4.9. The range input type in Safari

The default value of a range is the midpoint of the slider—in other words, halfway between the minimum and the maximum. Including the `list` attribute with an associated `datalist` enables creating little notches along the slider path showing the location of the suggested values.

The spec allows for a reversed slider (with values from right to left) if the maximum specified is less than the minimum; however, no browsers currently support this. Additionally, the spec allows for two thumbs with the inclusion of the `multiple` attribute. No browsers support this either.

`range` is supported in all browsers, starting with Firefox 23, Android 4.2, and Internet Explorer 10. `list` support on the `range` input type is currently only found in Chrome 20+, Opera, and Internet Explorer 10+.

Colors

The `color` input type (`type="color"`) provides the user with a color picker—or at least it does in some browsers, including BlackBerry 10, Firefox 29+, Safari 8+ for desktop, Chrome, Opera, and Android 4.4. WebKit for iOS 8 and Internet Explorer 11 are yet to support the `color` input type. The color picker returns a lower-case hexadecimal RGB color value, such as #ff3300, with the default value being #000000 (black).

If you want to use a color input, provide placeholder text indicating that a hexadecimal RGB color format is required, and use the `pattern` attribute to restrict the entry to only valid hexadecimal color values.

We don't use color in our form, but if we did, it would look a little like this:

```
<label for="clr">Color: </label>
<input id="clr" name="clr" type="color" placeholder="#ffffff"
➥pattern="#(?:[0-9A-Fa-f]{6})">
```

The resulting color picker is shown in Figure 4.10. Clicking the **Other...** button brings up a full color wheel, allowing the user to select any hexadecimal color value. If you're after other colors, use the `list` attribute with an associated `datalist` to define each color you want to suggest as individual options. This is currently supported in Blink browsers only.

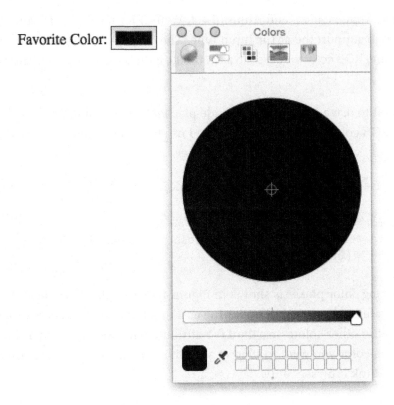

Figure 4.10. Chrome's color picker control for the color input type

Dates and Times

There are new date and time input types, some of which are included in the HTML5 specification, as well as a few others that are still listed in the HTML Living Standard and the HTML5.1 draft that may be at risk. The date and time input types made it into the HTML5 W3C Recommendation, while datetime, datetime-local, month, and week are at risk of being dropped. All date and time inputs accept data formatted according to the ISO 8601 standard.[7]

Here are the available date and time input types:

▨ date: comprises the date (year, month, and day), but no time; for example, 2004-06-24.

---

[7] http://en.wikipedia.org/wiki/ISO_8601

- `time`: signifies a time of day using the military format (24-hour clock); for example, 22:00 instead of 10.00 p.m.

- `month`: only includes the year and month; for example, 2012-12.

- `week`: covers the year and week number (from 1 to 52); for example, 2011-W01 or 2012-W52.

- `datetime`: includes both the date and time, separated by a "T", and followed by either a "Z" to represent UTC (Coordinated Universal Time) or by a time zone specified with a + or - character; for example, "2011-03-17T10:45-5:00" represents 10:45 a.m. on the 17th of March, 2011 in the UTC minus five hours time zone (Eastern Standard Time). This value has been removed from the spec and then added back in. It is currently without support.

- `datetime-local`: is identical to `datetime`, except that it omits the time zone; the main difference is that `datetime-local` is supported in browsers that support `date` and `time`, while `datetime` is not.

The most commonly used of these types is `date`. The specifications call for the browser to display date controls. At the time of writing, WebKit for iOS, Chrome 20+, and Opera provide calendar controls for most of these values. Internet Explorer 11, Safari for desktop, and Firefox 37 still do not.

Let's change our subscription start date field to use the `date` input type:

```
<label for="startdate">Please start my subscription on:</label>
<input type="date" min="1904-03-17" max="1904-05-17"
➥id="startdate" name="startdate" required aria-required="true"
➥placeholder="1904-03-17">
```

Now, we'll have a calendar control when we view our form in Opera, Chrome, or iOS WebKit, as shown in Figure 4.11. Unfortunately, it's unable to be styled with CSS at present.

Figure 4.11. A calendar control

For the month and week types, browsers display a similar UI as the date input type, but only allow the user to select full months or weeks. In those cases, individual days are unable to be selected; instead, clicking on a day selects the whole month or week. While datetime-local is supported in these browsers, datetime is not. datetime has been deprecated. month, week, and datetime-local are at risk as well, but have yet to fall to the same fate. Chrome lost support for datetime in version 26, Opera in version 15, and Safari in iOS7. Instead of using datetime since support should be deprecated, use date and time as two separate input types.

We recommend including a minimum and maximum when using the date input type. As with number and range, this is done with the min and max attributes.

The placeholder attribute that we added to our start date field earlier is made redundant in browsers supporting the datepicker interface, but it makes sense to leave it in place to guide users of IE, Safari, and Firefox until they implement the date and time controls. Until all browsers support the UI of the new input types, placeholders are a good way to hint to your users what kind of data is expected in those fields. Remember, they'll just look like regular text fields in nonsupporting browsers.

Dynamic Dates

In our example, we hardcoded the `min` and `max` values into our HTML. If you wanted the minimum to be the day after the current date—which makes sense for a newspaper subscription start date—this would require updating the HTML every day. The best way to handle it is to dynamically generate the minimum and maximum allowed dates on the server side. A little PHP can go a long way:

```php
<?php
function daysFromNow($days){
  $added = ($days * 24 * 3600) + time();
  return date("Y-m-d", $added);
}
?>
```

In our markup where we had static dates, we now dynamically create them with the above function:

```html
<li>
  <label for="startdate">Please start my subscription on:
➥</label>
  <input type="date" min="<?php echo(daysFromNow(1)); ?>"
➥max="<?php echo(daysFromNow(91)); ?>" id="startdate"
➥name="startdate" required aria-required="true"
➥placeholder="<?php echo(daysFromNow(1)); ?>">
</li>
```

This way, the user is limited to entering dates that make sense in the context of the form.

You can also include the `step` attribute with these input types. For example, `step="7"` on `date` will limit the user to selecting only one day per week: the particular weekday depends on the `min` if one is present, or is the current day of the week if none is present. On `time` input, the `step` attribute must be expressed in seconds, so adding `step="900"` on the `time` input type will cause the input to step in increments of 15 minutes.

Additional New Form Controls in HTML5

We've covered the new values for the input element's `type` attribute, along with some attributes that are valid on most form elements. But HTML5 web forms still have more to offer us! There are five new form elements in the HTML5 forms spe-cification: `datalist`, `output`, `keygen`, `progress`, and `meter`. We covered `datalist` above. We introduced you to `progress` and `meter` in the last chapter as they are often useful outside of forms. So let's recap and take a look at the other two elements.

The progress and meter Elements

Two of the most well-known HTML5 elements are the `progress` and `meter` elements.

The `meter` element provides for a gauge, displaying a general value within a range. You provide minimum (`min`) and maximum (`max`) values, and the required `value` that falls between those minimum and maximum values. While many think it's a form control with attributes similar to some numeric input types, it has no `name` attribute and won't be submitted on form submission.

The `meter` will default the minimum value to `0`, or the meter's `value`, whichever is lower. The maximum value defaults to `1` or the meter's `value`, whichever is higher. Use `meter` when there is a minimum value, a maximum value, and optimal values, and the value can go up and down like a test grade, gas tank level, or blood pressure. With these three attributes, browsers that support meter including Android 4.4+ (but not iOS7 or IE11) will show a green gauge.

`meter` enables us to show when a value is in the right range with the `low`, `high`, and `optimum` values. If the `value` is between `min` and `low`, the meter is yellow. If the value is between the `low` and `high` value the meter is green. If the `value` is between `high` and `max`, it will be red. Currently the `optimum` value has no noticeable effect.

The `meter` element should not be used to indicate progress; instead, use a `progress` bar to indicate the percentage of how complete a task is.

Progress attributes include `max` and `value`, with progress always being between 0 and 100% complete. The browser calculates what percentage the value is of the maximum and adjusts the length of the progress bar accordingly. It displays a par-tially filled gray to blue progress bar where it is fully gray at 0% and fully blue at 100%.

If no `value` is included, the progress bar is indeterminate. Chrome, Opera, Safari, and Firefox display indeterminate progress as animated bars, with IE styling it as animated dots.

Unlike `meter`, `progress` heads only in the direction of 100% of the `max` value. The presentation defaults to inline-block so you can set `width` and `height` on `progress` elements. Height will not change the actual height of the stylized bar (unlike `meter`) but will add space below it.

The `output` Element

The purpose of the `output` element is to accept and display the result of a calculation. The `output` element should be used when the user can see the value, but not directly manipulate it, and when the value can be derived from other values entered in the form. An example use might be the total cost calculated after shipping and taxes in a shopping cart.

The `output` element's value is contained between the opening and closing tags. Generally, it will make sense to use JavaScript in the browser to update this value. The `output` element has a `for` attribute, which is used to reference the IDs of form fields whose values went into the calculation of the `output` element's value.

The `output` element's `name` and `value` are submitted along with the form.

The `keygen` Element

The `keygen` element is a control for generating a public-private key pair[8] and for submitting the public key from that key pair. Opera, Chrome, Safari, Android, and Firefox all support this element, rendering it as a drop-down menu with options for the length of the generated keys; all provide different options, though. There is still no support in iOS7 and IE11.

The `keygen` element introduces two new attributes: the `challenge` attribute specifies a string that is submitted along with the public key, and the `keytype` attribute specifies the type of key generated. At the time of writing, the only supported `keytype` value is `rsa`, a common algorithm used in public-key cryptography.

The `contenteditable` Attribute

While it is always best to use the most appropriate form element for its intended purpose, sometimes the existing form elements fall short of our needs; for example, no form control makes for a good inline WYSIWYG text editor.

---

[8] http://en.wikipedia.org/wiki/Public-key_cryptography

There is a roundabout solution for that, though. Any element in an HTML5 document can be made editable with the `contenteditable` attribute. The `contenteditable` attribute, written simply as `contenteditable` or `contenteditable="true"`, makes the element on which it is included editable. You will usually find this attribute on divs, but you can even make a `style` element that's set to `"display:block"` editable, and change CSS on the fly. While any element that is not natively a form control will not by default be sent to the server with the rest of the form data on form submission, you can use JavaScript to send user edited content to the server asynchronously or on form submission.

If you've ever seen an editable profile where the element to click doesn't look like a form control at all, there is a chance that you were actually editing a `contenteditable` element. Any edits made on `contenteditable` components actually update the DOM.

Simply adding `contenteditable` to an element makes that element editable in all browsers. In addition, its descendents will also be editable unless `contenteditable="false"` is explicitly applied to them. While this does update the DOM client side, you do have to add JavaScript to explicitly save it.

Changes to Existing Form Controls

There have been a few other changes to form controls in HTML5.

The `form` Element

Throughout this chapter, we've been talking about attributes that apply to various form field elements; however, there are also some new attributes specific to the `form` element itself.

First, as we've seen, HTML5 provides a number of ways to natively validate form fields; certain input types such as `email` and `url`, for example, as well as the `required` and `pattern` attributes. You may, however, want to use these input types and attributes for styling or semantic reasons without preventing the form being submitted. The new Boolean `novalidate` attribute allows a form to be submitted without native validation of its fields.

Next, forms no longer need to have the `action` attribute defined. You no longer need to explicitly state the URL to use it for form submission. If omitted, the form will behave as though the `action` were set to the current page. You can write or override the URL defined in the form's `action` attribute with the `formaction` attribute of the button input types that activate form submission.

Lastly, the `autocomplete` attribute we introduced earlier can also be added directly to the `form` element; in this case, it will apply to all fields in that form unless those fields override it with their own `autocomplete` attribute.

The `optgroup` Element

In HTML5, you can have an `optgroup` as a child of another `optgroup`, which is useful for multilevel `select` menus.

The `textarea` Element

In HTML 4, we were required to specify a `textarea` element's size by specifying values for the `rows` and `cols` attributes. In HTML5, these attributes are no longer required; you should use CSS to define a `textarea`'s width and height.

New in HTML5 is the `wrap` attribute. This attribute applies to the `textarea` element, and can have the values `soft` (the default) or `hard`. With `soft`, the text is submitted without line breaks other than those actually entered by the user, whereas `hard` will submit any line breaks introduced by the browser due to the size of the field. If you set the `wrap` to hard, you need to specify a `cols` attribute.

In Conclusion

Unfortunately, we weren't able to cover everything—that should be a book in itself. This was, however, a fairly in-depth introduction. As support for HTML5 input elements and attributes grows, sites will require less and less JavaScript for client-side validation and user interface enhancements, while browsers handle most of the heavy lifting. Legacy user agents are likely to stick around for the foreseeable future, but there is no reason to avoid moving forward and using HTML5 web forms, with appropriate polyfills and fallbacks filling the gaps where required.

In the next chapter, we'll continue fleshing out The HTML5 Herald by adding what many consider to be HTML5's killer feature: native video and audio.

HTML5 Video and Audio

No book on HTML5 would be complete without an examination of the new video and audio elements. These groundbreaking new elements have already been utilized on the Web, and more developers and content creators are starting to incorporate them into their projects in place of technologies such as Flash and Silverlight.

For *The HTML5 Herald*, we're going to place a video element in the first column of our three-column layout. Before we explore the details of the video element and its various features, though, we'll take a brief look at the state of video on the Web today.

For the most part, this chapter will focus on the video element, since that's what we're using in our sample project. Note that the audio element behaves nearly identically: almost all the features that we'll be using for video also apply to audio. Where there are exceptions, we'll do our best to point them out.

A Bit of History

Up until the late 2000s and early 2010s, multimedia content on the Web was for the most part placed in web pages by means of third-party plugins or applications that integrated with the web browser. Some examples of such software include QuickTime, RealPlayer, and Silverlight.

At that time, by far the most popular way to embed video and audio on web pages was by means of Adobe's Flash Player plugin. The Flash Player plugin was originally developed by Macromedia and is now maintained by Adobe as a result of their 2005 buy out of the company. The plugin has been available since the mid-90s, but did not really take off as a way to serve video content until well into the 2000s.

Before HTML5, there was no standard way to embed video into web pages. A plugin such as Adobe's Flash Player is controlled solely by Adobe, and is not open to community development. The introduction of the `video` and `audio` elements in HTML5 resolves this problem and makes multimedia a seamless part of a web page, the same as the `img` element. With HTML5, there's no need for the user to download third-party software to view your content, and the video or audio player is easily accessible via scripting.

The Current State of Play

Unfortunately, as sublime as HTML5 video and audio sounds in theory, it's less simple in practice. A number of factors need to be considered before you decide to include HTML5's new multimedia elements on your pages.

First, you'll have to understand the state of browser support. HTML5 audio and video is supported in all in-use browsers except Internet Explorer versions 8 and earlier. Many websites still receive some traffic from those earlier browsers, so you'll have to take that into consideration.

The good news is even if you need to support those older browsers, you can still use HTML5 video on your pages today. Later on, we'll show you how the `video` element has been designed with backwards compatibility in mind so that users of non-supporting browsers will still have access to your multimedia content.

Video Container Formats

Video on the Web is based on container formats and codecs. A **container** is a wrapper that stores all the necessary data that comprises the video file being accessed, much like a ZIP file wraps or contains files. Some examples of well-known video containers include Flash Video (.flv), MPEG-4 (.mp4 or .m4v), and AVI (.avi).

The video container houses data, including a video track, an audio track with markers that help synchronize the audio and video, language information, and other bits of metadata that describe the content. The video container formats relevant to HTML5 are MPEG-4, Ogg, and WebM.

Video Codecs

A video **codec** defines an algorithm for encoding and decoding a multimedia data stream. A codec can encode a data stream for transmission, storage, or encryption, or it can decode it for playback or editing. For the purpose of HTML5 video, we're concerned with the decoding and playback of a video stream. The video codecs that are relevant to HTML5 video are H.264, Theora, and VP8.

Audio Codecs

An audio codec in theory works the same as a video codec, except that it's dealing with the streaming of sound rather than video frames. The audio codecs that are relevant to HTML5 video are AAC, Vorbis, and MP3.

Licensing Issues

The new `video` element itself is free to use in any context, but the containers and codecs are not always as simple. For example, while the Theora and VP8 (WebM) codecs are not patent-encumbered, the H.264 codec is, so licensing for it is provided by the MPEG-LA group.

Currently for H.264, if your video is provided to your users for free, there's no requirement for you to pay royalties; however, detailed licensing issues are far beyond the scope and intent of this book, so just be aware that you may have to do some research before using any particular video format when including HTML5 video in your pages.

The Markup

After that necessary business surrounding containers, codecs, and licensing issues, it's time to examine the markup of the `video` element and its associated attributes.

The simplest way to include HTML5 video in a web page is as follows:

```
<video src="example.webm"></video>
```

As you've probably figured out from the preceding sections, this will only work in a limited number of browsers. It is, however, the minimum code required to have HTML5 video working to some extent. In a perfect world, it would work everywhere—the same way the img element works everywhere—but that's a little way off just yet.

Similar to the img element, the video element can also include width and height attributes:

```
<video src="example.webm" width="375" height="280"></video>
```

Even though the dimensions can be set in the markup, they'll have no effect on the aspect ratio of the video. For example, if the video in the previous example was actually 375×240 and the markup was as shown, the video would be centered vertically inside the 280-pixel space specified in the HTML. This stops the video from stretching unnecessarily and looking distorted.

The width and height attributes accept integers only, and their values are always in pixels. Naturally, these values can be overridden via scripting or CSS.

Enabling Native Controls

No embedded video would be complete without giving the user the ability to play, pause, stop, seek through the video, or adjust the volume. HTML5's video element includes a controls attribute that does just that:

```
<video src="example.webm" width="375" height="280" controls></video>
```

controls is a Boolean attribute, so no value is required. Its inclusion in the markup tells the browser to make the controls visible and accessible to the user.

Each browser is responsible for the look of the built-in video controls. Figure 5.1 to Figure 5.4 show how these controls differ in appearance from browser to browser.

Figure 5.1. The native video controls in Chrome

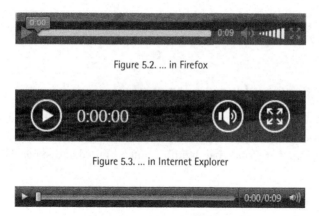

Figure 5.2. ... in Firefox

Figure 5.3. ... in Internet Explorer

Figure 5.4. ... and in Opera

The `autoplay` Attribute

We'd love to omit reference to this particular attribute, since using it will be undesirable for the most part; however, there are cases where it can be appropriate. The Boolean `autoplay` attribute does exactly what its name implies: it tells the web page to play the video immediately as soon as possible.

Normally, this is a bad practice; most of us know too well how jarring it can be if a website starts playing video or audio as soon as it loads—especially if our speakers are turned up. Usability best practice dictates that sounds and movement on web pages should only be triggered when requested by the user. But this doesn't mean that the `autoplay` attribute should never be used.

For example, if the page in question contains nothing but a video—that is, the user clicked on a link to a page for the sole purpose of viewing a specific video—it may be acceptable for it to play automatically, depending on the video's size, surrounding content, viewing platform, and audience.

Here's how you'd use this attribute:

```
<video src="example.webm" width="375" height="280" controls
➥autoplay></video>
```

 Mobile Browsers Ignore `autoplay`

Many, if not all, mobile browsers will ignore the `autoplay` attribute, so the video will always wait for the user to press the play button before starting. This is sensible, given that mobile bandwidth is often limited and expensive.

The `loop` Attribute

Another available attribute that you should think twice before using is the Boolean `loop` attribute. Again, it's fairly self-explanatory: according to the spec, this attribute will tell the browser to "seek back to the start of the media resource upon reaching the end."

So if you created a web page whose sole intention was to annoy its visitors, it might contain code such as this:

```
<video src="example.webm" width="375" height="280" controls autoplay
➥loop></video>
```

Autoplay and an infinite loop! We'd just need to remove the native controls and we'd have a trifecta of worst practices.

Of course, as with `autoplay`, there are some situations where `loop` can be useful: a browser-based game in which ambient sounds and music should play continuously when the page is open, for example.

The `preload` Attribute

In contrast to the two previously discussed attributes, `preload` is certainly handy in a number of cases. The `preload` attribute accepts one of three values:

- `auto`: indicates that the video and its associated metadata will start loading before the video is played. This way, the browser can start playing the video more quickly when the user requests it.

- `none`: indicates that the video shouldn't load in the background before the user presses play.

■ `metadata`: works like `none`, except that any metadata associated with the video (for example, its dimensions, duration, and the like) can be preloaded, even though the video itself won't be.

The `preload` attribute has no spec-defined default in cases where it's omitted; each browser decides which of those three values should be the default state. This makes sense, as it allows desktop browsers on good connections to preload the video and/or metadata automatically, having no real adverse effect; yet it permits mobile browsers to default to either `metadata` or `none`, as many mobile users have restricted bandwidth and will prefer to have the choice of whether or not to download the video.

The `poster` Attribute

When you attempt to view a video on the Web, usually a single frame of the video will be displayed in order to provide a teaser of its content. The `poster` attribute makes it easy to choose such a teaser. This attribute, similar to `src`, will point to an image file on the server by means of a URL.

Here's how our `video` element would look with a `poster` attribute defined:

```
<video src="example.webm" width="375" height="280" controls
➥poster="teaser.jpg"></video>
```

If the `poster` attribute is omitted, the default "poster" will be the first frame of the video, which displays as soon as it's loaded.

The `muted` Attribute

The `muted` attribute, a Boolean, controls the default state of the audio track for the `video` element.

Adding this attribute will cause the video's audio track to default to muted, potentially overriding any user preferences. This will only control the default state of the element—a user interacting with the controls or JavaScript can change this.

Here it is added to our `video` element:

```
<video src="example.webm" width="375" height="280" poster=
➥"teaser.jpg" muted></video>
```

In previous versions of the HTML5 spec, there was an attribute called `audio` that took a value of `muted`. The new `muted` attribute replaces the `audio` attribute, which is now obsolete.

Adding Support for Multiple Video Formats

As we've discussed, there is currently no option to use a single container format to serve your video, even though that's really the idea behind having the `video` element, and one which we hope will be realized in the near future. To include multiple video formats, the `video` element allows `source` elements to be defined so that you can allow each browser to display the video using the format of its choice. These elements serve the same function as the `src` attribute on the `video` element, so if you're providing `source` elements, there's no need to specify an `src` for your `video` element.

To achieve full browser support, here's how we'll declare our `source` elements:

```
<source src="example.mp4" type="video/mp4">
<source src="example.webm" type="video/webm">
<source src="example.ogv" type="video/ogg">
```

The `source` element (oddly enough) takes an `src` attribute that specifies the location of the video file. It also accepts a `type` attribute that specifies the container format for the resource being requested. This latter attribute enables the browser to determine if it can play the file in question, thus preventing it from unnecessarily downloading an unsupported format.

The `type` attribute allows also a codec parameter to be specified, which defines the video and audio codecs for the requested file. Here's how our `source` elements will look with the codecs specified:

```
<source src="example.mp4" type='video/mp4; codecs="avc1.42E01E,
➥mp4a.40.2"'>
<source src="example.webm" type='video/webm; codecs="vp8, vorbis"'>
<source src="example.ogv" type='video/ogg; codecs="theora, vorbis"'>
```

You'll notice that the syntax for the **type** attribute has been slightly modified to accommodate the container and codec values. The double quotes surrounding the values have changed to single quotes, and another set of nested double quotes is included specifically for the codecs.

This can be a tad confusing at first glance, but in most cases you'll just be copying and pasting those values once you have a set method for encoding the videos (which we'll touch on later in this chapter). The important point is that you define the correct values for the specified file to ensure that the browser can determine which (if any) file it can play.

Which formats do you need?

Depending on your website's target audience, you may not require three **source** elements for full browser support. Support for video and audio codecs and containers is excellent, and you might only need one or two combinations. To help you decide which formats to use, be sure to check out the latest browser support info on Can I use.[1]

Source Order

The three **source** elements are placed as children of the **video** element, and the browser being used to render the HTML will choose whichever container/codec format it recognizes—downloading only the resources it needs and ignoring the others. With our three file formats declared, our code will now look like this:

```
<video width="375" height="280" poster="teaser.jpg" audio="muted">
  <source src="example.mp4" type='video/mp4; codecs="avc1.42E01E,
➥mp4a.40.2"'>
  <source src="example.webm" type='video/webm; codecs="vp8,
➥vorbis"'>
```

---

[1] http://caniuse.com/

```
  <source src="example.ogv" type='video/ogg; codecs="theora,
➥vorbis"'>
</video>
```

You'll notice that our code is now without the `src` attribute on the `video` element. As mentioned, as well as being redundant, including it would override any video files defined in the `source` elements, so it's necessary in this case to leave it out.

What about browsers without support for HTML5 video?

The three `source` elements that we included inside our `video` element will cover all modern browsers, but we're yet to ensure that our video will play for older browsers. As has been mentioned, you might still have a significant percentage of users utilizing browsers without native support for HTML5 video. Most of those users are on some version of Internet Explorer prior to version 9.

In keeping with the principle of graceful degradation, the `video` element has been designed so that older browsers can access the video by some alternate means. Any browsers that fail to recognize the `video` element will simply ignore it, along with its `source` children. But if the `video` element contains content that the browser recognizes as valid HTML, it will read and display that content instead.

What kind of content can we serve to those non-supporting browsers? According to Adobe,[2] over one billion desktop users have the Flash Player plugin installed on their systems. And most of those instances of the Flash plugin are version 9 or later, which offer support for the MPEG-4 video container format. With this in mind, to allow Internet Explorer 8 and earlier (and other older browsers without support for HTML5 video) to play our video, we can declare an embedded Flash video to use as a fallback. Here's the completed code for the video on *The HTML5 Herald* with the Flash fallback code included:

```
<video width="375" height="280" poster="teaser.jpg" audio="muted">
  <source src="example.mp4" type='video/mp4; codecs="avc1.42E01E,
➥mp4a.40.2"'>
  <source src="example.webm" type='video/webm; codecs="vp8,
➥vorbis"'>
```

---

[2] http://www.adobe.com/ca/products/flashruntimes/statistics.html

```
  <source src="example.ogv" type='video/ogg; codecs="theora,
➥vorbis"'>
  <!-- fallback to Flash: -->
  <object width="375" height="280" type="application/x-shockwave-
➥flash" data="mediaplayer-5.5/player.swf">
    <param name="movie" value="mediaplayer-5.5/player.swf">
    <param name="allowFullScreen" value="true">
    <param name="wmode" value="transparent">
    <param name="flashvars" value="controlbar=over&amp;image=images/
➥teaser.jpg&amp;file=example.mp4">
    <!-- fallback image -->
    <img src="teaser.jpg" width="375" height="280" alt="" title="No
➥video playback capabilities">
  </object>
</video>
```

We'll skip going into all the details of how this newly added code works (this isn't a Flash book, after all!), but here are a few points to note about this addition to our markup:

- The `width` and `height` attributes on the `object` element should be the same as those on the `video` element.

- To play the file, we're using the open-source JW Player by LongTail Video,[3] which is free for non-commercial use, but you can use whichever video player you prefer.

- The Flash video code has a fallback of its own—an image file that displays if the code for the Flash video fails to work.

- The fourth `param` element defines the file to be used (`example.mp4`). As has been mentioned, most instances of the Flash player now support video playback using the MPEG-4 container format, so there's no need to encode another video format.

- HTML5-enabled browsers that support HTML5 video are instructed by the spec to ignore any content inside the `video` element that's not a `source` tag, so the fallback is safe in all browsers.

---

[3] http://www.longtailvideo.com/players/jw-flv-player/

In addition to the Flash fallback content, you could also provide an optional **download video** link that allows the user to access a local copy of the video and view it at their leisure. This would ensure that nobody is left without a means to view the video.

The last point to mention here is that, as is the case with the extra `source` elements, you may have no visitors from browsers without HTML5 video support on your website, or you might not be concerned about the small percentage using older browsers. In either of such cases, you could easily leave out the Flash fallback content and thus simplify the code.

Setting MIME Types

If you find that you've followed our instructions closely and your HTML5 video still fails to play from your server, the issue could be related to the content-type information being sent.

Content-type, also known as the **MIME type**, tells the browser the kind of content it's looking at. Is this a text file? If so, what kind? HTML? JavaScript? Is this a video file? The content-type answers these questions for the browser. Every time your browser requests a page, the server sends "headers" to your browser before sending any files. These headers tell your browser how to interpret the file that follows. Content-type is an example of one of the headers the server sends to the browser.

The MIME type for each video file that you include via the `source` element is the same as the value of the `type` attribute (minus any codec information). For the purpose of HTML5 video, we're concerned with three MIME types. To ensure that your server is able to play all three types of video files, place the following lines of code in your **.htaccess** file (or the equivalent if you're using a web server other than Apache):

```
AddType video/ogg .ogv
AddType video/mp4 .mp4
AddType video/webm .webm
```

If this fails to fix your problem, you may have to talk to your host or server administrator to find out if your server is using the correct MIME types. To learn more about configuring other types of web servers, read the excellent article "Properly Configuring Server MIME Types" from the Mozilla Developer Network.[4]

More on .htaccess

An .htaccess file provides a way to make configuration changes on a per-directory basis when using the Apache web server. The directives in an .htaccess file apply to the directory it lives in and all subdirectories. For more on .htaccess files, see the Apache documentation.[5]

Encoding Video Files for Use on the Web

The code we've presented for *The HTML5 Herald* is virtually bullet-proof, and will enable the video to be viewed by nearly everyone that sees the page. Because we need to encode our video in at least two formats (possibly three, if we want to), we need an easy way to encode our original video file into these HTML5-ready formats. Fortunately, there are some online resources and desktop applications that allow you to do exactly that.

Miro Video Converter[6] is free software with a super-simple interface that can encode your video into all the necessary formats for HTML5 video. It's available for Mac and Windows.

Simply drag a file to the window, or browse for a file in the customary way. A drop-down box gives options for encoding your video in a number of formats, including various platform- and device-specific presets (Apple iPad, Android, and so on).

There are a number of other choices for encoding HTML5 video, but Miro should suffice to help you create the two (or three) files necessary for embedding video that 99% of users can view.

---

[4] https://developer.mozilla.org/en-US/docs/Web/Security/Securing_your_site/Configuring_server_MIME_types
[5] http://httpd.apache.org/docs/current/howto/htaccess.html
[6] http://www.mirovideoconverter.com/

Creating Custom Video Controls

There's another huge benefit to using HTML5 video compared to the customary method of embedding video with a third-party technology. As discussed earlier in this chapter, with HTML5 video the `video` element becomes a real part of the web page, rather than just an inaccessible plugin. It's as much a part of the web page as an `img` element or any other native HTML element. This means that we can target the `video` element and its various parts using JavaScript—and even style the `video` element with CSS.

As we've seen, each browser that supports HTML5 video embeds a native set of controls to help the user access the video content. These controls have a different appearance in each browser, which may vex those concerned with a site's branding. No problem: by using the JavaScript API available with the `video` element, we can create our own custom controls and link them to the video's behavior.

Custom controls are created using whichever elements you want—images, plain HTML and CSS, or even elements drawn using the Canvas API—the choice is yours. To harness this API, create your own custom controls, insert them into the page, and then use JavaScript to convert those otherwise static graphic elements into dynamic, fully functioning video controls.

Some Markup and Styling for Starters

For our sample site, we're going to build a simple set of video controls to demonstrate the power of the new HTML5 video API. To start off, Figure 5.5 shows a screenshot of the set of controls we'll be using to manipulate the video.

Figure 5.5. Our set of video controls that we'll be building

Both of those buttons have alternate states: Figure 5.6 shows how the controls will look if the video is playing and the sound has been muted.

Figure 5.6. Our controls with the sound muted and the video playing

Our controls have three components:

- play/pause button
- timer that counts forward from zero
- mute/unmute button

In most cases, your custom video controls should have all the features of the default controls that various browsers natively provide. If your set of controls introduces fewer or inferior features, it's likely you'll frustrate your users.

For the purpose of introducing the API rather than trying to mimic what the browsers natively do, we want to introduce the important parts of the video API gradually. This will allow you to get your feet wet while establishing a foundation from which to work.

We'll be creating a simple, yet usable, set of controls for our video. The main feature missing from our set of controls is the seek bar that lets the user "scrub" through the video to find a specific part, so there will be no way of going back to the start of the video aside from refreshing the page or waiting for the video to end. Other than that, the controls will function adequately—they'll allow the user to play, pause, mute, or unmute the video.

Here's the HTML we'll use to represent the different parts of the video controls:

```
<div id="controls" class="hidden">
  <a id="playPause">Play/Pause</a>
  <span id="timer">00:00</span>
  <a id="muteUnmute">Mute/Unmute</a>
</div>
```

We'll skip going into the CSS in great detail, but here's a summary of what we've done (you can view the demo page's source in the code archive if you want to see how it's all put together):

- The text in the play/pause and mute/unmute buttons is removed from view using the text-indent property.

- A single CSS sprite image is used as a background image to represent the different button states (play, pause, mute, unmute).

- CSS classes are being used to represent the different states; those classes will be added and removed using JavaScript.

- The "controls" wrapper element is absolutely positioned and placed to overlay the bottom of the video.

- We've given the controls a default opacity level of 50%, but on mouseover the opacity increases to 100%.

- By default, the controls wrapper element is set to display: none using a class of "hidden", which we'll remove with JavaScript.

If you're following along building the example, go ahead and style the three elements however you like. You might even want to use icon fonts or SVG graphics to create the interface. Whatever you choose, the appearance of the controls is really secondary to what we're accomplishing here, so feel free to fiddle until you have a look that you're happy with.

Introducing the Media Elements API

Let's go through the steps needed to create our custom controls, and in the process we'll introduce you to the relevant aspects of the video API. Afterwards, we'll summarize some other features from the API that we won't be using in our controls, so that you have a good overview of what the API includes.

In order to work with our new custom controls, we'll first cache them by placing them into JavaScript variables. Here are the first few lines of our code:

```
var videoEl = document.getElementsByTagName('video')[0],
    playPauseBtn = document.getElementById('playPause'),
    vidControls = document.getElementById('controls'),
    muteBtn = document.getElementById('muteUnmute'),
    timeHolder = document.getElementById('timer');
```

Of course, caching our selections in variables is optional, but it's always best practice (for maintainability and performance) to work with cached objects, rather than needlessly repeating the same code to target various elements on the page. We're using a comma to separate our variable definitions, which means we're using a single var statement.

The first line is targeting the `video` element itself. We'll be using this `videoEl` variable quite a bit when using the API—since most API methods need to be called from the media element. The next four lines of code should be familiar to you if you took note of the HTML that comprises our controls. Those are the four elements on the page that we'll be manipulating based on user interaction.

Our first task is to make sure the video's native controls are hidden. We could do this easily by simply removing the `controls` attribute from the HTML. But since our custom controls are dependent on JavaScript, visitors with JavaScript disabled would be deprived of any way of controlling the video. So to follow the principle of progressive enhancement, we're going to remove the `controls` attribute using JavaScript:

```
videoEl.removeAttribute('controls');
```

The next step is to make our own custom controls visible. As has been mentioned, we've used CSS to remove our controls from view by default. By using JavaScript to enable the visibility of the custom controls, we ensure that the user will never see two sets of controls.

Our next chunk of code will look like this:

```
videoEl.addEventListener('canplaythrough', function () {
  vidControls.classList.remove('hidden');
}, false);
```

This is the first place we've used a feature from the HTML5 video API. First, take note of the `addEventListener` method. This method does exactly what its name implies: it listens for the specified event occurring on the targeted element.

addEventListener Isn't Cross-browser

If you're familiar with cross-browser JavaScript techniques, you probably know that the `addEventListener` method isn't cross-browser. In this case, it poses no problem. The only browsers in use that have no support for `addEventListener` are versions of Internet Explorer prior to version 9—and those browsers have no support for HTML5 video anyway. All we need do is use Modernizr (or some equivalent JavaScript) to detect support for the HTML5 video API, and then only run the code for supporting browsers—all of which support `addEventListener`.

In this case, we're targeting the video element itself. The event we're registering to listen for is the canplaythrough event from the video API. According to the definition of this event in the spec:[7]

> The user agent estimates that if playback were to be started now,
> the media resource could be rendered at the current playback rate
> all the way to its end without having to stop for further buffering.

There are other events we can use to check whether the video is ready, each of which has its own specific purpose. We'll touch on some of those other events later in the chapter. This particular one ensures continuous playback, so it's a good fit for us as we'd like to avoid choppy playback.

Playing and Pausing the Video

When the canplaythrough event fires, a callback function is executed. In that function, we've put a single line of code that removes the hidden class from the controls wrapper, so now our controls are visible. Now we want to add some functionality to our controls. Let's bind a click event handler to our play/pause button:

```
playPauseBtn.addEventListener('click', function () {
  if (videoEl.paused) {
    videoEl.play();
  } else {
    videoEl.pause();
  }
}, false);
```

When the button is clicked, we run an if/else block that's using three additional features from the video API. Here's a description of all three:

- The paused property is being accessed to see if the video is currently in the "paused" state. This doesn't necessarily mean the video has been paused by the user; it could represent the start of the video before it's been played. This property will return true if the video isn't currently playing.

---

[7] http://www.w3.org/html/wg/drafts/html/master/single-page.html#event-media-canplaythrough

■ Since we've now determined that the play/pause button has been clicked, and the video is not currently playing, we can safely call the `play()` method on the `video` element. This will play the video from its last paused location.

■ Finally, if the `paused` property doesn't return `true`, the `else` portion of our code will execute and this will trigger the `pause()` method on the `video` element, pausing the video.

You may have noticed that our custom controls have no "stop" button (customarily represented by a square icon), which would not only stop playback but also send the video to the beginning. You could add such a button if you feel it's necessary, but many video players don't use it since the seek bar can be used to move to the beginning of the video. The only catch is that the video API has no "stop" method; to counter this, you can cause the video to mimic the traditional "stop" behavior by pausing it and then sending playback to the beginning (more on this later).

You'll notice that something's missing from our `if`/`else` construct. Earlier, we showed you a couple of screenshots displaying the controls in their two states. We'll use JavaScript to alter the background position of our sprite image, and change the button from visually representing "play me" to "pause me."

This is how we'll do it:

```
videoEl.addEventListener('play', function () {
  playPauseBtn.classList.add('playing');
}, false);

videoEl.addEventListener('pause', function () {
  playPauseBtn.classList.remove('playing');
}, false);
```

Here we have two more uses of the `addEventListener` method (you'll need to become accustomed to this method if you're going to use the video and audio APIs!). The first block is listening for `play` events, so if the `click` handler we wrote triggers the `play()` method (or if something else causes the video to play, such as other code on the page), the `play` event will be detected by the listener and the callback function will execute. The second block of code is listening for the `pause` event (not to be confused with the `paused` property).

If the element has been played, the first block will add the class `playing` to our play/pause button. This class will change the background position of the sprite on the play/pause button to make the "pause me" icon appear. Similarly, the second block of code will remove the `playing` class, causing the state of the button to go back to the default (the "play me" state).

You're probably thinking, "Why not just add or remove the `playing` class in the code handling the button click?" While this would work just fine for when the button is clicked (or accessed via the keyboard), there's another behavior we need to consider here, demonstrated in Figure 5.7.

Figure 5.7. Some video controls are accessible via the context menu

This menu appears when you bring up the video's context menu (accessed via right-clicking on the video). As you can see, clicking the controls on the `video` element isn't the only way to play/pause or mute/unmute the video.

To ensure that the button states are changed no matter how the `video` element's features are accessed, we instead listen for `play` and `pause` events (and, as you'll see in a moment, sound-related events) to change the states of the buttons.

Save Video As...

You may be concerned that the `video` element's context menu has an option for **Save Video As...**. There's been discussion online about how easy it is to save HTML5 video, and this could affect how copyrighted videos will be distributed. Some content producers might feel like avoiding HTML5 video for this reason alone.

Whatever you choose to do, just recognize the realities associated with web video. Most users who are intent on copying and distributing copyrighted video will find ways to do it, regardless of any protection put in place. There are many web apps and software tools that can easily rip even Flash-based video. You should also be aware that even if you do disable the context menu on the `video` element, the user can still view the source of the page and find the location of the video file(s).

Some sites, like YouTube, have already implemented features to combat this when using HTML5 video. YouTube has a page that allows you to opt in to HTML5 video[8] if your browser doesn't use HTML5 video by default. After opting in, when you view a video and open the `video` element's context menu, there's a custom context menu without the **Save Video As...** option. YouTube also dynamically adds the `video` element to the page, and deeply nests the element with an indecipherable `src` attribute. So you do have options, and it is possible to make it more difficult (but not impossible) for users to rip your copyrighted videos. But recognize that there are drawbacks to changing user expectations, in addition to the performance and maintainability issues associated with convoluting your scripts and markup for what could be little, if any, gain.

Muting and Unmuting the Video's Audio Track

The next bit of functionality we want to add to our script is the mute/unmute button. This piece of code is virtually the same as what was used for the play/pause button, except that this time we've bound the `click` event to the mute/unmute button, following with a similar `if`/`else` construct:

```
muteBtn.addEventListener('click', function () {
  if (videoEl.muted) {
    videoEl.muted = false;
  } else {
    videoEl.muted = true;
  }
}, false);
```

This block of code introduces a new part of the API: the `muted` property. After the mute button is clicked, we check to see the status of the `muted` property. If it's `true` (meaning the sound is muted), we set it to `false` (unmuting the sound); if it's `false`, we set its status to `true`.

---

[8] http://www.youtube.com/html5

Again, we've avoided any button-state handling here for the same reasons mentioned earlier when discussing the play/pause buttons; the context menu allows for muting and unmuting, so we want to change the mute button's state depending on the actual muting or unmuting of the video, rather than the clicking of the button.

Unlike the play/pause button, we lack the ability to listen for "mute" and "unmute" events. Instead, the API offers the `volumechange` event:

```
videoEl.addEventListener('volumechange', function () {
  if (videoEl.muted) {
    muteBtn.classList.add('muted');
  } else {
    muteBtn.classList.remove('muted');
  }
}, false);
```

Again, we're using an event listener to run some code each time the specified event (in this case, a change in volume) takes place. As you can probably infer from its name, the `volumechange` event isn't limited to detecting muting and unmuting; it can detect any change in volume.

Once we've detected the change in volume, we check the status of the `video` element's `muted` property and change the class on the mute/unmute button accordingly.

Responding When the Video Ends Playback

The code we've written so far will allow the user to play and pause the video, as well as mute and unmute the sound. All of this is done using our custom controls.

At this point, if you let the video play to the end it will stop on the last frame. Instead of leaving it on the last frame, we think it's best to send the video back to the first frame, ready to be played again. This gives us the opportunity to introduce two new features of the API:

```
videoEl.addEventListener('ended', function () {
  videoEl.currentTime = 0;
}, false);
```

This block of code listens for the `ended` event, which tells us that the video has reached its end and stopped. Once we detect this event, we set the video's `current-`

`Time` property to zero. This property represents the current playback position, expressed in seconds (with decimal fractions).

This brings us to the next step in our code.

Updating the Time as the Video Plays

Now for the last step: we want our timer to update the current playback time as the video plays. We've already introduced the `currentTime` property, which we can use to update the content of our `#timeHolder` element (which is the cached element with an ID of `"timer"`). Here's how we do it:

```
videoEl.addEventListener('timeupdate', function () {
  timeHolder.innerHTML = secondsToTime(videoEl.currentTime);
}, false);
```

In this case, we're listening for `timeupdate` events. The `timeupdate` event fires each time the video's time changes, which means that even a fraction of a second's change will fire this event.

This alone would suffice to create a bare-bones timer. Unfortunately, it would be unhelpful and ugly on the eyes because you'd see the time changing every millisecond to numerous decimal places, as shown in Figure 5.8.

Figure 5.8. Using the `currentTime` property directly in our HTML is less than ideal

In addition, instead of hours or minutes the timer in this state will only display seconds—which could end up being in the hundreds or thousands, depending on the length of the video. That's impractical, to say the least.

To format the seconds into a more user-friendly time, we've written a function called `secondsToTime()`, and called it from our `timeupdate` handler. We want to avoid showing the milliseconds in this case, so our function rounds the timer to the nearest second. Here's the start of our function:

```
var h = Math.floor(s / (60 * 60)),
    dm = s % (60 * 60),
    m = Math.floor(dm / 60),
    ds = dm % 60,
    secs = Math.ceil(ds);
```

After those five lines of code, the final variable secs will hold a rounded number of seconds, calculated from the number of seconds passed into the function.

Next, we need to ensure that a single digit amount of seconds or minutes is expressed with a preceding zero; that is, employing "05" instead of just "5". The next code block will take care of this:

```
if (secs === 60) {
  secs = 0;
  m = m + 1;
}

if (secs < 10) {
  secs = '0' + secs;
}

if (m === 60) {
  m = 0;
  h = h + 1;
}

if (m < 10) {
  m = '0' + m;
}
```

Finally, we return a string that represents the current time of the video in its correct format:

```
if (h === 0) {
  fulltime = m + ':' + secs;
} else {
  fulltime = h + ':' + m + ':' + secs;
```

```
}

return fulltime;
```

The `if`/`else` construct is included to check if the video is one hour or longer; if so, we'll format the time with two colons. Otherwise, the formatted time will use a single colon that divides minutes from seconds, which will be the case in most circumstances.

Remember where we're running this function: we've included this inside our `timeupdate` event handler. The function's returned result will become the content of the `timeHolder` element:

```
timeHolder.innerHTML = secondsToTime(videoEl.currentTime);
```

Because the `timeupdate` event is triggered with every fraction of a second's change, the content of the `timeHolder` element will change rapidly. But because we're rounding the value to the nearest second, the *visible* changes will be limited to a time update every second, even though technically the content of the timer element is changing more rapidly.

And that's it, our custom controls are done! The buttons work as expected and the timer runs smoothly. As has been stated, this falls a little short of being a fully functional set of controls, but you should at least have a good handle on the basics of interacting with HTML5 video using JavaScript, so have a tinker and see what else you can add.

Further Features of the Media Elements API

The Media Elements API has much more to it than what we've covered here. Here's a summary of some events and properties that you might want to use when building your own custom controls, or when working with `video` and `audio` elements.

One point to remember is that these API methods and properties can be used anywhere in your JavaScript—they don't need to be linked to custom controls. If you'd like to play a video when the mouse hovers over it, or use `audio` elements to play various sounds associated with your web application or game, all you have to do is call the appropriate methods.

API Events

We've already seen the `canplaythrough`, `play`, `pause`, `volumechange`, `ended`, and `timeupdate` events. Here are some of the other events available to you when working with HTML5 video and audio:

- `canplay`: this is similar to `canplaythrough`, but will fire as soon as the video is playable, even if it's just a few frames (this contrasts with `canplaythrough`, which only fires if the browser thinks it can play the video all the way to the end without rebuffering)

- `error`: this event is sent when an error has occurred; there's also an `error` property

- `loadeddata`: the first frame of the media has loaded

- `loadedmetadata`: this event is sent when the media's metadata has finished loading; the metadata would include dimensions, duration, and any text tracks (for captions)

- `playing`: this indicates that the media has begun to play; the difference between `playing` and `play` is that `play` will not be sent if the video loops and begins playing again, whereas `playing` will

- `seeking`: this is sent when a seek operation begins; it might occur when a user starts to move the seek bar to select a new part of the video or audio

- `seeked`: this event fires when a seek operation is completed

API Properties

In addition to the properties we've already seen, here's a number of useful ones that are available to use:

- `playbackRate`: the default playback rate is 1, which can be changed to speed up or slow down playback; this is naturally of practical use if you're creating a fast-forward or rewind button, or a slow-motion or slow-rewind button

- `src`: as its name implies, this property returns the URL that points to the video being played, but only works if you're using the `src` attribute on the `video` element

▨ `currentSrc`: this will return the value of the URL pointing to the video file being played, whether it's from the `video` element's `src` attribute or one of the `source` elements

▨ `readyState`: this property returns a numeric value from 0 to 4 with each state representing the readiness level of the media element; for example, a value of 1 indicates that the media's metadata is available, while a value of 4 is virtually the same as the condition for firing the `canplaythrough` event, meaning the video is ready to play and won't be interrupted by buffering or loading

▨ `duration`: this returns the length of the video in seconds

▨ `buffered`: this represents the time ranges of the video that have buffered and are available for the browser to play

▨ `videoWidth`, `videoHeight`: these properties return the intrinsic dimensions of the video—the actual width and height as the video was encoded, not what's declared in the HTML or CSS; if you want the HTML- or CSS-defined values, these can be accessed through the customary `width` and `height` properties

You can also access attributes that can be declared directly in the HTML such as `preload`, `controls`, `autoplay`, `loop`, and `poster`.

What about audio?

Much of what we've discussed in relation to HTML5 video and its API also applies to the `audio` element, the obvious exceptions being those related to visuals.

Similar to the `video` element, the `preload`, `autoplay`, `loop`, and `controls` attributes can be used (or not) on the `audio` element.

The `audio` element won't display anything unless controls are present, but even if the element's controls are absent, the element is still accessible via scripting. This is useful if you want your site to use sounds not tied to controls presented to the user. The `audio` element nests `source` tags, similar to video, and will also treat any child element that's not a `source` tag as fallback content for non-supporting browsers.

Accessible Media

In addition to their status as first-class citizens of the page—making them intrinsic- ally more keyboard accessible (using `tabindex`, for example)—the HTML5 media elements also give you access to the `track` element to display captions or a transcript of the media file being played. Like `source` elements, `track` elements should be placed as children of the `video` or `audio` element.

If the `track` element is included as a child of the `video` element, it would look like the example shown here (similar to an example given in the spec):

```
<video src="example.webm">
  <track kind="subtitles" src="example.en.vtt" srclang="en" label=
➥"English" default>
  <track kind="captions" src="example.en.hoh.vtt" srclang="en" label
➥="English for the Hard of Hearing">
  <track kind="subtitles" src="example.fr.vtt" srclang="fr"
➥lang="fr"label="Français">
  <track kind="subtitles" src="example.de.vtt" srclang="de"
➥lang="de" label="Deutsch">
</video>
```

The code here has four `track` elements, each referencing a text track for captions in a different language (or, in the case of the second one, alternating content in the same language).

The `kind` attribute can take one of five values: `subtitles`, `captions`, `descriptions`, `chapters`, and `metadata`. The `src` attribute is required, and points to an external file that holds the track information. The `srclang` attribute specifies the language. The `label` attribute gives a user-readable title for the track. Finally, the Boolean `default` attribute defines which of the tracks will be used if the others are unsuitable.

The `track` element has excellent browser support, being available in all modern browsers. For an in-depth explanation of the `track` element and its many features, check out this article on the SitePoint website by Ankul Jain.[9]

---

[9] http://www.sitepoint.com/comprehensive-look-html5-track-element/

It's Showtime

Video and audio on the Web have long been the stronghold of Flash, but, as we've seen, HTML5 has changed that. While the codec and format landscape is still somewhat fragmented, the promises of fully scriptable multimedia content—along with the performance benefits of running audio and video natively in the browser instead of in a plugin wrapper—are hugely appealing to web designers, developers, and content providers.

Because of excellent browser support and easy-to-implement fallback techniques, there's no reason not to start using these elements and their associated APIs today.

We've now covered just about everything on HTML5 proper (that is, the bits that are in the HTML5 spec). In the next few chapters, we'll turn our attention to CSS3 and start to make *The HTML5 Herald* look downright fancy. Then we'll finish by looking at some of the new JavaScript APIs that are frequently bundled with the term "HTML5."

Introducing CSS3

The content layer is done. Now it's time to make it pretty. The next four chapters focus on presentation. In this one, we'll start by covering some basics: we'll first do a quick overview of CSS selectors, and see what's been added to our arsenal in CSS3. Then, we'll take a look at a few new ways of specifying colors. We'll dive into rounded corners, drop shadows, and text shadows—tips and tricks enabling us to style pages without having to make dozens of rounded-corner and text images to match our designs.

But first, we need to ensure older browsers recognize the new elements on our page, so that we can style them.

Getting Older Browsers on Board

As we mentioned back in Chapter 2, styling the new HTML5 elements in older versions of Internet Explorer requires a snippet of JavaScript called an HTML5 shiv. If you're using the Modernizr library detailed in Appendix A you'll have the option to include the shiv, so in that case you'll be fine.

Even with this JavaScript in place, though, you're not quite ready to roll. IE through version 8 will now be aware of these new elements, but these archaic browsers will still be without any default styles. In fact, this will be the case for previous versions of other browsers as well; while they may allow arbitrary elements, they've no way of knowing, for example, that `article` should be displayed as block-level and `mark` should be displayed inline. Because elements render as inline by default, it makes sense to tell these browsers which elements should be block-level.

This can be done with the following CSS rule:

```
article, aside, figure, footer, header, main, nav, section {
  display: block;
}
```

With this CSS and the required JavaScript in place, all browsers will start off on an even footing when it comes to styling HTML5 elements.

CSS3 Selectors

Selectors are at the heart of CSS. Without selectors to target elements on the page, the only way to modify the CSS properties of an element would be to use the element's `style` attribute and declare the styles inline, which is awkward and unmaintainable. So we use selectors. Originally, CSS allowed the matching of elements by type, class, and/or ID. This required adding class and ID attributes to our markup to create hooks and differentiate between elements of the same type. CSS2.1 added pseudo-elements, pseudo-classes, and combinators. With CSS3, we can target almost any element on the page with a wide range of selectors.

In the descriptions that follow, we'll be including the selectors provided to us in earlier versions of CSS. They are included because, while we can use CSS3 selectors, selectors that predate CSS3 are also part of the CSS Selectors Level 3 specification and are still supported, as CSS Selectors Level 3 expands on them. Even for those selectors that have been around for quite some time, it's worth going over them here, as there are some hidden gems in the old spec that few developers know. Note that all modern browsers, including IE9 and above, support all CSS3 selectors.

Relational Selectors

Relational selectors target elements based on their relationship to another element within the markup. All of these are supported since IE7+, and in all other major browsers:

Descendant combinator (E F)   You should definitely be familiar with this one. The descendant selector targets any element F that is a descendant (child, grandchild, great grandchild, and so on) of an element E. For example, ol li targets li elements that are inside ordered lists. This would include li elements in a ul that's nested in an ol, which might not be what you want.

Child combinator (E > F)   This selector matches any element F that is a *direct child* of element E—any further nested elements will be ignored. Continuing the example, ol > li would only target li elements directly inside the ol, and would omit those nested inside a ul.

Adjacent sibling, or next sibling selector (E + F)   This will match any element F that shares the same parent as E, and comes *directly after* E in the markup. For example, li + li will target all li elements except the first li in a given container.

General sibling or following sibling selector (E ~ F)   This one's a little trickier. It will match any element F that shares the same parent as any E and comes after it in the markup. So, h1 ~ h2 will match any h2 that follows an h1, as long as they both share the same direct parent—that is, as long as the h2 is not nested in any other element.

Let's look at a quick example:

```
<article>
  <header>
    <h1>Main title</h1>
```

```
    <h2>This subtitle is matched </h2>
  </header>
  <p> blah, blah, blah …</p>
  <h2>This is not matched by h1 ~ h2, but is by header ~ h2</h2>
  <p> blah, blah, blah …</p>
</article>
```

The selector string h1 ~ h2 will match the first h2, because both the h1 and h2 are children, or direct descendants, of the header. The next h2 you'll see in the code snippet doesn't match, since its parent is article, not header. It would, however, match header ~ h2. Similarly, h2 ~ p only matches the last paragraph, since the first paragraph precedes the h2 with which it shares the parent article.

 Why is there no "parent" selector?

You'll notice that up to this point there has been no "parent" or "ancestor" selector, and there's also no "preceding sibling" selector. The performance of the browser having to go backwards up the DOM tree, or recurse into sets of nested elements before deciding whether or not to apply a style, prevented the ability to have native "up the DOM tree" selectors.

jQuery included :has() as an ancestral selector. This selector is being considered for CSS Selectors Level 4, but has yet to be implemented in any browser. If and when it is implemented, we will be able to use E:has(F) to find E that has F as a descendant, E:has(> F), to find E that has F as a direct child, E:has(+ F), to find E that directly precedes a sibling F, and similar.

Looking through the stylesheet for *The HTML5 Herald*, you'll see a number of places where we've used these selectors. For example, when determining the overall layout of the site, we want the three-column divs to be floated left. To avoid this style being applied to any other divs nested inside them, we use the child selector:

```
main > div {
  float: left;
  overflow: hidden;
}
```

As we add new styles to the site over the course of the next few chapters, you'll be seeing a lot of these selector types.

Attribute Selectors

CSS2 introduced several attribute selectors. These allow for matching elements based on their attributes. CSS3 expands upon those attribute selectors, allowing for some targeting based on pattern matching. CSS Selectors Level 4 adds a few more:

E[attr]   Matches any element E that has the attribute `attr` regardless of the attribute's value. We made use of this back in Chapter 4 to style required inputs; `input:required` works in the latest browsers, but `input[required]` has the same effect and works in IE7 and IE8 as well.

E[attr=val]   Matches any element E that has the attribute `attr` with the exact value `val`. While not new, it's helpful in targeting form input types; for instance, targeting checkboxes with `input[type=checkbox]`.

E[attr|=val]   Matches any element E whose attribute `attr` either has the value `val` or begins with `val-`. This is most commonly used for the `lang` attribute. For example, `p[lang|="en"]` would match any paragraph that has been defined as being in English whether it be UK or US English with `&lt;p lang="en-uk">` or `&lt;p lang="en-us">`.

E[attr~=val]   Matches any element E whose attribute `attr` has within its value the full word `val`, surrounded by whitespace. For example, `.info[title~=more]` would match any element with the class info that had a `title` attribute containing the word "more," such as "Click here for more information."

E[attr^=val]   Matches any element E whose attribute `attr` starts with the value `val`. In other words, the `val` matches the beginning of the attribute value.

E[attr$=val]   Matches any element E whose attribute `attr` *ends* in `val`. In other words, the `val` matches the end of the attribute value.

E[attr*=val]   Matches any element E whose attribute `attr` matches `val` anywhere within the attribute. It is similar to E[attr~=val], except the `val` can be part of a word. Using the same example as before, `.fakelink[title~=info] {}` would match any element with the class `fakelink` that has a `title` attribute containing the string `info`, such as "Click here for more information."

In these attribute selectors, the value of `val` is case-sensitive for values that are case sensitive in HTML. For example, `input[class^="btn"]` is case sensitive as class names are case sensitive, but `input[type="checkbox"]` is not case sensitive, as the `type` value is case-insensitive in HTML.

The value does not have to be quoted if the value is alphanumeric, with some exceptions. Empty strings, strings that begin with a number, two hyphens, and other quirks need to be quoted. Because of the exceptions, it's a good idea to make a habit of always including quotes for those times when you do need them.

In CSS Selectors Level 4, we can have case insensitivity by including an `i` before the closing bracket, `E[attr*=val i]`.

Pseudo-classes

It's likely that you're already familiar with some of the user interaction pseudo-classes, namely `:link`, `:visited`, `:hover`, `:active`, and `:focus`.

 Key Points to Note

There are security issues the `:visited` pseudo-class can pose, so browsers do not support all CSS properties on visited links. Without these limitations, malicious sites could apply a style to a `visited` link, such as a unique background image for each visited link, to check whether popular sites or banks have been visited by the user. This allows the attacker to glimpse the user's browsing history without their permission. As a result, modern browsers limit the styles that can be applied with `:visited`.

The spec explicitly condones these changes, saying: "UAs [User Agents] may therefore treat all links as unvisited links, or implement other measures to preserve the user's privacy while rendering visited and unvisited links differently."

For better accessibility, add `:focus` wherever you include `:hover` as not all visitors will use a mouse to navigate your site.

■ :hover can apply to any element on the page—not just links and form controls.

■ :focus and :active are relevant to links, form controls, content editable elements, and any element with a tabindex attribute.

While it's likely you've been using these basic pseudo-classes for some time, there are many others available. Several of these pseudo-classes have been in the specification for years, but weren't supported (or commonly known) until browsers started supporting the new HTML5 form attributes that made them more relevant.

The following pseudo-classes match elements based on attributes, user interaction, and form control state:

:enabled
A user interface element that's enabled, which is basically any form control that supports the disabled attribute but doesn't currently have it applied.

:disabled
Conversely, a user interface element that is disabled: any form control that supports the disabled attribute and currently has it applied.

:checked
For radio buttons or checkboxes that are selected or ticked.

:indeterminate
For form elements that are neither checked nor unchecked. For example, if you tick a **check all** checkbox to select a group of checkboxes, then deselect some but not all of the checkboxes in the group, the **check all** could be set to the indeterminate state (with JavaScript) to indicate that it's neither checked nor unchecked.

:target
This selector singles out the element that is the target of the currently active intrapage anchor. That sounds more complicated than it is: you already know that you can have links to anchors within a page by using the # character with the ID of the target. For example, you may have <a href="#content">Skip to content</a> link in your page that, when clicked, will jump to the element with an ID of content.

This changes the URL in the address bar to `thispage.html#content`—and the `:target` selector now matches the element in the document that has `content` as its ID. It's as if you had included, temporarily, the selector `#content`. We say temporarily because as soon as the user clicks on a different anchor, `:target` will match the new target.

`:default`

Applies to one or more UI elements that are the default among a set of similar elements. For example, the one radio button in a group of same-named radio buttons that was checked on page load will continue to match `:default` after another radio button in the same-named group is selected. Similarly, checkboxes that are selected on page load will continue to match `:default` after they are unchecked.

`:valid`

Applies to elements that are valid, based on the `type`, `pattern`, or other input attributes (as we discussed in Chapter 4).

`:invalid`

Applies to empty required elements and elements failing to match the requirements defined by the `type` or `pattern` attributes.

`:in-range`

Applies to elements with range limitations where the value is within those limitations. This applies, for example, to date/time, `number`, and `range` input types with `min` and `max` attributes. When the value is `null`, it is `:in-range`.

`:out-of-range`

The opposite of `:in-range`: elements whose value is *outside* the limitations of their range. Missing values are not out of range, as they are empty.

`:required`

Applies to form controls that have the `required` attribute set.

`:optional`

Applies to all form controls that *do not* have the `required` attribute.

`:read-only`

Applies to elements whose contents are unable to be altered by the user. This is most elements other than those with the `contenteditable` attribute set and form fields.

`:read-write`   Applies to elements whose contents are user-alterable, such as `contenteditable` components and writable input fields.

Browser support for these attributes is complete in browsers that support the attributes in their form controls; in other words, browsers that support `required` and `pattern` also support the associated `:valid` and `:invalid` pseudo-classes.

IE8 and earlier lack support for `:checked`, `:enabled`, `:disabled`, and `:target`. The good news is that IE9 *does* support these selectors, but not the user-interface selectors. IE10 and IE11 support `:indeterminate`, `:required`, and `:optional`, but not `:default`, `:in-range`, `:out-of-range`, `:read-only`, or `:read-write`.

While support is still lacking, JavaScript libraries such as Selectivizr[1] can help in targeting these pseudo-classes in Internet Explorer.

Structural Pseudo-classes

So far, we've seen how we can target elements based on their attributes and states. CSS3 also enables us to target elements based simply on their location in the markup. These selectors are grouped under the heading structural pseudo-classes.[2]

These might seem complicated right now, but they'll make more sense as we look at ways to apply them later on. These selectors are supported in IE9 and newer, as well as current and older versions of all the other browsers—but not in IE8 and below:

`:root`   The root element, which is the `html` element in our HTML files.

`E:nth-child(n)`   The element E that is the nth child of its parent. The n parameter is explained in the note below.

`E:nth-last-child(n)`   The element F that is the nth child of its parent E, counting backwards from the last one. `li:nth-last-child(1)` would match the last item in any list—this is the same as `li:last-child` (see the note below).

---

[1] http://selectivizr.com/

[2] http://www.w3.org/TR/css3-selectors/#structural-pseudos

`E:nth-of-type(n)`

The element that is the nth element of its type in a given parent element. The difference between :nth-child and :nth-of-type is explained in the note below.

`E:nth-last-of-type(n)`

Like nth-of-type(n), except counting backwards from the last element in a parent.

 Parameters of Structural Selectors

There are four pseudo-classes that take the equation **an+b** as a parameter in parentheses, or the keywords **odd** and **even**. The structural pseudo-classes include :nth-child(an + b), :nth-last-child(an + b), :nth-of-type(an + b), and :nth-last-of-type(an + b). In the equation **an+b**, **a** is the multiplier as an integer, **b** is the offset as an integer, and **n** is always the variable **n**.

In the simplest case, you can pass an integer. For example, E:nth-of-type(3) will target the third E element child of a single parent element. You can pass one of the two keywords **odd** or **even**, targeting every other element. You can also, more powerfully, pass a number expression such as E:nth-of-type(3n+1). 3n means every third element, defining the frequency, and +1 is the offset. The default offset is zero, so where :nth-of-type(3n) would match the 3rd, 6th, and 9th elements in a series, :nth-of-type(3n+1) would match the 1st, 4th, 7th, and so on.

Negative offsets are also allowed. CSS is based on linguistic languages, not programming languages, so the count starts at 1 not 0. There can be no space between the multiplier **a** and the variable **n**, and the offset must come last.

With these numeric pseudo-classes, you can pinpoint which elements you want to target without adding classes to the markup. The most common example is a table where every other row is a slightly darker color to make it easier to read. We used to have to add odd or even classes to every `tr` to accomplish this. Now, we can simply declare `tr:nth-of-type(odd)` to target every odd line without touching the markup. You can even take it a step further with three-colored striped tables: target `tr:nth-of-type(3n)`, `tr:nth-of-type(3n+1)`, and `tr:nth-of-type(3n+2)` and apply a different color to each.

`E:first-child`	The element E if E is the first child of its parent. This is the same as `E:nth-child(1)`.
`E:last-child`	The element E if E is the last child of its parent, same as `E:nth-last-child(1)`.
`E:first-of-type`	The same as `:nth-of-type(1)`.
`E:last-of-type`	The same as `:nth-last-of-type(1)`.
`E:only-child`	Element E if E is the only child of its parent.
`E:only-of-type`	Element E if E is the only element of type E that is a direct child of its parent element.

 Child versus Type

In employing the structural selectors of `nth-of-type` and `nth-child`, it's important to understand what "child" and "type" mean in this case. "Child" looks at all the child elements that match the count and check if the precursor is a match. "Type" looks at all the elements that match the precursor first, then matches based on the count.

In the case of `p:nth-child(3n)`, the browser looks at every third child of a parent. If that child is a `p`, there is a match; if not, no match. In the case of `p:nth-of-type(3n)`, the browser looks at all the `p` children of the parent, and matches every third `p`.

Structural pseudo-classes are based on the parent, and restart counting for each new parent. They only look at elements that are the direct children of the parent. Text nodes are not part of the equation.

`E:empty`

An element that has no children; this includes text nodes, so `<p>hello</p>` and `<p> </p>` will not be matched by `p:empty`, but `<p></p>` and `<p><!-- comment --></p>` will be. This selector also matches empty or void elements, such as `<br>` and `<input>`. In CSS Selectors Level 4, we'll get `p:blank` that will match `<p> </p>`.

`E:lang(en)`

An element in the language denoted by the two-letter abbreviation, such as en. Unlike `E:[lang|=en]`, where the `lang` attribute must be present as an attribute of element E, `E:lang(en)` will match E if the language was declared on the element itself or any ancestor.

`E:not(exception)`

This is a particularly useful one: it will select elements that *don't* match the selector in the parentheses.

Selectors with the `:not` pseudo-class match everything to the left of the colon, and then exclude from that matched group the elements that also match what's to the right of the colon. The left-hand side matching goes first. For example, `p:not(.copyright)` will match all the paragraphs in a document first, and then exclude all the paragraphs from the set that also have the class of `copyright`. You can string several `:not` pseudo-classes together. `input:not([type=check-box]):not([type=radio])` will match all `input` elements on a page except those that are of type `checkbox` or `radio`.

Pseudo-elements and Generated Content

In addition to pseudo-classes, CSS gives us access to pseudo-elements. **Pseudo-elements** allow you to target text that is part of the document, but not otherwise targetable in the document tree. Pseudo-classes enable us to target existing elements. Pseudo-elements, on the other hand, enable us to target content based on the structure of the document when there are no actual elements or DOM nodes to target.

For example, all text nodes have a first letter and a first line, but how can you target them without wrapping them in a `span`, especially when you don't know exactly where the first line will wrap? CSS provides the `::first-letter` and `::first-line` pseudo-elements that match the first letter and first line of a text node respectively. These can alternatively be written with just a single colon: `:first-line` and `:first-letter`.

Why bother with the double colon?

The double colon is the correct syntax, but the single colon is what IE supported through IE8. All other browsers support both. Even though `:first-letter`, `:first-line`, `:first-child`, `:before`, and `:after` have been around since CSS2, these pseudo-elements in CSS3 have been redefined using double colons to differentiate them from pseudo-classes.

Generated Content

The `::before` and `::after` pseudo-elements don't refer to content that exists in the markup, but rather to a location where you can insert additional content, generated right there in your CSS. While this generated content won't become part of the DOM, it can be styled.

To generate content for a pseudo-element, use the `content` property. For example, let's say when printing a document that you wanted all external links on your page to be followed by the link's URL in parentheses, enabling users to know where the links led even when they're unclickable as they're looking at a printed page. Rather than hardcoding the URLs into your markup, you can use the combination of an attribute selector and the ::after pseudo-element:

```
a[href^=http]:after {
  content: " (" attr(href) ")";
}
```

attr() allows you to access any attribute of the selected element, coming in handy here for displaying the link's target. And you'll remember from the attribute selectors section that a[href^=http] means "any a element whose href attribute begins with http"; in other words, external links. To be more precise, we could have written a[href^="http://"], a[href^="https://"].

Here's another example:

```
a[href$=".pdf"] {
  background: transparent url(pdficon.gif) 0 50% no-repeat;
  padding-left: 20px;
}
a[href$=".pdf"]:after {
  content: " (PDF)";
}
```

Those styles will add a PDF icon and the text " (PDF)" after links to PDFs. Remember that the [attr$=val] selector matches the end of an attribute—so document.pdf will match but pdf.html won't.

::selection

The ::selection pseudo-element matches user-selected or highlighted text.

This is supported in all browsers since IE9, but requires the -moz vendor prefix for Firefox. Let's use it on *The HTML5 Herald* to bring the selection background and text color in line with the monochrome style of the rest of the site:

```
::-moz-selection {
  background: #484848;
  color: #fff;
}
::selection {
```

```
    background: #484848;
    color: #fff;
}
```

CSS3 Colors

We know you're probably champing at the bit to put the *really* cool stuff from CSS3 into practice, but before we do there's one more detour we need to take. CSS3 brings with it support for some new ways of describing colors on the page. Since we'll be using these in examples over the next few chapters, it's important we cover them now.

Prior to CSS3, we almost always declared colors using the hexadecimal format (#FFF, or #FFFFFF for white). It was also possible to declare colors using the rgb() notation, providing either integers (0–255) or percentages. For example, white is rgb(255, 255, 255) or rgb(100%, 100%, 100%). In addition, we had access to several named colors such as purple, lime, aqua, red, and the like. While the color keyword list has been extended in the CSS3 color module[3] to include 147 additional keyword colors (that are generally well supported), CSS3 also provides us with a number of other options: HSL, HSLA, and RGBA. The most notable change with these new color types is the ability to declare semitransparent colors.

RGBA

RGBA works just like RGB, except that it adds a fourth value: alpha, the opacity level or alpha transparency level. The first three values still represent red, green, and blue. For the alpha value, 1 means fully opaque, 0 is fully transparent, and 0.5 is 50% opaque. You can use any number between 0 and 1 inclusively.

Unlike RGB, which can also be represented with hexadecimal notation as #RRGGBB, there is no hexadecimal notation for RGBA. An eight-character hexadecimal value for RGBA as #RRGGBBAA has been proposed and added to the draft CSS Color Module Level 4,[4] but is yet to be supported.

For example, let's look at our registration form. We want the form to be a darker color, while still preserving the grainy texture of the site's background. To accom-

---

[3] http://www.w3.org/TR/css3-color/

[4] http://dev.w3.org/csswg/css-color-4/#hex-notation

plish this, we'll use an RGBA color of 0,0,0,0.2—in other words, solid black that's 80% transparent:

```
form {
    ⋮
    background: url(../images/bg-form.png) no-repeat bottom center
➥rgba(0, 0, 0, 0.2);
}
```

Since Internet Explorer 8 and below lack support for RGBA, if you declare an RGBA color, make sure you *precede* the property value pair with the same property that includes as its value a color IE can understand. IE will render the last color it can make sense of, so it will just skip the RGBA color. Other browsers will understand both colors, but thanks to the CSS cascade, they'll overwrite the IE color with the RGBA color as it comes later.

In the aforementioned example, we're actually fine with older versions of IE having no background color, because the color we're using is mostly transparent anyway.

HSL and HSLA

HSL stands for hue, saturation, and lightness. Unlike RGB, where you need to manipulate the saturation or brightness of a color by changing all three color values in concert, with HSL you can tweak either just the saturation or the lightness while keeping the same base hue. The syntax for HSL comprises an integer value for hue, and percentage values for saturation and lightness.[5]

Although monitors display colors as RGB, the browser simply converts the HSL value you give it into one the monitor can display.

The `hsl()` declaration accepts three values:

- The hue in degrees from 0 to 359. Some examples are: 0 = red, 60 = yellow, 120 = green, 180 = cyan, 240 = blue, and 300 = magenta. Of course, feel free to use everything in between.

---

[5] A full exploration of color theory—along with what is meant by the terms "saturation" and "lightness"—is beyond the scope of this book. If you want to read more, *The Principles of Beautiful Web Design* (SitePoint: Melbourne, 2014) [https://learnable.com/books/the-principles-of-beautiful-web-design-3rd-edition] includes a great primer on color.

- The saturation as a percentage with 100% being the norm. Saturation of 100% will be the full hue, and saturation of 0 will give you a shade of gray—essentially causing the hue value to be ignored.

- A percentage for lightness with 50% being the norm. Lightness of 100% will be white, 50% will be the actual hue, and 0% will be black.

HSL also allows for an opacity value. For example, `hsla(300, 100%, 50%, 0.5)` is magenta with full saturation and normal lightness, which is 50% opaque.

HSL mimics the way the human eye perceives color, so it can be more intuitive for designers to understand and, as mentioned, make adjustments a bit quicker and easier. Feel free to use whatever syntax you're most comfortable with—but remember that if you need to support IE8 or below, you'll generally want to limit yourself to hexadecimal notation.

Let's sum up with a review of all the ways to write colors in CSS. A shade of dark red can be written as:

- `#800000`
- `maroon`
- `rgb(128,0,0)`
- `rgba(128,0,0,1.0)`
- `hsl(0,100%,13%)`
- `hsla(0,100%,13%,1.0)`

Last, but certainly not least, CSS Color Module Level 3 provides us with `current-Color`. The `currentColor` keyword is equal to the current element's color property.

In CSS Colors Level 4, we get four- and eight-digit hex colors with the last digit(s) specifying transparency, `hwb()` and `hwba()` to specify colors by hue, whiteness and blackness, plus a `gray()` function to enable a shorter method for declaring shades of gray.

Opacity

In addition to specifying transparency with HSLA and RGBA colors (and soon, eight-digit hexadecimal values), CSS3 provides us with the `opacity` property. `opacity` sets the opaqueness of the element on which it's declared. Similar to alpha transparency, the opacity value is a floating point number between (and including) 0 and 1. An opacity value of 0 defines the element as fully transparent, whereas an opacity value of 1 means the element is fully opaque.

Let's look at an example:

```
div.halfopaque {
    background-color: rgb(0, 0, 0);
    opacity: 0.5;
    color: #000000;
}

div.halfalpha {
    background-color: rgba(0, 0, 0, 0.5);
    color: #000000;
}
```

Though the two declaration blocks may seem identical at first glance, there's actually a key difference. While opacity sets the opacity value for an element *and all of its children*, a semitransparent RGBA or HSLA color has no impact on the element's other CSS properties or descendants, other than inherited properties such as text color.

Looking at the example, any text in the `halfopaque` div will be 50% opaque (most likely making it difficult to read!). The text on the `halfalpha` div, though, will still be black and 100% opaque. Only the background color of that single element will be slightly opaque, as `background-color` is not an inherited property.

While the `opacity` property is a quick and easy solution for creating semitransparent elements, you should be aware of this consequence.

Putting It into Practice

Now that we've been through all the available CSS selectors and new color types, we're ready to really start styling.

For the rest of the chapter, we'll style a small section of *The HTML5 Herald* front page; this will demonstrate how to add rounded corners, text shadow, and box shadow.

In the right-hand sidebar of *The HTML5 Herald*'s front page are a series of whimsical advertisements—we marked them up as `article` elements within an `aside` way back in Chapter 2. The first of these is an old "Wanted" poster-style ad, advising readers to be on the lookout for the armed and dangerous HTML5 and CSS3. The ad's final appearance is depicted in Figure 6.1.

Figure 6.1. Our "Wanted" ad

You'll notice that the dark gray box in the center of the ad has a double border with rounded corners, as well as a three-dimensional "pop" to it. The text that reads "<HTML5> & {CSS3}" also has a shadow that offsets it from the background. Thanks to CSS3, all these effects can be achieved with some simple code and with no reliance on images or JavaScript. Let's learn how it's done.

The markup for the box is simply `<a href="…">&lt;HTML5&gt; &amp; {CSS3}</a>`. Other than the HTML entities, it's as straightforward as it gets!

Before we can apply any styles to it, we need to select it. Of course, we could just add a `class` attribute to the markup, but where's the fun in that? We're here to learn CSS3, so we should try and use some fancy new selectors instead.

Our box isn't the only a element on the page, but it might be the only a immediately following a paragraph in the sidebar. In this case, that's good enough to single out the box. We also know how to add some pre-CSS3 styling for the basics, so let's do that:

```
aside p + a {
  display: block;
  text-decoration: none;
  border: 5px double;
  color: #ffffff;
  background-color: #484848;
  text-align: center;
  font-size: 1.75rem;
  margin: 5px 5px 9px 5px;
  padding: 15px 0;
  position: relative;
}
```

Not bad! As Figure 6.2 shows, we're well on our way to the desired appearance. This will also be the appearance shown to IE8 and below except for the font styling, which we'll be adding in Chapter 9.

Figure 6.2. The basic appearance of our ad link, which will be seen by older browsers

IE6 lacks support for the adjacent sibling selector—so if you really need to provide support to that browser, you can add an `id` or `class` to the HTML and select it that way.

This presentation is fine and should be acceptable—there's no need for web pages to look identical in all browsers. Users with Internet Explorer 9 and older will be unaware that they're missing anything. But we can still provide treats to better browsers. Let's go ahead and add a bit of polish.

Rounded Corners: `border-radius`

The `border-radius` property lets you create rounded corners without the need for images or additional markup. To add rounded corners to our box, we simply add:

```
border-radius: 25px;
```

Safari, Chrome, Opera, IE9+, and Firefox all support rounded corners without a vendor prefix (just `border-radius`).

Figure 6.3 shows what our link looks like with the addition of these properties.

Figure 6.3. Adding rounded corners to our link

The `border-radius` property is actually a shorthand. For our a element, the corners are all the same size and symmetrical. If we had wanted different-sized corners, we could declare up to four unique values—`border-radius: 5px 10px 15px 20px;`, for example. Just like `padding`, `margin`, and `border`, you can adjust each value individually:

```
border-top-left-radius: 5px;
border-top-right-radius: 10px;
border-bottom-right-radius: 15px;
border-bottom-left-radius: 40px;
```

The resulting off-kilter box is shown in Figure 6.4.

Figure 6.4. It's possible to set the radius of each corner independently

When using the shorthand `border-radius`, the order of the corners is top-left, top-right, bottom-right, and bottom-left. You can also declare only two values, in which case the first is for top-left and bottom-right, and the second is for top-right and bottom-left. If you declare three values, the first refers to top-left, the second sets both the top-right and bottom-left, and the third is bottom-right.

We recommend using the shorthand—because it's much shorter.

You can also create asymmetrical corners with a different radius on each side. Rather than being circular, these will appear elliptical. If two values are supplied to any of the four longhand values, you'll be defining the horizontal and vertical radii of a quarter ellipse respectively. For example, `border-bottom-left-radius: 20px 10px;` will create an elliptical bottom-left corner.

When using the shorthand for elliptical corners, separate the value of the horizontal and vertical radii with a slash. `border-radius: 20px / 10px;` will create four equal elliptical corners, and `border-radius: 5px 10px 15px 20px / 10px 20px 30px 40px;` will create four unequal elliptical corners. That last example will create corners seen in Figure 6.5. Interesting? Yes. Aesthetically pleasing? Not so much.

Figure 6.5. Four interesting unequal elliptical corners

There's only one other element on *The HTML5 Herald* that uses rounded corners: the registration form's submit button. Let's round those corners now:

```
input[type=submit] {
  border-radius: 10%;
  background-clip: padding-box;
}
```

You'll note two things about this CSS: we've used an attribute selector to target the `submit` input type, and we've used percentages instead of pixel values for the rounded corners. This will come in handy if we need to add more forms to the site later; other submit buttons might be smaller than the one on the registration page, and by using percentages, rounded corners will scale in proportion to the size of the button.

Note that if a `border-radius` declaration is larger than 50% of the width or height of the box, the browser will round the corners proportionally based on the values provided. We also included `background-clip: padding-box;` to ensure that the background color doesn't bleed through the rounded border.

The `border-radius` property can be applied to all elements except the `table` element when the `border-collapse` property is set to `collapse`.

 Older Browsers

Generally speaking, there's no need to provide an identical look in older browsers, but sometimes a client may insist on it. There are some JavaScript solutions such as CSS3 PIE[6] that provide CSS3 decorations to older versions of IE without requiring additional images or markup. For Android 2.3, you can prefix the property as `-webkit-border-radius`. For performance reasons, we recommend against providing rounded corners to Android 2.3, IE8, and earlier versions of those browsers.

Drop Shadows

CSS3 provides the ability to add drop shadows to elements using the `box-shadow` property. This property lets you specify the color, height, width, blur, and offset of one or multiple inner and/or outer drop shadows on your elements.

We usually think of drop shadows as an effect that makes an element look like it's hovering over the page and leaving a shadow; however, with such fine-grained control over all those variables, you can be quite creative. For our advertisement link, we can use a box-shadow with no blur to create the appearance of a 3D box.

The `box-shadow` property takes a comma-separated list of shadows as its value. Each shadow is defined by two to four size values, a color, and the key term `inset` for inset—or internal—shadows. If you fail to specify `inset`, the default is for the shadow to be drawn outside of the element:

Let's look at the shadow we're using on our element, so that we can break down what each value is doing:

---

[6] http://css3pie.com/

```
box-shadow: 2px 5px 0 0 rgba(72,72,72,1);
```

The first value is the horizontal offset. A positive value will create a shadow to the right of the element, a negative value to the left. In our case, our shadow is two pixels to the right of the a.

The second value is the vertical offset. A positive value pushes the shadow down, creating a shadow on the bottom of the element. A negative value pushes the shadow up. In our case, the shadow is five pixels below the a.

The third value, if included, is the blur distance of the shadow. The greater the value, the more the shadow is blurred. Only positive values are allowed. Our shadow is not blurred — being opaque throughout — so we can either include a value of zero (0), or omit the value altogether.

The fourth value determines the spread distance of the shadow. A positive value will cause the shadow shape to expand in all directions. A negative value contracts the shadow. Our shadow has no spread, so again we can either include a value of zero (0), or omit the value altogether.

The fifth value is the shadow's color. You will generally want to declare the color of the shadow. If it's omitted, the spec states that it should default to the same as the `color` property of the element, or `currentColor`. In the example, we used an RGBA color. In this particular design the shadow is a solid color, so we could just have used the hex value. Most of the time, though, shadows will be partially transparent, so you'll typically be using RGBA or HSLA.

The drop shadow created by these declarations is shown in Figure 6.6.

Figure 6.6. Adding a drop shadow to our box gives it the illusion of depth

By default, the shadow is a drop shadow—occurring on the outside of the box. You can create an inset shadow by adding the word `inset` to the start or end of your shadow declaration.

The `box-shadow` property is well supported, with IE support starting at IE9.

Drop Shadows on Transparent Images

Drop shadows look good on rectangular elements, following the curve of the corners. Keep in mind, though, that the shadow follows the *edges* of your element, rather than the pixels of your content. So, if you try to use drop shadows on semitransparent images, you'll receive an ugly surprise: the shadow follows the rectangular borders of the image box instead of the contour of the image's content. To create drop shadows that work for alpha transparent images, use the `filter` property's `drop-shadow()` function—`filter: drop-shadow(2px 5px rgb(72,72,72))`—which works in Firefox 35, with the `-webkit-` prefix in Chrome 31+, Safari 7+, Opera, Android 4.4+, and iOS6+. The filter property is significantly different from and incompatible with Microsoft's older `filter` property, and is without support in IE 11.

To include more than one box shadow on an element, define a comma-separated list of shadows. When more than one shadow is specified, the shadows are layered front to back as if the browser drew the last shadow first and the previous shadow on top of that.

Like an element's outline, box shadows are *supposed* to be invisible in terms of the box model. In other words, they should have no impact on the layout of a page—they'll overlap other boxes and their shadows if necessary. We say "supposed to," because there are bugs in some browsers, though these are few and will likely be fixed fairly quickly.

Inset and Multiple Shadows

The registration form for *The HTML5 Herald* has what looks like a gradient background around the edges, but it's actually a few inset box shadows.

To create an inset box shadow, add the `inset` key term to your declaration. In our case, we have to include two shadows so that we cover all four sides: one shadow for the top left, and one for the bottom right:

```
form {
 box-shadow:
   inset 1px 1px 84px rgba(0,0,0,0.24),
   inset -1px -1px 84px rgba(0,0,0,0.24);
}
```

As you can see, to add multiple shadows to an element repeat the same syntax again, separated with a comma.

WebKit and Inset Shadows

Older versions of WebKit-based browsers that are still found on many mobile devices suffer from *very* slow performance when rendering inset box shadows with a large `blur` value, such as the one we're using on *The HTML5 Herald*'s registration form. For this reason, we recommend against using the vendor-prefixed property. It's very simple to not give older mobile browser users a bad experience: avoid adding the `-webkit-` prefix on shadow and border radii.

Text Shadow

Where `box-shadow` lets us add shadows to boxes, `text-shadow` adds shadows to individual characters in text nodes. Added in CSS2, `text-shadow` has been supported in Safari since version 1 and finally received support in IE10, unprefixed in all browsers.

The syntax of the `text-shadow` property is very similar to `box-shadow`, including prefixes, offsets, and the ability to add multiple shadows; the exceptions are that there's no spread, and inset shadows aren't permitted:

```
/* single shadow */
text-shadow: topOffset leftOffset blurRadius color;

/* multiple shadows */
text-shadow: topOffset1 leftOffset1 blurRadius1 color1,
             topOffset2 leftOffset2 blurRadius2 color2,
             topOffset3 leftOffset3 blurRadius3 color3;
```

Like `box-shadow`, when multiple shadows are declared, they're painted from front to back with the first shadow being the topmost. Text shadows appear behind the text itself. This is different from `box-shadow`, which starts on the outside of the box (or is displayed only on the inside in the case of `inset`). If a shadow is so large that it touches another letter, it will continue behind that character.

Our text has a semi-opaque shadow to the bottom right:

```
text-shadow: 3px 3px 1px rgba(0, 0, 0, 0.5);
```

This states that the shadow extends three pixels below the text, three pixels to the right of the text, is slightly blurred (one pixel), and has a base color of black at 50% opacity.

With that style in place our ad link is nearly complete, as Figure 6.7 shows. The finishing touch—a custom font—will be added in Chapter 9.

Figure 6.7. Our ad link is looking quite snazzy!

 Color-matching Your Shadow

Use the keyword `currentColor` if you want your text's shadow to match the color of your text. A single-pixel text shadow can make very thin fonts, such as Helvetica Neue Light, more legible:

```
text-shadow: 0 0 1px currentColor;
```

More Shadows

We now know how to create drop shadows on both block-level elements and text nodes. But so far, we've only styled a fraction of our page—only one link in one advertisement, in fact. Let's do the rest of the shadows before moving on.

Looking back at the site design, we can see that all the h1 elements on the page are uppercase and have drop shadows. The text is dark gray with a very subtle solid-white drop shadow on the bottom right, providing a bit of depth.[7] The tagline in the site header also has a drop shadow, but is all lowercase. The taglines for the articles, meanwhile, have no drop shadow.

We know that we can target all these elements without using classes. Let's do that without any additional markup:

```css
h1, h2 {
  text-transform: uppercase;
  text-shadow: 1px 1px #FFFFFF;
}
:not(article) > header h2 {
  text-transform: lowercase;
  text-shadow: 1px 1px #FFFFFF;
}
```

The first declaration targets all the h1 and h2 elements on the page. The second targets all the h2 elements that are in a header, but only if that header is not nested in an article element.

Our text shadows are a solid white, so there's no need to use alpha transparent colors or a blur radius.

Up Next

Now that we have shadows and rounded corners under our belt, it's time to have some more fun with CSS3. In the next chapter, we'll be looking at CSS3 gradients and multiple background images.

---

[7] See http://twitter.com/#!/themaninblue/status/27210719975964673.

7

CSS3 Gradients and Multiple Backgrounds

In Chapter 6, we learned a few ways to add decorative styling features—such as shadows and rounded corners—to our pages without the use of additional markup or images. The next most common feature frequently added to websites that used to require images is gradients. CSS3 provides us with the ability to include multiple background images on any element including multiple radial and linear gradients that we can make the browser create for us. With CSS3, there's no need to create the multitudes of JPEGs of years past, or add nonsemantic hooks to our markup.

Browser support for gradients and multiple backgrounds has fully evolved, with IE9 supporting multiple background images and IE10 supporting gradients.

We'll start by looking at CSS3 gradients. But first, what *are* gradients about? **Gradients** are smooth transitions between two or more specified colors. In creating gradients, you can specify multiple in-between color values called **color stops**. Each color stop is made up of a color and a position; the browser fades the colors from each stop to the next to create a smooth gradient. Gradients can be utilized anywhere a CSS image can be used. This means that in your CSS, a gradient can be theoretically employed anywhere a `url()` value can be used, such as `background-image`, `border-image`, and even `list-style-type`.

By using CSS gradients to replace images, you save your users from having to download extra images. Furthermore, CSS gradients are fully responsive, and so you avoid pixelation when you zoom in, unlike with images.

Linear and radial gradients are both well-supported types of gradients. Let's go over them in turn.

Linear Gradients

Linear gradients are those where colors transition across a straight line: from top to bottom, left to right, or along any arbitrary axis. If you've spent any time with image-editing tools such as Photoshop and Fireworks, you should be familiar with linear gradients—but as a refresher, Figure 7.1 shows some examples.

Figure 7.1. Linear gradient examples

Similar to image-editing programs, to create a linear gradient you specify a direction, the starting color, the end color, and any color stops you want to add along the gradient line. The browser takes care of the rest, filling the entire element by painting lines of color perpendicular to the gradient line. It produces a smooth fade from one color to the next, progressing in the direction you specify.

When it comes to browsers and linear gradients, it becomes a little messy. WebKit first introduced gradients several years ago using a particular and—many argued—convoluted syntax. After that, Mozilla implemented gradients using a simpler and more straightforward syntax. Then, in January of 2011, the W3C included a proposed syntax in CSS3. The final W3C syntax, which is slightly different from the previous prefixed implementation, is supported by all major browsers starting with IE10. It is supported without prefixes, though you may want to use the intermediate syntax with the `-webkit-` prefix to target some mobile WebKit browsers that are still in play, such as Android 4 to 4.3, Blackberry 10, and UC Browser for Android 9.

That still leaves us with the question of how to handle gradients in IE9 and earlier. Fortunately, IE9 supports scalable vector graphics (SVG) backgrounds—and it's fairly simple to create gradients in SVG. (We'll be covering SVG in more detail in Chapter 12.) In addition, IE8 supports a proprietary filter that enables the creation of basic linear gradients.

Confused? Don't be. While gradients are important to understand, memorizing all the browser syntaxes is unnecessary. We'll cover the final syntax, as well as the soon-to-be-forgotten old-style syntax, but first we'll let you in on a little secret: there are tools that will create all the required styles for you, so there's no need to remember all the specifics of each syntax. Let's get started.

There's one linear gradient in *The HTML5 Herald*, in the second advertisement block shown in Figure 7.2 (which happens to be advertising this very book!). You'll note that the gradient starts off dark at the top, lightens, then darkens again as if to create a road under the cyclist, before lightening again.

Figure 7.2. A linear gradient in *The HTML5 Herald*

To create a cross-browser gradient for our ad, we'll start with the standard syntax. Then we'll cover how to tweak it slightly to target older WebKit browsers.

The W3C Syntax

Here's the basic syntax for linear gradients:

```
background-image: linear-gradient( … );
```

Inside those parentheses, you specify the direction of the gradient and then provide some color stops. For the direction, you can provide either the angle along which the gradient should proceed, or the side or corner to which it should end—in which case it will proceed towards the opposite side or corner.

For angles, you use values in degrees (deg). 0deg points upward, 90deg points toward the right, and so on in a clockwise rotation. For a side or corner, use to top, to bottom, to left, to right, to top left, to bottom left, to top right, or to bottom right direction key phrases.

After specifying the direction, provide your color stops; these are made up of a color and a percentage or length specifying how far along the gradient that stop is located.

That's a lot to take in, so let's look at some gradient examples. For the sake of illustration, we'll use a gradient with just two color stops: #FFF (white) to #000 (black).

To have the gradient go from top to bottom of an element, as shown in Figure 7.3, you could specify any of the following:

```
background-image: linear-gradient(180deg, #FFF 0%, #000 100%);
background-image: linear-gradient(to bottom, #FFF 0%, #000 100%);
background-image: linear-gradient(#FFF 0%, #000 100%);
```

Figure 7.3. A white-to-black gradient from the top center to the bottom center of an element

The last declaration works because `to bottom` is the default in the absence of a specified direction.

Because the first color stop is assumed to be at 0%, and the last color stop is assumed to be at 100%, you could also omit the percentages from that example and achieve the same result:

```
background-image: linear-gradient(#FFF, #000);
```

While all of these examples are functionality-equivalent, we recommend that you select a preferred way of declaring your gradients for consistency and markup legibility.

Now let's put our gradient on an angle and place an additional color stop. Let's say we want to go from black to white, and then back to black again:

```
background-image: linear-gradient(60deg, #000, #FFF 75%, #000);
```

We've placed the color stop 75% along the way, so the white band is closer to the gradient's end point than its starting point, as shown in Figure 7.4.

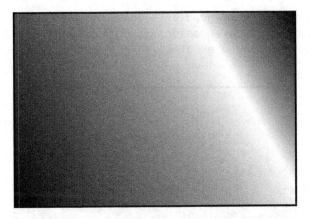

Figure 7.4. A gradient with three color stops

You can place your first color stop somewhere other than 0%, and your last color stop at a place other than 100%. All the space between 0% and the first stop will be the same color as the first stop, and all the space between the last stop and 100% will be the color of the last stop. Here's an example:

```
background-image: linear-gradient(60deg, #000 50%, #FFF 75%,
➥#000 90%);
```

The resulting gradient is shown in Figure 7.5.

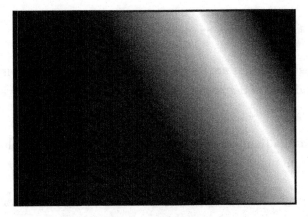

Figure 7.5. A gradient confined to a narrow band by offsetting the start and end color stops

There's no need to actually specify positions for any of the color stops. If you omit them, the stops will be evenly distributed. Here's an example:

```
background-image:
  linear-gradient(45deg,
    #FF0000 0%,
    #FF6633 20%,
    #FFFF00 40%,
    #00FF00 60%,
    #0000FF 80%,
    #AA00AA 100%);

background-image:
  linear-gradient(45deg,
    #FF0000,
    #FF6633,
    #FFFF00,
    #00FF00,
    #0000FF,
    #AA00AA);
```

Each of the previous declarations makes for a fairly unattractive angled rainbow. Note that we've added line breaks and indenting for ease of legibility—they are not essential.

Colors transition smoothly from one color stop to the next; however, if two color stops are placed at the same position along the gradient, the colors won't fade, but will stop and start on a hard line. This is a way to create a striped background effect, such as the one shown in Figure 7.6.

Figure 7.6. Careful placement of color stops can create striped backgrounds

Here are the styles used to construct that example:

```
background-image:
  linear-gradient(45deg,
    #000000 30%,
    #666666 30%,
    #666666 60%,
    #CCCCCC 60%,
    #CCCCCC 90%
);
```

At some point in the reasonably near future, you can expect this hopefully final, non-prefixed version of the syntax to be the only one you'll need to write—but we're not quite there yet.

The Prefixed Syntax

If you intend targeting gradients to older mobile WebKit browsers, you need to include a prefixed gradient declaration with slightly different syntax.

In the prefixed rendition of linear gradients, the angles were different: 0deg pointed to the right, and angles went counterclockwise instead of clockwise, so 90deg was up, and so on. In addition, the key phrases were different: we declared where the gradient was coming from instead of where it was going to. For a side or corner, in the prefixed syntax use top, bottom, left, right, top left, bottom left, top right, or bottom right.

In this intermediate syntax, the corner gradients didn't necessarily go from corner to corner like the new syntax: instead, they went at a 45 degrees angle through the center of the element on which it was applied.

These three declarations are the same as our three default declarations listed, but with the -webkit- prefix.

```
background-image: -webkit-linear-gradient(270deg, #FFF 0%, #000
➥100%);
background-image: -webkit-linear-gradient(top, #FFF 0%, #000 100%);
background-image: -webkit-linear-gradient(#FFF 0%, #000 100%);
```

This -webkit- prefixed syntax works for Safari 5.1-6, iOS 5-6.1, Chrome 10-25, Android 4.0-4.3, and Blackberry 10. Microsoft, other than for its developer preview, never released a browser with prefixed linear gradients.

The Old WebKit Syntax

Older versions of Webkit for Safari 4 and 5, Android 2.3 to 3, iOS 3.2 to 4.3, Blackberry 7, and Chrome through version 9 supported the original syntax. If you still need to support these browsers, you have to understand the syntax. But think twice before including it as the performance and memory consumption of this old syntax on old devices that require it may not make the gradient worth the effort.

Let's look at this original syntax, using our first white-to-black gradient example again:

```
background-image:
  -webkit-gradient(linear, 0% 0%, 0% 100%, from(#FFFFFF),
➡to(#000000));
```

Rather than use a specific `linear-gradient` property, there's a general-purpose `-webkit-gradient` property where you specify the type of gradient (`linear` in this case) as the first parameter. The linear gradient then needs both a start and end point to determine the direction of the gradient. The start and end points can be specified using percentages, numeric values, or the keywords `top`, `bottom`, `left`, `right`, or `center`.

The next step was to declare color stops of the gradients. You can include the originating color with the `from` keyword and the end color with the `to` keyword. Then you can include any number of intermediate colors using the `color-stop` function to create a color stop. The first parameter of the `color-stop()` function is the position of the stop expressed as a percentage, and the second parameter is the color at that location.

Here's an example:

```
background-image:
  -webkit-gradient(linear, left top, right bottom,
    from(red),
    to(purple),
    color-stop(20%, orange),
```

```
            color-stop(40%, yellow),
            color-stop(60%, green),
            color-stop(80%, blue));
```

With that, we've recreated our angled rainbow, reminiscent of GeoCities circa 1996.

This syntax is more complicated than what was finally adopted by the W3C. Fortunately, tools exist to generate all the required code for a given gradient automatically. We'll be looking at some of them at the end of this section, but first we'll see how to use both syntaxes to create a cross-browser gradient for *The HTML5 Herald*. The good news is that since the three WebKit syntaxes use different property values, you can use them side by side without conflict. The old syntax is still supported in newer browsers, so the browser will just use whichever one was declared last. We've included it here mainly for legacy purposes, as you might come across this still-supported old syntax in legacy code.

Putting It All Together

Now that you have a fairly good understanding of how to declare linear gradients, let's declare ours.

If your designer included a gradient in the design, it's likely to have been created in Photoshop or another image-editing program. You can use this to your advantage; if you have the original files, it's fairly easy to replicate exactly what your designer intended.

If we open Photoshop and inspect the gradient we want to use for the ad (shown in Figure 7.7), we see that our gradient is linear, with five color stops that change the opacity of a single color (black).

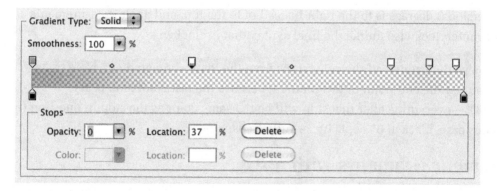

Figure 7.7. An example linear gradient in Photoshop

You'll note via the Photoshop screengrab that the first color stop's location is at 37% with an opacity of 0%. We can use this tool to grab the data for our CSS declaration, beginning with the `-webkit-` prefixed version for older browsers, and followed by the W3C non-prefixed syntax:

```
.ad-ad3 {
  ⋮
  background-image:
    -webkit-linear-gradient(
      270deg,
      rgba(0,0,0,0.4) 0,
      rgba(0,0,0,0) 37%,
      rgba(0,0,0,0) 83%,
      rgba(0,0,0,0.06) 92%,
      rgba(0,0,0,0) 98%
    );
  background-image:
    linear-gradient(
      180deg,
      rgba(0,0,0,0.4) 0,
      rgba(0,0,0,0) 37%,
      rgba(0,0,0,0) 83%,
      rgba(0,0,0,0.06) 92%,
      rgba(0,0,0,0) 98%
    );
}
```

We want the gradient to run from the very top of the ad to the bottom, so we set the angle to 180deg, which is toward bottom, or 180 degrees clockwise from the top of 0 degrees. The prefixed syntax has a different angle with 270deg: as in the older version 0 degrees is to the right instead of to the top, and angle measurements are counterclockwise unlike the final syntax that is clockwise.

We've then added all the color stops from the Photoshop gradient. Note that we've omitted the end point of the gradient, because the last color stop is at 98%—everything after that stop will be the same color as the stop in question (in this case, black at 0% opacity, or fully transparent).

Linear Gradients with SVG

We still have a few more browsers to add our linear gradient to. For IE9, which lacks support for gradients, we can declare SVG files as background images. By creating a gradient in an SVG file and declaring that SVG as the background image of an element, we can recreate the same effect we achieved with CSS3 gradients.

 SVG

SVG stands for **Scalable Vector Graphics**. It's an XML-based language for defining vector graphics using a set of elements—like what you use in HTML to define the structure of a document. We'll be covering SVG in much more depth in Chapter 12, but for now we'll just skim over the basics, since all we're creating is a simple gradient.

An SVG file sounds scary, but for creating gradients it's quite straightforward. Here's our gradient in SVG form:

```
<?xml version="1.0" standalone="no"?>
<!DOCTYPE svg PUBLIC "-//W3C//DTD SVG 1.0//EN"
  "http://www.w3.org/TR/2001/REC-SVG-20050904/DTD/svg10.dtd">
<svg xmlns="http://www.w3.org/2000/svg"
     xmlns:xlink="http://www.w3.org/1999/xlink" version="1.1">
<title>Module Gradient</title>
 <defs>
  <linearGradient id="grad" x1="0" y1="0" x2="0" y2="100%">
    <stop offset="0" stop-opacity="0.3" color-stop="#000000" />
    <stop offset="0.37" stop-opacity="0" stop-color="#000000" />
    <stop offset="0.83" stop-opacity="0" stop-color="#000000" />
    <stop offset="0.92" stop-opacity="0.06" stop-color="#000000" />
    <stop offset="0.98" stop-opacity="0" stop-color="#000000" />
  </linearGradient>
 </defs>
</defs>
```

```
<rect x="0" y="0" width="100%" height="100%"
➥style="fill:url(#grad)" />
</svg>
```

Looking at the SVG file, you should notice that it's quite similar to the syntax for linear gradients in CSS3. We declare the gradient type and the orientation in the `linearGradient` element, then add color stops. Like in the oldest WebKit syntax, the orientation is set with start and end coordinates, from x1, y1 to x2, y2. The color stops are fairly self-explanatory, having an offset between 0 and 1 determining their position and a stop-color for their color. After declaring the gradient, we then have to create a rectangle (the `rect` element) and fill it with our gradient using the `style` attribute.

So, we've created a nifty little gradient, but how do we use it on our site? Save the SVG file with the **.svg** extension. Then in your CSS declare the SVG as your background image with the same syntax, as if it were a JPEG, GIF, or PNG:

```
.ad-ad3 {
  ⋮
  background-image: url("../images/gradient.svg");
  ⋮
}
```

The SVG background should be declared before the CSS3 gradients, so browsers that understand both will use the latter. Browsers that support gradients are even smart enough not to download the SVG if it's overwritten by another `background-image` property later on in your CSS.

The major difference between our CSS linear gradients and the SVG version is that the SVG background image won't default to 100% of the height and width of the container the way CSS gradients do. To make the SVG fill the container, declare the height and width of your SVG rectangle as 100%.

Linear Gradients with IE Filters

For Internet Explorer prior to version 9, we can use the proprietary IE filter syntax to create simple gradients. The IE gradient filter doesn't support color stops, gradient angle, or, as we'll see later, radial gradients. All you have is the ability to specify whether the gradient is horizontal or vertical, as well as the "to" and "from" colors.

It's fairly basic, but if you need a gradient on these older browsers, it can provide the solution.

The filter syntax for IE is:

```
filter:progid:DXImageTransform.Microsoft.gradient(GradientType=0,
➥startColorstr='#COLOR', endColorstr='#COLOR); /* IE6 & IE7 */
-ms-filter:"progid:DXImageTransform.Microsoft.gradient(GradientType=
➥0,startColorstr='#COLOR', endColorstr='#COLOR')"; /* IE8 */
```

The `GradientType` parameter should be set to 1 for a horizontal gradient, or 0 for a vertical gradient.

Since the gradient we're using for our ad block requires color stops, we'll skip using the IE filters. The ad still looks fine without the gradient, so it's all good.

As we've mentioned before, IE's filters can have a significant impact on performance, so use them sparingly if at all. Calculating the display of filter effects takes processing time, with some effects being slower than others. We recommend against using Microsoft filters: sites do *not* need to look the same in all browsers.

Tools of the Trade

Now that you understand how to create linear gradients and have mastered the intricacies of their convoluted syntax, there's no need to worry if you forget the specifics of the syntax you just learned. There are some very cool tools to help you create linear gradients without having to recreate your code for the old and new syntaxes.

John Allsop's CSS3 Sandbox[1] is a tool that enables you to create gradients with color stops, with separate tabs for radial and linear gradients. The tool only creates gradients with hexadecimal color notation, but it does provide you with copy-and-paste code, so you can copy it and then switch the hexadecimal color values to RGBA or HSLA if you prefer.

Damian Galarza's Gradient Generator[2] provides for both color stops and RGB. It even lets you set colors with an HSL color picker, but converts it to RGB in the code.

---

[1] http://www.westciv.com/tools/gradients/

[2] http://gradients.glrzad.com/

It does not provide for alpha transparency, but since the code generated is in RGB, it's easy to update. This gradient generator is more powerful than John Allsop's one, but may be a bit overwhelming for a newbie.

Radial Gradients

Radial gradients are circular or elliptical gradients. Rather than proceeding along a straight axis, colors blend out from a starting point in all directions. To create a radial gradient you define the center of the gradient, its size and shape, and the color stops, like we do for linear gradients. The color stops start at the center and progress outwards. Similar to linear gradients, radial gradients are supported in all browsers (beginning with IE10). As with linear gradients, they can be created in SVG so support can be provided to IE9. Radial gradients are entirely unsupported in IE8 and earlier—not even with filters.

The W3C Syntax

Let's start with a basic circular gradient to illustrate the standard syntax:

```
background-image: radial-gradient(circle farthest-corner at center,
➥#FFF, #000);
```

This will result in the gradient shown in Figure 7.8. We've declared the shape of the gradient as a circle: the default radial gradient is an ellipse whose height and width has the same aspect ratio as the container on which it is set, unless the size is declared in length units with differing proportions. We've declared the size as farthest-corner, which means that the end of the gradient is at the corner furthest from the center of the gradient. We set the center of the gradient to be at the center of the containing block, which is the default. We then defined two color stops of white and black. Color stops are declared the same way as linear gradients.

Figure 7.8. A centered radial gradient

Let's now play with the position:

```
background-image: radial-gradient(circle farthest-corner at 30px
➡30px, #FFF, #000);
```

This will place the center of the gradient 30 pixels from the top and 30 pixels from the left of the element, as you can see in Figure 7.9. As with background-position, you can use values, percentages, or keywords to set the gradient's position.

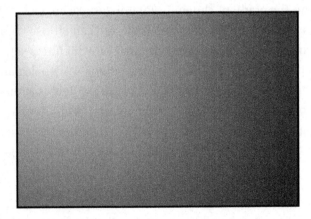

Figure 7.9. A radial gradient positioned off-center

Now let's look at the shape and size parameter. The shape can take one of two values, circle or ellipse, with the latter being the default.

For the size parameter, you can use one of the following values (and you can see example results in Figure 7.10):

closest-side	The gradient's shape meets the side of the box closest to its center (for circles), or meets both the vertical and horizontal sides closest to the center (for ellipses). It creates the smallest gradient of the four key terms.
`closest-corner`	The gradient's shape is sized so that it meets exactly the closest corner of the box from its center.
`farthest-side`	Similar to `closest-side`, except that the shape is sized to meet the side of the box farthest from its center—or the farthest vertical and horizontal sides in the case of ellipses.
`farthest-corner`	The gradient's shape is sized so that it meets exactly the farthest corner of the box from its center. Creates the largest gradient of the four key terms.
lengths	For the size we could have used a length unit instead of one of the four key terms mentioned, with percentage values being supported for elliptical declarations, but not for circles. If you declare lengths, the circle gradient only supports one value; for ellipses, the length unit requires both the horizontal and vertical radii be declared, with the width coming before the height.

The length or key term determines where the 100% color stop will be located. Any points beyond that color stop will be the same color as that color stop.

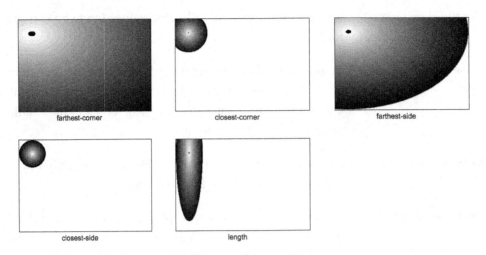

Figure 7.10. Radial gradient sizing

The color stop syntax is the same as for linear gradients: a color value followed by an optional stop position. Let's look at one last example:

```
background-image: radial-gradient(circle farthest-side at 30px 30px,
➥#FFF, #000 30%, #FFF);
```

This will create a gradient like the one in Figure 7.11.

Figure 7.11. A radial gradient with a modified size and shape, and an extra color stop

The Prefixed WebKit Syntax

To create the example in Figure 7.11 using the prefixed WebKit syntax currently in iOS up to 5.1, Android up to 4.3, and BlackBerry 10, we need to prefix the value and reorder the value components:

```
background-image: -webkit-radial-gradient(30px 30px,
➥ circle farthest-side, #FFF, #000 30%, #FFF);
```

We prefix the property value with `-webkit-`. The location is declared first, without the `at` key term. Otherwise, the prefixed version is similar to the unprefixed syntax.

Making Our Own Radial Gradient

Let's take all that we've learned and implement a radial gradient for *The HTML5 Herald*. You may not have noticed, but the form submit button has a radial gradient in the background. The center of the radial gradient is outside the button area, towards the left and a little below the bottom, as Figure 7.12 shows.

Figure 7.12. A radial gradient on a button in *The HTML5 Herald*'s sign-up form

We'll want to declare at least three background images: an SVG file for IE9, the older WebKit syntax for mobile Webkit, and the unprefixed version for modern browsers:

```
input[type=submit] {
  ⋮
  background-color: #333;
  /* SVG for IE9 */
  background-image: url(../images/button-gradient.svg);
  /* prefixed for Android 4 to 4.3, Blackberry and UC Browser
  background-image: -webkit-radial-gradient(30% 120%, circle,
    rgba(144,144,144,1) 0%,
    rgba(72,72,72,1) 50%);
  background-image: radial-gradient(circle at 30% 120%,
```

```
    rgba(144,144,144,1) 0%,
    rgba(72,72,72,1) 50%);
}
```

The center of the circle is 30% from the left, and 120% from the top, so it's actually *below* the bottom edge of the container. We've included two color stops for the color #484848—or rgba(72,72,72)—and #909090—or rgba(144,144,144).

And here's the SVG file used as a fallback:

```
<?xml version="1.0" standalone="no"?>
<!DOCTYPE svg PUBLIC "-//W3C//DTD SVG 1.0//EN"
➥"http://www.w3.org/TR/2001/REC-SVG-20050904/DTD/svg10.dtd">
<svg xmlns="http://www.w3.org/2000/svg" xmlns:xlink="
➥http://www.w3.org/1999/xlink" version="1.1">
<title>Button Gradient</title>
 <defs>
  <radialGradient id="grad" cx="30%" cy="120%" fx="30%" fy="120%"
➥r="50%" gradientUnits="userSpaceOnUse">
    <stop offset="0" stop-color="#909090" />
    <stop offset="1" stop-color="#484848" />
  </radialGradient>
</defs>
<rect x="0" y="0" width="100%" height="100%"
➥style="fill:url(#grad)" />
</svg>
```

The syntax is fairly explanatory, but we'll cover SVG in Chapter 12 anyway. Keep in mind that you can also leverage background-position and background-size for your design.

Repeating Gradients

Sometimes you'll find yourself wanting to create a gradient pattern that repeats over the background of an element. While recurring linear gradients can be created by repeating the background image (with background-repeat), there's no equivalent way to easily create repeating radial gradients. Fortunately, CSS3 comes to the rescue with both a repeating-linear-gradient and a repeating-radial-gradient syntax. The vendor-prefixed repeating-linear-gradient syntax is supported in Firefox 3.6+, Safari 5.0.3+, Chrome 10+, and Opera 11.10+, and unprefixed since IE10,

Firefox 16, Safari 6.1, iOS 7.1, Opera 12.1, Chrome 26 (though it can be quirky) and even Opera Mobile 12.1.

In terms of color stops and angles, gradients with `repeating-linear-gradient` and `repeating-radial-gradient` have the same syntax as the non-repeating versions.

Here are examples of what can be created with just a few lines of CSS:

```css
.repeat_linear_1 {
  background-image:
    repeating-linear-gradient(to right,
      rgba(0,0,0,0.5) 10%,
      rgba(0,0,0,0.1) 30%);
}
.repeat_radial_2 {
  background-image:
    repeating-radial-gradient(circle at top left,
      rgba(0,0,0,0.9),
      rgba(0,0,0,0.1) 10%,
      rgba(0,0,0,0.5) 20%);
}
.multiple_gradients_3 {
  background-image:
    repeating-linear-gradient(to right,
      rgba(0,0,0,0.5) 10%,
      rgba(0,0,0,0.1) 30%),
    repeating-radial-gradient(circle at top left,
      rgba(0,0,0,0.9),
      rgba(0,0,0,0.1) 10%,
      rgba(0,0,0,0.5) 20%);
}
```

The resulting gradients are shown in Figure 7.13.

Figure 7.13. A few examples of repeating gradients

The important difference to remember is that the color-stop placement values matter in repeating gradients. In regular gradients, the last color stop location is simply the end point of the color transition. In repeating gradients, the first color stop is the beginning of the gradient, and the last color stop location is the end of the gradient: it starts repeating with the first color stop at that location. In our example our two color stops are at10% and 30%. This means the gradient will repeat five times, as each is 20% of the width of the containing object (30% - 10% = 20%). In our radial example, the first color stop has no location, so it defaults to 0%.

Multiple Background Images

You probably noticed that our advertisement with the linear gradient is incomplete: we're missing the bicycle. Prior to CSS3, adding the bicycle would have required placing an additional element in the markup to contain the new background image. In CSS3, there's no need to include an element for every background image; it provides us with the ability to add more than one background image to any element, even to pseudo-elements.

To understand multiple background images, you need to understand the syntax and values of the various background properties. The syntax for the values of all the background properties, including `background-image` and the shorthand `background` property, are the same whether you have one background image or many. To make a declaration for multiple background images, simply separate the values for each individual image with a comma. For example:

```
background-image:
  url(firstImage.jpg),
  url(secondImage.gif),
  url(thirdImage.png);
```

This works just as well if you're using the shorthand `background` property:

```
background:
  url(firstImage.jpg) no-repeat 0 0,
  url(secondImage.gif) no-repeat 100% 0,
  url(thirdImage.png) no-repeat 50% 0;
```

The background images are layered one on top of the other with the first declaration on top, as if it had a higher `z-index`. The final image is drawn under all the images preceding it in the declaration, as if it had a low `z-index`. Basically, think of the images as being stacked in reverse order with the last one being drawn first, and each previous image being drawn on top of it.

IE8 doesn't support multiple background images. If you're still supporting IE8, declare a single background image before the multiple background image declaration.

If you want to declare a background color—which you should, especially if it's light-colored text on a dark-colored background image—declare it last. It's often simpler and more readable to declare it separately using the `background-color` property.

As a reminder, the shorthand `background` property is short for eight longhand `background` properties. If you use the shorthand, any longhand `background` property value that's omitted from the declaration will default to the longhand property's default (or initial) value. The default values for the various `background` properties are listed:

- `background-color: transparent;`

- `background-image: none;`

- `background-position: 0 0;`

- `background-size: auto;`

- `background-repeat: repeat;`

- `background-clip: border-box;`

- `background-origin: padding-box;`

- `background-attachment: scroll;`

The heading on our sign-up form has two background images. While we could attach a single extra-wide image in this case, spanning across the entire form, there's no need! With multiple background images, CSS3 allows us to attach two separate small images, or a single image sprite twice with different background positions. This saves on bandwidth, of course, but it's also beneficial if the heading needed to stretch; a single image would be unable to accommodate differently sized elements. This time, we'll use the `background` shorthand:

```
background:
  url("../images/bg-formtitle-left.png") left 13px no-repeat,
  url("../images/bg-formtitle-right.png") right 13px no-repeat;
```

Using the Shorthand

In browsers that support all the available `background` properties and the shorthand, the following two statements are equivalent:

```
div {
  background: url("tile.png") no-repeat scroll center
➥bottom / cover rgba(0, 0, 0, 0.2);
}

div {
  background-color: rgba(0,0,0,0.2);
  background-position: 50% 100%;
  background-size: cover;
  background-repeat: no-repeat;
  background-clip: border-box;
  background-origin: padding-box;
```

```
    background-attachment: scroll;
    background-image: url(form.png);
}
```

If you declare the shorthand, remember that all omitted properties reset themselves to each longhand property's default value. When using both shorthand with a property override, remember to declare the shorthand *before* the longhand property.

 Multiple Background Images in IE8

If you still need to support IE8, which does not support multiple background images, you can leverage generated content to access three hooks to use for single background images: adding a single background image to the element, the `:before` content and the `:after` content as shown:

```
div {
  position: relative;
  background: url(secondImage.gif) no-repeat 100% 0;
}
div:before, div:after {
  position: absolute;
  top: 0; left: 0; right: 0; bottom: 0;
  content: '';
}
div:after { background: url(firstImage.jpg) no-repeat 0 0;}
div:before { background: url(thirdImage.png) no-repeat 50%
➡0;}
```

Remember to use single-colon notation as IE8 doesn't understand double-colon notation.

Background Size

The `background-size` property allows you to specify the size you want your background images to have. Include `background-size` within the shorthand background declaration by adding it after the background's position, separated with a slash (/). This syntax is confusing to many. As a result, many developers use the `background-size` property as a separate declaration instead. Support for `background-size` is fairly universal, starting with IE9, and unprefixed starting with Firefox 4 and Android 3.

The `background-size` value takes a length, a percentage, or one of the key terms `cover`, `contain`, or `auto`, with `auto` being the default.

If you include a single length or percentage value, that will define the width of the image, with the height set to maintain the image's aspect ratio. If you prefer to base the size on the height of the image, use two values with the first (or width) being `auto` and the second being the height preference, as the first value is the width and the second, the height. If you have multiple background images, separate the sizes for each image with a comma.

Both these lines have the same meaning:

```
background-size: 100px auto, auto auto;
background-size: 100px, auto;
```

As with all background properties, use commas to separate values for each image declared. If you only include one size, all the background images will be of that size. If we wanted our bicycle to be really big, we could declare:

```
background-size: 100px auto, cover;
```

By default, a background image is the actual size of the image. Sometimes the image is just a bit smaller or larger than its container. You can define the size of your background image in pixels (as shown) or percentages, or you can use the `contain` or `cover` keyterms.

The `contain` value scales the image while preserving its aspect ratio, which may leave uncovered space. The `cover` value scales the image so that it completely covers the element, also maintaining the image's aspect ratio. This can result in clipping the image if the background image has a different aspect ratio than the element.

 Background Image Performance

In terms of performance, it's best to use `auto` with the `background-size` property if you can, especially when animating. All other values require the image to be decoded twice, with `cover` requiring the most time and CPU.

Working with HiDPI Devices

The `background-size` property comes in handy for devices that have different pixel densities, such as HiDPI devices like the many mobile devices and Apple laptops that have a pixel density four times higher than the average inexpensive laptop or monitor. To prevent pages designed for older devices from looking tiny, the browsers on these HiDPI devices *behave* as though they had a regular display. The iPhone 5, for example, has a screen resolution of 640×960 but behaves as if it has a 320×480 display. On this device, every pixel in your CSS corresponds to four screen pixels. Images are scaled up to compensate, but this means they can sometimes look a little rough compared to the smoothness of the text displayed.

To deal with this, you can provide higher-resolution images to HiDPI devices. For example, if we were providing a high-resolution image of a bicycle for the iPad, it would measure 74×90px instead of 37×45px. However, we don't actually want it to be twice as big! We only want it to take up 37×45px worth of space. We can use `background-size` to ensure that our high-resolution image still takes up the right amount of space:

```
background-size: 37px 45px, cover;
```

In this scenario, you can use media queries to define which device receives what based on the viewport size and pixel density, with `min-resolution` replacing the `min-device-pixel-ratio`:

```
<link rel="stylesheet" media="screen and (max-device-width:
➥520px) and (min-resolution: 2dppx)" />
```

In the Background

That's all for CSS3 backgrounds and gradients. In the next chapter, we'll be looking at transforms, animations, and transitions. These allow you to add dynamic effects and movement to your pages without relying on bandwidth- and processor-heavy JavaScript.

CSS3 Transforms and Transitions

Our page is fairly static. Actually, it's completely static. In Chapter 4 we learned a little about how to alter a form's appearance based on its state with the :invalid and :valid pseudo-classes. But what about really moving things around? What about changing the appearance of elements, such as rotating or skewing them?

For years, the only way to display text on an angle was to use an image of text created in an image-editing program and the only way to animate was to change positioning with JavaScript. This is far from ideal. Enter CSS3: without a line of JavaScript or a single JPEG, you can tilt, scale, move, and even flip your elements with ease.

Let's see how it's done.

Transforms

The CSS3 transform property lets you lets you translate, rotate, scale, and/or skew any element on the page. While some of these effects were possible using previously existing CSS features (such as translating with relative and absolute positioning), CSS3 gives you unprecedented control over many more aspects of the element's appearance.

We can manipulate an element's appearance using **transform functions**. The value of the `transform` property is one or more transform functions (separated by spaces) that will be applied in the order they're provided. In this book, we'll cover all the two-dimensional transform functions. All modern browsers, starting with IE10 and Android 3, also support the transformation of elements in 3D space, but 3D transforms are beyond the scope of this book.

To illustrate how transforms work, we'll be working on another advertisement block from *The HTML5 Herald*, shown in Figure 8.1.

Figure 8.1. This block will serve to illustrate CSS3 transforms

Translation

Translation functions allow you to move elements left, right, up, or down. These functions are similar to the behavior of `position: relative`; when declaring `top` and `left`, moving elements up and down or left and right along the x and y axes. When you employ a translation function, you're moving elements without impacting the flow of the document. Unlike `position: relative`, which allows you to position an element either against its current position or against a parent or other ancestor, a translated element can only be moved relative to its current position.

The `translate(x,y)` function moves an element x from the left, and y from the top:

```
transform: translate(45px, -45px);
```

 Transforms and Older Browsers

Transforms require vendor prefixing for IE9, Android up to 4.4.3, iOS8, and Blackberry 10. To make the aforementioned code work in IE9 and older mobile WebKit browsers, you would include the following:

```
-webkit-transform: translate(45px,-45px); /* iOS8, Android
➥4.4.3, BB10 */
-ms-transform: translate(45px,-45px); /* IE9 only */
transform: translate(45px,-45px);
```

If you only want to move an element vertically or horizontally, you can use the translatex or translatey functions respectively. To move 45px to the right along the x axis, include:

```
transform: translateX(45px);
```

To move up along the y axis by 30px, include:

```
transform: translateY(-30px);
```

For our ad, we want to move the word "dukes" over to the right when the user hovers over it, as if it had been punched by our mustachioed pugilist. In the markup, we have:

```
<h1>Put your <span>dukes</span> up, sire</h1>
```

Let's apply the style whenever the user hovers over the h1. This will make the effect more likely to be stumbled across than if it was only triggered by hovering over the span itself:

```
.ad-ad2 h1:hover span {
  color: #484848;
  transform: translateX(40px);
}
```

Wait—this doesn't work. What gives?

Transforms don't work on inline elements. But that's easy enough to fix. We'll just add display: inline-block; to our span:

```
.ad-ad2 h1 span {
  font-size: 30px;
  color: #999999;
  display: inline-block;
  ⋮
```

The result is shown in Figure 8.2.

Figure 8.2. The result of our `translate` transform

It's nice, but we can still do better! Let's look at how we can scale our text to make it bigger as well.

Scaling

The `scale(x,y)` function scales an element by the defined factors horizontally then vertically. If only one value is provided, it will be used for both the x and y values, growing or shrinking your element or pseudo-element while maintaining the original aspect ratio. For example, `scale(1)` would leave the element the same size, `scale(2)` would double its proportions, `scale(0.5)` would halve them, and so on. Providing different values will distort the element, as you'd expect:

```
transform: scale(1.5, 0.25);
```

As with `translate`, you can also use the `scaleX(x)` or `scaleY(y)` functions. These functions will scale only the horizontal dimensions or only the vertical dimensions respectively.

A scaled element will grow outwards from or shrink inwards towards its center; in other words, the element's center will stay in the same place as its dimensions change. To change this default behavior, you can include the `transform-origin` property, which we'll be covering a bit later.

Let's add a `scale` transform to our span:

```
.ad-ad2 h1:hover span {
  color: #484848;
  transform: translateX(40px) scale(1.5);
}
```

Note that you shouldn't declare a new `transform`: because of the cascade, a second `transform` would override the first. To declare multiple transformations, provide a space-separated list of `transform` functions. We simply add our `scale` to the end of that space-separated list.

It's also worth remembering that scaling, like translation, has no impact on the document flow. This means that if you scale `inline-block` elements, text around it will fail to accommodate it with reflowing. Figure 8.3 shows an example of how this might be a problem. In cases where this is an issue, you may consider adjusting the element's `height`, `width`, or `font-size` instead of using a `scale()` transform. Changing those properties will alter the space allocated to the element by the browser, but will also cause a reflow, recalculating the elements in the document to re-rendering part or all of the page. Transforming does not cause a reflow.

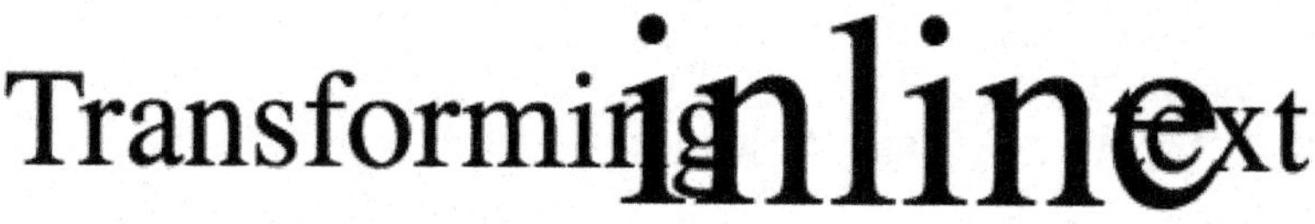

Transformi**in line**xt

Figure 8.3. Using the `scale` function on inline text can have unwanted results

In our example, however, we want the text to pop out of the ad without reflowing the surrounding text, so the scale does exactly what we need it to do. Figure 8.4 shows what our hover state looks like with the scale added to the existing translation.

Figure 8.4. Our ad now has plenty of pop

It's looking good, but there's still more to add.

Rotation

The `rotate()` function rotates an element around the point of origin by a specified angle value. As with `scale`, by default the point of origin is the element's center. Generally, angles are declared in degrees, with positive degrees moving clockwise and negative moving counterclockwise. In addition to degrees, values can be provided in grads, radians, or turns, but we'll just be sticking with degrees.

Let's add a `rotate` transform to our "dukes":

```
.ad-ad2 h1:hover span {
  color: #484848;
  transform: rotate(10deg) translateX(40px) scale(1.5);
}
```

We're rotating our `span` by ten degrees clockwise—adding to the effect of text that's just been dealt a powerful uppercut. We are declaring the rotation *before* the `translate` so that it's applied first—remember that transforms are applied in the order provided. In this case, the `span` will be rotated 10 degrees, and then moved 40px along the rotated x axis.

The final transformed text is shown in Figure 8.5.

Figure 8.5. Our text has now been translated, scaled, and rotated—that's quite a punch!

There's one more type of `transform` we're yet to visit. It won't be used on *The HTML5 Herald*, but let's take a look anyway.

Skew

The `skew(x,y)` function specifies a skew along the x and y axes. As you'd expect, the x specifies the skew on the x axis, and the y specifies the skew on the y axis. If the second parameter is omitted, the `skew` will only occur on the x axis:

```
transform: skew(15deg, 4deg);
```

Applying these styles to a heading, for example, results in the skew shown in Figure 8.6.

A Skewed Perspective

Figure 8.6. Some text with a skew transform applied

As with `translate` and `scale`, there are axis-specific versions of the skew transform: `skewX()` and `skewY()`.

Changing the Origin of the Transform

As we hinted at earlier, you can control the origin from which your transforms are applied. This is done using the `transform-origin` property. It has the same syntax as the `background-position` property, and defaults to the center of the object (so that scales and rotations will be around the center of the box by default).

Let's say that you were transforming a circle. Because the default `transform-origin` is the center of the circle, applying a `rotate()` transform to a circle would have no visible effect—a circle rotated 90 degrees still looks exactly the same as it did before being rotated. An ellipse rotated 180 degrees around its center would also look the same as it did before being rotated upside down. However, if you gave your circle or ellipse a `transform-origin` of 10% 10% or `top center`, you would notice the rotation as Figure 8.7 illustrates.

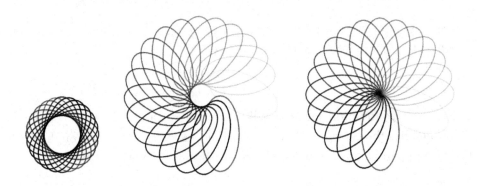

Figure 8.7. Rotating an ellipse[1] is more noticeable if the `transform-origin` is set to something other than the default 50% 50%

Browser support for the `transform-origin` property is the same as for `transform`—prefixing being required when the `transform` property requires it:

```
transform-origin: 0 0;
```

 Choose Your Ordering Carefully

The order of `transform` functions does matter: if you rotate before translating, your translate direction will be on the rotated axis. The rightmost square in Figure 8.8 was translated then rotated with `transform: translateX(200px) rotate(135deg);`. The leftmost square was rotated first then translated along the newly rotated axis: `transform: rotate(135deg) translateX(200px);`.

---

[1] http://codepen.io/estelle/pen/myXGGe

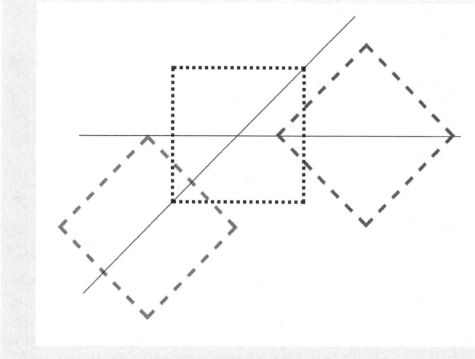

Figure 8.8. The order of transform functions makes a difference

Support for Internet Explorer 8 and Earlier

While CSS3 transforms are unsupported in IE before version 9, you can mimic these effects with other CSS properties, including filters. To mimic translation use `position: relative;`, and `top` and `left` values:

```
.translate {
  position: relative;
  top: 200px;
  left: 200px;
}
```

You can also scale an element by altering its `width` and `height`, or changing the `font-size`. Remember, though, that while transformed elements still take up the space they did before being scaled, altering a `width`, `height` or `font-size` alters the space allocated for the element and can affect the layout.

You can use filters to rotate an element in older versions of Internet Explorer, but it's ugly and performs poorly:

```
.rotate {
  transform: rotate(15deg);
  filter: progid:DXImageTransform.Microsoft.Matrix(
      sizingMethod='auto expand', M11=0.9659258262890683,
      M12=-0.25881904510252074, M21=0.25881904510252074,
      M22=0.9659258262890683);
  -ms-filter: "progid:DXImageTransform.Microsoft.Matrix(
      M11=0.9659258262890683, M12=-0.25881904510252074,
      M21=0.25881904510252074, M22=0.9659258262890683,
      sizingMethod='auto expand')";
  zoom: 1;
}
```

This filter's syntax isn't worth going into here. If you want to rotate an element in Internet Explorer, go to http://www.useragentman.com/IETransformsTranslator/ for cross-browser code for a given transform. Just edit the original transform expression; the older IE version will be updated accordingly. This page provides prefixed transform declarations that are outdated, but the IE filter is accurate.

Transitions

Animation has certainly been possible for some time with JavaScript, but native CSS transitions generally require less client-side processing, so they'll usually appear smoother. On mobile devices with limited computing power, this can be a lifesaver.

As much fun as it's been to have a feature work in IE9, it's time to again leave that browser behind. IE10 and all other browsers support CSS transitions, and transitions are UI enhancements, and fail accessibly, so we need not worry about archaic IE browsers.

Transitions allow the values of CSS properties to change over time, essentially providing simple animations. For example, if a link changes color on hover, you can have it gradually fade from one color to the other instead of a sudden change. They're both transitions, but with the CSS transition property the color transition can be gradual. If the browser lacks support for transitions, the change will be immediate instead of gradual, which is fine and accessible.

We can animate any of the transforms we've just seen, so that our pages feel more dynamic.

CSS transitions are declared along with the regular styles on an element. Whenever the target properties change, the browser will apply the transition making the change gradual. Often the change will be due to different styles applied to a hover state; however, transitions will work equally well if the property in question is changed by adding a class, or otherwise using JavaScript to change state. This is significant: rather than writing out an animation in JavaScript, you can simply switch a property value and rely on the browser to do all the heavy lifting.

Here are the steps to create a simple transition using only CSS:

1. Declare the original state of the element in the default style declaration.

2. Declare the final state of your transitioned element; for example, a `:hover` state.

3. Include the transition functions in your default style declaration using the transition properties, including: `transition-property`, `transition-duration`, `transition-timing-function`, and `transition-delay`. We'll look at each of these and how they work shortly.

The important point to note is that the `transition` is declared in the default or originating state. The `-webkit-` vendor prefix is still needed for older mobile devices, including iOS6.1, BlackBerry10, Android 4.3 and UC Browser for Android. All other browsers, including IE10 and Android 4.4 browser support the unprefixed syntax.

This may be a lot to grasp, so let's go over the various transition properties. As we go, we'll apply a transition to the transforms we added to our ad in the last section, so that the word "dukes" moves smoothly into its new position when hovered.

transition-property

The `transition-property` property defines the CSS properties of the element that should be transitioned, with `all` for all properties being the default.

Any property changing from one value to another for which you can find a valid midpoint can be transitioned. For example, in transitioning from a 1px red border to a 15px blue border, we transition the `color` and `width` of the border. The midpoint of 1px and 15px is obvious (8px), so we know that is a transitionable property value. The midpoint between red and blue might not seem obvious, but the browser converts named colors to their numeric values, which have a midpoint. If the `border-style` were declared as changing from solid to dashed, that would not be a transitionable property as there is no midpoint between these key terms.

It is important to include a pre-state and a post-state. For example, to transition from rectangular corners to rounded corners, set the original state to `border-radius: 0;`.

The exception to this "if there is a valid midpoint, it can be transitioned" rule is visibility: although there is no valid midpoint between the values `visible` and `hidden`, when transitioned, the value changes at the endpoint of the transition. The list of properties that can be animated is found at https://developer.mozilla.org/en-US/docs/Web/CSS/CSS_animated_properties.

You can provide any number of CSS properties to the `transition-property` declaration, separated by commas. Alternatively, you can use the keyword `all` to indicate that every supported property should be animated as it transitions.

In the case of our ad, we'll apply the transition to the `transform` property:

```
.ad-ad2 h1 span {
  transition-property: transform;
}
```

 Supporting Older Browsers

To support older WebKit browsers, you need to include the `-webkit-` prefix for all of your transition properties. You may also need to specify the `-webkit-`prefixed forms of properties. For example, you're unable to animate `transform` in a browser that only understands `-webkit-transform`:

```
.ad-ad2 h1 span {
  -webkit-transition-property: -webkit-transform;
  transition-property: transform;
}
```

Include the `-webkit-` prefix for all the transition properties, not just the `transition-property` property. There's no need to include `-ms-transform:;` al-

> though IE9 does understand prefixed transforms, it doesn't understand transitions. IE9 will get the transformed look, but will not animate it as it transitions to the new value.

As new properties gain browser transition support, be careful what you include as the value for the `transition-property`: it's possible that a property that doesn't animate at the time you're writing your page eventually will, so be selective in the properties you specify, and only use or default to `all` if you really want to animate every property. If you want to transition more than one property, but not all, comma-separate them:

```
.foo {
  transition-property: transform, color;
}
```

In itself, the `transition-property` property has no effect; that's because we still need to specify the duration of the transition.

The `transition-duration` Property

The `transition-duration` property sets how long the transition will take: the duration of time it takes to go from the default state to the transitioned state. You can specify this either in seconds (`s`) or milliseconds (`ms`). We'd like our animation to be fairly quick, so we'll specify 0.2 seconds (`0.2s`), or 200 milliseconds (`200ms`):

```
transition-duration: 0.2s;
```

200ms is generally considered the optimum time for a transition: anything slower will make the website seem slow, drawing generally unwanted attention to what was supposed to be a subtle effect. Anything faster may be too subtle.

With those styles in place, our `span` will transition on hover. Notice that by default the "reverse" transition also takes place over the same duration—the element returns to its previous position.

 Automatic Graceful Degradation

> While transitions are supported in all modern browsers, the fact that they're de-clared separately from the properties that are changing means that those changes

will still be apparent in older browsers without support for transitions. Those browsers will still apply the :hover (or other) state, except that the changes will happen instantly rather than transitioning over time.

The `transition-timing-function` Property

The `transition-timing-function` lets you control the pace of the transition in even more granular detail. Do you want your animation to start off slow and become faster, start off fast and end slower, advance at an even keel, or some other variation?

The most common timing functions include the key terms `ease`, `linear`, `ease-in`, `ease-out`, or `ease-in-out`. The default `ease` has a slow start, then it speeds up, and ends slowly. `ease-in-out` is similar to `ease`, but accelerates more sharply at the beginning. `linear` creates a transition that animates at a constant speed. `ease-in` creates a transition that is slow to start but gains speed, then stops abruptly. The opposite, `ease-out`, starts at full speed, then slows progressively as it reaches the conclusion of the transition. The best way to familiarize yourself with them is to play around and try them all. Most often, one will just feel right for the effect you're aiming to create. It's helpful to set a relatively long `transition-duration` when testing timing functions—if it's too fast, you may not be able to tell the difference.

You can also describe your timing function more precisely by defining your own `cubic-bezier` function. It accepts four numeric parameters; for example, `linear` is the same as `cubic-bezier(0, 0, 1, 1)`. If you've studied six years of calculus, the method of writing a cubic Bézier function might make sense; otherwise, it's likely you'll want to stick to one of the five basic timing functions. You can also look at online tools that let you play with different values, such as http://cubic-bezier.com/, which lets you compare the common key terms against each other or against your own cubic Bézier function. Another document, http://estelle.github.io/animation/files/cubicbezierprint.html, allows you to set the timing function and time to watch it, visualizing how Bézier curves work.

In addition to the predefined timing functions and developer-defined cubic Bézier function, you can divide the transition over equidistant steps. With the `steps` function, you define the number of steps and the direction of either `start` or `end`, where either the first step happens at the animation start, or the last step happens at the animation end respectively. For example, `steps(5, start)` would jump through the equidistant steps of 0%, 20%, 40%, 60%, and 80%, and `steps(5, end)` would jump throught the equidistant steps of 20%, 40%, 60%, 80%, and 100%. We will use the `steps(n, end)` timing function when we animate our bicycle with CSS animation later on in this chapter.

For our transition, we'll use `ease-out`:

```
transition-timing-function: ease-out;
```

This makes the transition fast to start with, becoming slower as it progresses. Of course, with a 0.2 second duration, the difference is barely perceptible.

The `transition-delay` Property

Finally, by using the `transition-delay` property, it's possible to introduce a delay before the transition begins. Normally a transition begins immediately, so the default is 0. Include the number of milliseconds (`ms`) or seconds (`s`) to delay the transition. We don't want our transition to start immediately, because that might be a bad user experience if the user accidentally mouses through our ad on the way from one part of the document to the next. A 50ms delay is enough time to wait to be sure they are intentionally hovering over our advertisement:

```
-webkit-transition-delay: 50ms;
transition-delay: 50ms;
```

 Negative Delays

Interestingly, a negative time delay that's less than the duration of the entire transition will cause it to start immediately, but it will start partway through the animation. For example, if you have a delay of -500ms on a 2s transition, the transition will start a quarter of the way through, and will last 1.5 seconds. On the way back, it will jump 75% of the way through the transition, and then transition back to the default state. This might be used to create some interesting effects, so it's worth being aware of.

The `transition` Shorthand Property

With four transition properties and a vendor prefix, you could wind up with eight lines of CSS for a single transition. Fortunately, as with other properties such as border, there's a shorthand available. The `transition` property is shorthand for the four transition properties just described.

Let's take another look at our transition so far:

```
.ad-ad2 h1 span {
  transition-property: transform;
  transition-duration: 0.2s;
  transition-timing-function: ease-out;
  transition-delay: 50ms;
}
```

Now let's combine all those values into a shorthand declaration:

```
.ad-ad2 h1 span {
  transition: transform 0.2s ease-out 50ms;
}
```

Note that the properties in the shorthand syntax can be in any order, however, if a delay is included, you must also include a duration, and the duration must precede the delay.

Multiple Transitions

The `transition` properties allow for multiple transitions in one call. For example, if we want to change the color at the same time as changing the rotation and size, we can.

Let's say instead of just transitioning the rotation, we transition the text's `color` property as well. We'd have to first include a `color` property in the transitioned style declaration, and then either add the `color` property in the `transition-property` value list, or use the key term `all`:

```
transition-property: transform, color;
transition-duration: 0.2s;
transition-timing-function: ease-out;
transition-delay: 50ms;
```

If you want your properties to transition at different rates, or if you just want a select few to have a transition effect, include them as a comma-separated list containing, at minimum, the `transition-property` and `transition-duration` for each. Simply include each value in a comma-separated list using the same order as the `transition-property` for all your longhand `transition` property declarations:

```
transition-property: transform, color;
transition-duration: 0.2s, 0.1s;
transition-timing-function: ease-out, linear;
transition-delay: 50ms;
```

These properties will apply an `ease-out` transition over 0.2 seconds to the `transform`, but a `linear` transition over 0.1 seconds to the `color`. Both have a delay of 50ms before transition initiation.

You can also use the shorthand to specify multiple transitions at different durations, delays, and timing functions. In this case, specify all the transition values as a shorthand for each transition, and separate each property's transition with a comma:

```
transition: transform 0.2s ease-out 50ms, color 0.1s linear 50ms;
```

If you want to change both properties at the same rate and delay, you can include both property names or—since you are transitioning all the properties listed in the hover state anyway—you can employ the `all` keyword.

When using the `all` keyword, all the properties transition at the same rate, speed, and delay:

```
transition: all 0.2s ease-out 50ms;
```

How do we know when a transition has ended? A `transitionend` event—prefixed and camel-cased as `webkitTransitionEnd` for older mobile browsers—is fired upon completion of a CSS transition in both directions. The event is fired once per direction for each completed transformed property. In the case where the transition fails to complete, such as if you mouseout before our 250ms transition is over in the example above, it will not fire when it has only partially moved and started changing color, but will fire when it returns to the original default state. If you have more than one property being transitioned, the `transitionend` event will fire multiple times. In our case, it will fire twice when both the `color` and `transform` reach their transitioned state, and twice again when `color` and `transform` return to the original state.

Animations

Transitions animate elements over time; however, they're limited in what they can do. You can define starting and ending states, but there's no fine-grained control over any intermediate states. **CSS animations**, unlike transitions, allow you to control each step of an animation via keyframes.

If you've ever worked with Flash, you're likely very familiar with the concept of keyframes; if not, don't worry, it's fairly straightforward. A **keyframe** is a snapshot that defines a starting or end point of any smooth transition. With CSS transitions, we're essentially limited to defining a first and a last keyframe. CSS animations allow us to add any number of keyframes in between, to guide our animation in more complex ways.

All modern browsers support CSS animation, starting with IE10, though we still require the `-webkit-` prefix in iOS8, Android 4.4.3, and BlackBerry 10. IE10 is unprefixed. Firefox 16, Chrome 39, and Opera 26 dropped their need for a prefix for CSS animations.

The lack of powerful processors on many mobile devices makes CSS animations a great alternative to weighty, CPU-intensive JavaScript animation. Generally, it is best to use CSS for simple-state changes in a mobile environment. But it's still better to employ JavaScript for intricate, stateful UIs, and when you do, you'll likely want to use a JavaScript animation library to help with manageability and performance.

We do have a subtle animation in our *Herald*, so we'll use CSS for our animations.

Keyframes

To animate an element in CSS, you first create a named animation, then attach it to an element in that element's property declaration block. Animations in themselves don't do anything; in order to animate an element, you'll need to associate the animation with that element.

To create an animation, use the `@keyframes` rule for IE10+ and FF16+. Include `@-webkit-keyframes` for all WebKit implementations followed by a name of your choosing, which will serve as the identifier for the animation. Then, you can specify your keyframes.

For an animation called `myAnimation`, the `@keyframes` rule would look like this:

```
@-webkit-keyframes myAnimation {
  /* put animation keyframes here */
}
@keyframes myAnimation {
  /* put animation keyframes here */
}
```

Do not quote the animation name.

Each keyframe looks like its own nested CSS declaration block. Instead of a traditional selector, though, you use a percentage value, or a comma-separated list of percentage values. There are two keyterms—`from` and `to`—which evaluate to 0% and 100% respectively. These values specify how far along the animation each keyframe is located.

Inside each keyframe include the properties you want to animate, along with the animated values. The values will be smoothly interpolated by the browser's animation engine between each keyframe.

Keyframes can be specified in any order; it's the percentage values rather than the order of the declarations that determine the sequence of keyframes in the animation.

Here are a few simple animations:

```
@keyframes moveRight {
  from {
    transform: translateX(-50%);
  }
  to {
    transform: translateX(50%);
  }
}

@keyframes appearDisappear {
  0%, 100% {
    opacity: 0;
  }
```

```
  20%, 80% {
    opacity: 1;
  }
}

@keyframes bgMove {
  100% {
    background-position: 120% 0;
  }
}
```

The second animation is worth paying extra attention to: we've applied the same styles to 0% and 100%, and to 20% and 80%. In this case, it means the element will start out invisible (opacity: 0;), fade in to visible by 20% of the way through the duration, remain visible until 80%, then fade out.

We've created three animations, but nothing in our document will animate yet. An element must have at minimum an animation name for there to be an animation, and must also have a duration declared for the animation to be perceptible. Once we have defined our keyframe animations, the next step is to apply it to one or more elements using the various animation properties.

Animation Properties

The animation properties, remembering that you will need two declarations for each property as the -webkit- prefix is still needed in WebKit browsers, are as follows:

animation-name

This property is used to attach an animation (previously defined using the @keyframes syntax) to an element:

```
animation-name: appearDisappear;
```

Note that you should not put quotes around the animation name in either the property value or the @keyframes at-rule, as the specifications state the name is an identifier and not a string, so browsers don't support quoted animation names.

animation-duration

The `animation-duration` property defines the length of time (in seconds or milliseconds) an animation takes to complete one iteration (all the way through, from 0% to 100%):

```
animation-duration: 300ms;
```

While `animation-name` is the only required animation property to create an animation, the `animation-duration` *should* be considered required to animate an element. Without declaring the duration it defaults to 0s, which is imperceptible, but still fires the `animationstart` and `animationend` events. The other animation properties, while they enable you to better control your animation, are optional.

animation-timing-function

Like the `transition-timing-function` property, the `animation-timing-function` determines how the animation will progress over its duration. The options are the same as for `transition-timing-function`: `ease`, `linear`, `ease-in`, `ease-out`, `ease-in-out`, a developer-defined `cubic-bezier()` function, `step-start`, `step-end`, or a developer-defined number of steps with the `steps(number, direction)` function:

```
animation-timing-function: linear;
```

The bicycle in the advertisement on the right is animated in browsers that support animation. The bicycle is a background image, and while background images aren't able to be animated, `background-position` is. We've created a sprite of four images with our silhouetted man pedaling, as shown in Figure 8.9.

Figure 8.9. The sprite image we'll use to create the animation

To make it look like he is pedaling along, we show the different images of the sprite in succession. To do this, we use the `steps()` function, moving the background image sprite through the sized background box in four steps. We move the background image to the left so that each image within the sprite is displayed in succession:

```
.ad-ad3 :after {
  content: '';
  width: 90px;
  height: 92px;
  background-image: url(../images/bike_sprite.png);
  display: block;
  margin: auto;
}

@keyframes bike {
  0% {
    background-position: 0 0;
  }
  100% {
    background-position: -360px 0;
  }
}
```

Our background image is 360px wide and our container is 90px wide. We want to show the background images in quick succession, with the `background-position` at 0 0, -90px 0, -180px 0, and -270px 0. Using `steps(4, direction)`, if the direction is `start` we'll see the 25%, 50%, 75%, and 100% keyframes. If the direction is `end` we'll see the 0%, 25%, 50%, and 75% keyframes. At the 100% keyframe, the background image is completely off to the left—we don't want to see this. At the 0% keyframe, the background image is at 0 0, which is the default value for `background-position`, and which will display the first image in our sprite. This is what we want:

```
animation-timing-function: steps(4, end);
```

animation-iteration-count

The `animation-iteration-count` property lets you define how many times the animation will play through. The value is generally an integer, but you can also use numbers with decimal points (in which case, the animation will end partway through an iteration), or the value `infinite` for endlessly repeating animations. If omitted, it will default to 1, in which case the animation will occur only once. The following is an example of using this property:

```
animation-iteration-count: infinite;
```

animation-direction

When the animation iterates, it normally goes from the 0% to the 100% keyframe, jumping back to the 0% when it starts a new iteration (if the `animation-iteration-count` is greater than 1). This is the default or `normal` value for `animation-direction`. You can use the `animation-direction` property to change this behavior.

The value of `reverse` will cause the animation to start at the 100% keyframe and work its way to the 0% keyframe for every iteration. With the `alternate` value, the initial iteration and odd-numbered iterations after that will go in the normal 0% to 100% direction, but the second iteration and every even iteration after that will go in the reverse direction of 100% to 0%. Similarly, the `alternate-reverse` anima-tion-direction value causes the animation to alternate direction at every iteration, but it starts in reverse.

An animation of a snowflake falling will always be `normal`, though, you could use the same "falling" animation and employ `alternate` to reverse it, making it bounce up on every second playthrough. If you were to animate two kids playing on a seesaw, one kid could be tagged `alternate` and the other, `alternate-reverse`:

```
animation-direction: alternate;
```

When animations are played in reverse, timing functions are also reversed; for example, `ease-in` becomes `ease-out`.

animation-delay

The `animation-delay` property is used to define how many milliseconds or seconds to wait before the browser begins the animation:

```
animation-delay: 50ms;
```

animation-fill-mode

The `animation-fill-mode` property defines what happens before the first animation iteration begins and after the last animation iteration concludes. By default, an animation has no effect on property values outside of when it's iterating, but we can override this default behavior of `animation-fill-mode: none`.

The available values are `none`, `forwards`, `backwards`, or `both`. The default is `none`, in which case the animation proceeds and ends as expected, not inheriting the initial keyframe properties until after the delay has expired; it reverts to no longer being impacted by any of the keyframe property values when the animation completes its final iteration.

We can tell the animation to sit and wait on the first keyframe from the moment the animation is applied to the element, through the duration of the animation delay, until the animation starts iterating with `animation-fill-mode: backwards`. We can also hold the element at the last keyframe, with last keyframe property values overriding the element's original property values, without reverting to the original values at the conclusion of the last animation iteration with `animation-fill-mode: forwards`. We can also achieve both of these with `animation-fill-mode: both`.

As an example, let's say we animate four green elements from red to blue over one second, include a one-second delay for each, and set each with a different value for the `animation-fill-mode` property. The elements with `animation-fill-mode` set to `backwards` or `both` will be set to red as soon as the animation is attached to the element. When the `animation-delay` expires, all four elements will be red, changing to blue over one second. When the animation ends, the elements with `animation-fill-mode` set to `forwards` and `both` will stay blue, but those without the property set, or if it's set to `none` or `backwards`, will jump back to green.

Table 8.1. Examples of `animation-fill-mode` in effect

Fill mode	page load	1s	2s	after 2s
none	green	red	blue	green
backwards	red	red	blue	green
forwards	green	red	blue	blue
both	red	red	blue	blue

When set to `forwards`, the animation continues to apply the values of the last key-frames after the animation ends. When set to `backwards`, the animation's initial keyframes are applied as soon as the animation style is applied to an element. As you'd expect, a value of `both` applies both the `backwards` and `forwards` effects:

```
animation-fill-mode: both;
```

`animation-play-state`

The `animation-play-state` property defines whether the animation is running or paused. A paused animation displays the current state of the animation statically. When a paused animation is resumed, it restarts from the current position. This provides a simple way to control CSS animations from within your CSS or with JavaScript.

The Shorthand `animation` Property

Fortunately, there's a shorthand for all of these animation properties, especially since we're still including the `-webkit-` prefix. The `animation` property takes as its value a space-separated list of values for the longhand `animation-name`, `animation-duration`, `animation-timing-function`, `animation-delay`, `animation-iteration-count`, `animation-direction`, `animation-fill-mode`, and `animation-play-state` properties:

```
.verbose {
  animation-name: appearDisappear;
  animation-duration: 300ms;
  animation-timing-function: ease-in;
  animation-iteration-count: 1;
  animation-direction: alternate;
  animation-delay: 5s;
```

```
    animation-fill-mode: backwards;
    animation-play-state: running;
}

/* shorthand */
.concise {
    animation: 300ms ease-in alternate 5s backwards appearDisappear;
}
```

Note that in the shorthand version, we've left out the `animation-iteration-count` and `animation-play-state` since both were set to default.

 Be Careful with Naming

> If using the shorthand property, be careful with your `animation-name`. You want to avoid accidentally using any animation property key term such as `forwards`, `running`, or `alternate`. Those three key terms in particular have caused many developers hours of debugging. If you include a key term, the browser will assume that the first occurrence of a valid value for any of the longhand properties is the value for that property, not the value for the `animation-name` property.

To declare multiple animations on an element, include a grouping for each animation name, with each shorthand grouping separated by a comma. For example:

```
.target {
  animation:
    animationOne 300ms ease-in backwards,
    animationTwo 600ms ease-out 1s forwards;
}
```

For our bicycle, we want to translate it to the right while animating the sprite to make it seem as if the man is pedaling, using the `steps()` timing function to change the background image:

```
@keyframes bike {
  0% {
    background-position: 0 0;
  }
  100% {
    background-position: -360px 0;
  }
```

```
}
@keyframes move {
  0% {
    transform: translateX(-100px);
  }
  100% {
    transform: translateX(100px);
  }
}

h1:after {
  content: '';
  width: 90px;
  height: 92px;
  background-image: url(../images/bike_sprite.png);
  display: block;
  margin: auto;
  animation:
      0.4s steps(4, end) infinite 50ms bike,
      8s linear infinite 50ms move;
  animation-play-state: paused;
}
h1:hover:after {
  animation-play-state: running;
}
```

We've created two keyframe animations: one to animate the bicycle pedals using an animated sprite, and a second to move the animated bicycle across the advertisement using translated `transform` functions.

In its default state we have paused the animation. On hover, the animation comes alive with `animation-play-state` of `running`. There's no need to include the `animation-fill-mode` property as our animations iterate infinitely, and there's a 50ms delay before the animation starts so that it doesn't start if the user accidentally mouses through the ad.

Moving On

With transforms, transitions, and animations, our site is looking more dynamic. Remember the old maxim, though: just because you can, doesn't mean you should. Animations were aplenty on the Web in the late 90s; a lot of us remember flashing banners and scrolling marquees, and animated gifs were less entertaining than those that are popular today. Use animations and transitions where it makes sense, enhancing the user experience—and skip it everywhere else.

We still have a few lessons to learn in CSS3 to make our website look more like an old-time newspaper. In the next chapter, we'll we'll learn about typography and how to include fancy fonts not installed by default on our users' computers. We'll also look at how you can span text across multiple columns without scripts or extra HTML.

9

Embedded Fonts and Multicolumn Layouts

We've added quite a lot of decoration to *The HTML5 Herald*, but we're still missing some key components to give it that old-fashioned feel. To look like a real newspaper, the text of the articles should be laid out in narrow columns, and we should use some suitably appropriate fonts.

In this chapter, we'll add to the look and feel of our website with `@font-face` and CSS3 columns.

Web Fonts with `@font-face`

Since the early days of the Web, designers have been dreaming of creating sites with beautiful typography. But, as we all know too well, browsers are limited to rendering text in just the fonts the user has installed on their system. In practical terms, this has limited most sites to a handful of fonts: Arial, Verdana, Times, Georgia, and a few others.

Over the years, web decelopers have come up with a number of clever workarounds for this problem. We created JPEGs and PNGs for site titles, logos, buttons, and navigation elements. When those elements required additional states or variants, we created even more images. We then converted our text images to image sprites to ensure the page stayed snappy and responsive. Whenever the design or text changed, all those images had to be recreated. By definition this was a bad idea, but it really caused problems when it came to site performance, accessibility, translations, and internationalization. For page elements that need to change frequently, or at all, and to maximize accessibility and minimize bandwidth usage, we were stuck with those same few fonts.

To fill this typographic void, a few font-embedding scripts were created such as the Flash- and JavaScript-based sIFR[1] methods, and the canvas-based Cufón[2]. While these methods were a useful stopgap measure, allowing us to include our own fonts, they had severe drawbacks. Sometimes they were tricky to implement. They required that JavaScript be enabled and, in the case of sIFR, the Flash plugin be installed. In addition, they significantly slowed the page's download and rendering.

@font-face rule

Fortunately, there's now a better way. @font-face is a pure CSS solution for embedding fonts—and it's supported on every modern browser.

We'll be including two embedded fonts on *The HTML5 Herald* site: League Gothic from The League of Movable Type,[3] and Acknowledgement Medium by Ben Weiner of Reading Type.[4] The two fonts are shown respectively in Figure 9.1 and Figure 9.2.

---

[1] http://en.wikipedia.org/wiki/Scalable_Inman_Flash_Replacement
[2] http://cufon.shoqolate.com/generate/
[3] http://www.theleagueofmoveabletype.com/
[4] http://www.readingtype.org/

League Gothic

Figure 9.1. League Gothic

ACKNOWLEDGEMENT

Figure 9.2. Acknowledgement Medium

We'll now look at how we can embed these fonts and use them to power any of the text on our site, just as if they were installed on our users' machines. While including multiple fonts may improve a site's appearance, it's important that your typography choices don't decimate your site's performance.

Implementing `@font-face`

`@font-face` is one of several CSS at-rules, like `@media`, `@import`, `@page`, and the one we've just seen, `@keyframes`.

At-rules are ways of encapsulating several rules together in a declaration to serve as instructions to the browser's CSS processor. We saw the `@keyframes` at-rule in the previous chapter. The `@font-face` at-rule allows us to specify custom fonts that we can then include with the `font-family` property in other declaration blocks.

To include fonts using `@font-face`, you have to:

1. load the font file onto your servers in a variety of formats required by all the different browsers

2. name, describe, and link to that font in an `@font-face` rule

3. include the font's name in a `font-family` property value in your CSS, just as you would for system fonts

You already know how to upload a file onto a server, so we'll discuss the details of the various file types in the next section. For now, we'll focus on the second and third steps so that you can become familiar with the syntax of `@font-face`.

Here are the rules that go into an `@font-face` block:

```css
@font-face {
  font-family: 'fontName';
  src: source;
  font-weight: weight;
  font-style: style;
  unicode-range: characters;
}
```

The `font-family` and `src` properties are required. The `font-weight`, `font-style`, and `unicode-range` are optional.

You need to include a separate `@font-face` at-rule for every font you include in your site. You'll also have to include a separate at-rule for each variation of the font: regular, thin, thick, italic, black, and so on. *The HTML5 Herald* will require two imported fonts, so we'll include two `@font-face` blocks:

```css
@font-face {
  ⋮
}

@font-face {
  ⋮
}
```

The `font-family` declaration part of the `@font-face` at-rule declaration is slightly different from the `font-family` property with which you are already familiar. In this case, we're *declaring* a name for our font, rather than assigning a font with a given name to an element. The font name can be anything you like—it's only a reference to a font file, so it need not even correspond to the name of the font. Of course, it makes sense to use the font's name, or an abbreviated version of it, to keep your CSS readable and maintainable. Whatever you decide to name your font, it's best to settle on a convention and stick to it for all your fonts. For our two fonts, we'll use camel case:

```css
@font-face {
  font-family: 'LeagueGothic';
}
```

```
@font-face {
  font-family: 'AcknowledgementMedium';
}
```

Declaring Font Sources

Now that we have a skeleton laid out for our `@font-face` rules and given each of them a name, it's time to link them up to the actual font files.

There are several different font formats, including EOT, OTF, TTF, WOFF, WOFF2, among others. EOT (Embedded Open Type) font is a proprietary format for Internet Explorer and the only file type understood by IE4 through IE8. TTF (TrueType Font) is an outline font that is the most common format for fonts on the Mac OS and Microsoft Windows operating systems. OTF (OpenType Font) is a scalable font built on TTF, with the same basic structure but added data structures for prescribing typographic behavior. The W3C recommendation is WOFF (Web Open Font Format), which is essentially an OpenType or TrueType font format with compression and additional metadata. The goal for WOFF was to improve performance, by minimizing the bandwidth needed to send the font file to the client. WOFF2 is the second W3C spec, improving compression and therefore performance.

The `src` property can take several formats. Additionally, you can declare more than one comma-separated source as the value of the source property.

Let's add some formats to our League Gothic declaration:

```
@font-face {
  font-family: 'LeagueGothicRegular';
  src: url('../fonts/League_Gothic-webfont.eot?#iefix')
           ↪format('embedded-opentype'),
       url('../fonts/League_Gothic-webfont.woff2') format('woff2'),
       url('../fonts/League_Gothic-webfont.woff') format('woff'),
       url('../fonts/League_Gothic-webfont.ttf') format('truetype');
}
```

There are four font sources listed in this code block. If the browser fails to locate or recognize the first source, it will try for the next one, and so on, until it either finds a source it supports (at which point it stops looking) or runs out of options.

The first declaration is the EOT font declaration for older versions of Internet Explorer.

Then we define WOFF2, which has the best compression but is yet to be well supported; then WOFF, which is a better-supported Web Open Font Format. We then declare the TTF (TrueType Font) and OTF (OpenType Font) fallback formats. We used to include an SVG (Scalable Vector Graphics) font file for the original iPhones. This format is being deprecated, but continues to be supported.

WOFF is supported in all newer browsers, so we could have simply included a single WOFF file; however, we have a new format in WOFF2, similar to WOFF but with better web font compression (leading to faster loading), and we still want to ensure some support for older Android browsers.

Here's a table showing current browser support for the various font formats.

Table 9.1. Browser support for font formats

	IE	Safari	Chrome	Firefox	Opera	iOS	Android
@font-face	6	3.2	4	3.5	10	3.2	2.1
WOFF	9	5.1	5	3.6	11.1	5.1	4.4
WOFF2			36	35?	23		(starting with Android 5.0, the WebView will be updated[5] so it will support WoFF2)
OTF	9	3.1	4	3.5	10.1	4.3	2.2
TTF	9	3.1	4	3.5	10.1	4.3	2.2
SVG		3.2	4–37[a]		9.6	3.2	3.0
EOT	4						

[a] To be precise, "SVG fonts are no longer supported, except on Windows systems older than Windows 7. Note that while the feature works on those systems, it is considered deprecated." [http://blog.chromium.org/2014/08/chrome-38-beta-new-primitives-for-next.html]

As you can see, WOFF is supported in all modern browsers. You may still want to provide fallbacks for older browsers, like we did with video in Chapter 5. Because of bandwidth issues, however, you may just want to include WOFF for newer browsers and EOT for IE8, and avoid forcing additional HTTP requests to older mobile devices. If a format hint is listed, browsers check to see if it is supported before downloading or advancing to the next format listed. If no format hint is included, the browser downloads the resource. While we list WOFF 2.0 for browsers that support it, WOFF for the majority of browsers, TTF for Android 4.4 and below, and EOT for IE8 and earlier, as long as we provide the format hint, only the font file the browser will use will be downloaded.

Adding these extra font formats ensures support for all browsers, but unfortunately it can cause problems in versions of IE older than IE9. They see everything between

[5] http://developer.telerik.com/featured/android-5-0s-auto-updating-webview-means-mobile-apps/

the first `url('` and the last `')` as one URL, so will fail to load the font. Fortunately, adding a query string to the end of the EOT URL is a quick fix, so no choice needs to be made between supporting IE or supporting all other browsers. This tricks the browser into thinking that the rest of the `src` property is a continuation of that query string, so it goes looking for the correct URL and loads the font:

```
@font-face {
  font-family: 'LeagueGothicRegular';
  src: url('../fonts/League_Gothic-webfont.eot?#iefix') format('
➥embedded-opentype'),
       url('../fonts/League_Gothic-webfont.woff2') format('woff2'),
       url('../fonts/League_Gothic-webfont.woff') format('woff'),
       url('../fonts/League_Gothic-webfont.ttf') format('truetype');
}
```

Font Property Descriptors

Font property descriptors—including `font-style`, `font-variant`, `font-weight`, and others—can optionally be added to define the characteristics of the font face, and are used to match styles to specific font faces. The values are the same as the equivalent CSS properties:

```
@font-face {
  font-family: 'LeagueGothicRegular';
  src: url('../fonts/League_Gothic-webfont.eot?#iefix')
➥format('embedded-opentype'),
       url('../fonts/League_Gothic-webfont.woff2') format('woff2'),
       url('../fonts/League_Gothic-webfont.woff') format('woff'),
       url('../fonts/League_Gothic-webfont.ttf') format('truetype');
  font-weight: bold;
  font-style: normal;
}
```

You are not telling the browser to make the font bold; rather, you're telling it that this *is* the bold variant of the font. This can be confusing, but there is a reason to use the `font-weight` or `font-style` descriptor in the `@font-face` rule declaration. You can declare several font sources for the same font-family name:

```
@font-face {
  font-family: 'CoolFont';
  font-style: normal;
```

```
  src: url(fonts/CoolFontStd.woff);
}

@font-face {
  font-family: 'CoolFont';
  font-style: italic;
  src: url(fonts/CoolFontItalic.woff);
}

.whichFont {
  font-family: 'CoolFont';
}
```

Notice that both at-rules use the same font-family name but different font styles. In this example, the `.whichFont` element will use the `CoolFontStd.woff` font, because it matches the style given in that at-rule; however, if the element were to inherit an italic font style, it would switch to using the `CoolFontItalic.woff` font instead.

The Unicode Range Descriptor

Also available is the `unicode-range` descriptor, which is employed to define the range of Unicode characters supported by the font. If this property is omitted, the entire range of characters included in the font file will be made available.

Here's an example of what it looks like:

```
unicode-range: U+000-49F, U+2000-27FF, U+2900-2BFF, U+1D400-1D7FF;
```

If you are including a Unicode range, it makes sense to create font files containing only the characters within your range to reduce bandwidth and memory consumption. Tools that convert your desktop fonts to EOT, WOFF, WOFF2, TTF, OTF, and SVG, such as Font Squirrel Generator,[6] are capable of creating very small font resources containing only the characters you need; however, you have to take care to include all the characters that may be required. Furthermore, if you want to enable your content to be translated while maintaining the desired look and feel, you'll likely need to include the characters for any translation. The process of creating

---

[6] http://www.fontsquirrel.com/tools/webfont-generator

these smaller files is described shortly. Unfortunately, this feature is yet to be well supported.[7].

Applying the Font

Once the font is declared using the `@font-face` syntax, you can then refer to it as you would any normal system font in your CSS: include it in a font stack as the value of a `font-family` property. It's a good idea also to declare a fallback font or two in case your embedded font fails to load.

Let's look at one example from *The HTML5 Herald*:

```
h1 {
  text-shadow: #ffffff 1px 1px;
  font-family: LeagueGothic, Tahoma, Geneva, sans-serif;
  text-transform: uppercase;
  line-height: 1;
}
```

Our two embedded fonts are used in a number of places in our stylesheet, but you get the idea.

Legal Considerations

We've included the markup for two fonts on our site, but we're yet to put the font files themselves in place. We found both of these fonts freely available online. They are both licensed as freeware; that is, they're free to use for both personal and commercial use. Generally, this is the only kind of font you should use for `@font-face`, unless you're using a third-party service.

How is `@font-face` any different from using a certain font in an image file? By having a website on the Internet, your font source files are hosted on publicly available web servers. In theory, anyone can download them. In fact, in order to render the text on your page, the browser *has* to download the font files. By using `@font-face`, you're distributing the font to everyone who visits your site. To include a font on your website, then, you need to be legally permitted to distribute the font.

---

[7] http://jakearchibald.com/2014/minimising-font-downloads/

Owning or purchasing a font doesn't give you the legal right to redistribute it—in the same way that buying a song on iTunes doesn't grant you the right to put it up on your website for anyone to download. Licenses that allow you to distribute fonts are more expensive (and rarer) than licenses allowing you to use a font on one computer for personal or even commercial use.

There are several websites that have free downloadable web fonts with Creative Commons,[8] shareware, or freeware licensing. Alternatively, there are paid and subscription services that allow you to purchase or rent fonts, generally providing you with ready-made scripts or stylesheets that make them easy to use with `@font-face`.

A few sites providing web font services include Typekit,[9] Typotheque,[10] Webtype,[11] Fontdeck,[12] and Fonts.com.[13]

Google's web fonts directory[14] has a growing collection of fonts provided free of charge and hosted at Google's servers. It simply provides you with a URL pointing to a stylesheet that includes all the required `@font-face` rules, so all you have to do is add a link element to your document and the font name in a font-family declaration in your CSS in order to start using a font.

When selecting a service, font selection and price are certainly important, but there are other considerations. Make sure any service you choose to use takes download speed into consideration. As has been mentioned, font files can be fairly large, potentially containing several thousand characters. Good services allow you to select character subsets, as well as font-style subsets, to decrease the file size. Bear in mind, also, that some services require JavaScript in order to function.

---

[8] If you're unfamiliar with Creative Commons licenses, you can find out more at http://creativecommons.org/.

[9] http://typekit.com/

[10] http://www.typotheque.com/

[11] http://www.webtype.com/

[12] http://fontdeck.com/

[13] http://webfonts.fonts.com

[14] http://code.google.com/apis/webfonts/

Creating Various Font File Types: Font Squirrel

If you have a font that you're legally allowed to redistribute, there'll be no need for you to use any of the font services mentioned. You will, however, have to convert your font into the various formats required to serve the most performant file format while supporting every browser on the market. So how do you go about converting your fonts into all of these formats?

One of the easiest tools for this purpose is Font Squirrel's `@font-face` generator.[15] This service allows you to select fonts from your desktop with a few clicks of your mouse and convert them to TTF, EOT, WOFF, WOFF2, SVG, SVGZ, and even a Base64 encoded version.[16]

By default, the **Optimal** option is selected for generating an `@font-face` kit; however, in some cases you can decrease the file sizes by choosing **Expert...** and creating a character subset. Rather than including every conceivable character in the font file, you can limit yourself to those you know will be used on your site.

For example, on *The HTML5 Herald* site the Acknowledgement Medium font is used only in specific ad blocks and headings, so we require just a small set of characters. All the text set in this font is uppercase, so let's restrict our font to uppercase letters, punctuation, and numbers, as shown in Figure 9.3.

---

[15] http://www.fontsquirrel.com/fontface/generator

[16] Base64 encoding is a way of including the entire contents of a font file directly in your CSS file. Sometimes this can provide performance benefits by avoiding an extra HTTP request, but that's beyond the scope of this book. Don't sweat it, though—the files generated by the default settings should be fine for most uses.

Subsetting:	◯ Basic Subsetting	◉ Custom Subsetting...	◯ No Subsetting
	Western languages	Custom language support	

Character Encoding:	☐ Mac Roman

Character Type:	☐ Lowercase	☐ Currency	☐ Lower Accents
	☑ Uppercase	☐ Typographics	☐ Upper Accents
	☑ Numbers	☐ Math Symbols	☐ Diacriticals
	☑ Punctuation	☐ Alt Punctuation	

Figure 9.3. Selecting a subset of characters in Font Squirrel's @font-face generator

Figure 9.4 shows how the file sizes of our subsetted fonts stack up against the default character sets. In our case, the uppercase- and punctuation-only fonts are 25 to 30% smaller than the default character sets. Font Squirrel even lets you specify certain characters for your subset, so there's no need to include all the letters of the alphabet if you know you won't use them. Just remember, if there's the possibility that your text might be translated, you may need to include characters not in your original content.

acknowledgement–subset.eot	12 KB
acknowledgement–subset.svg	25 KB
acknowledgement–subset.ttf	20 KB
acknowledgement–subset.woff	12 KB
Acknowledgement–webfont.eot	29 KB
Acknowledgement–webfont.svg	37 KB
Acknowledgement–webfont.ttf	29 KB
Acknowledgement–webfont.woff	16 KB

Figure 9.4. File sizes of subsetted fonts can be substantially smaller

For the League Gothic font, we'll need a more expanded character subset. This font is used for article titles, which are all uppercase like our ads, so we can again omit lowercase letters; however, we should consider that content for titles may include a wider range of possible characters. Moreover, users might use in-browser tools or Google Translate to translate the content on the page—in which case other characters might be required. So, for League Gothic, we'll go with the default **Basic Subsetting**—this will give you all the characters required for Western languages.

When employing `@font-face`, as a general rule minimize font file size as much as reasonably possible, while making sure to include enough characters so that a translated version of your site is still accessible.

Once you've uploaded your font for processing and selected all your options, press **Download Your Kit**. Font Squirrel provides an archive containing your font files with the extensions requested, a demo HTML file for each font face style, and a stylesheet from which you can copy and paste the code directly into your own CSS.

Font Squirrel's Font Catalog

In addition to the `@font-face` generator, the Font Squirrel site includes a catalog of hand-picked free fonts whose licenses allow for web embedding. In fact, both the fonts we're using on *The HTML5 Herald* can also be found on Font Squirrel, with ready-made `@font-face` kits to download without relying on the generator at all.

To target all browsers, make sure that you've created WOFF2, WOFF, TTF, and EOT font file formats, including SVG if you're still supporting really old mobile. Once you've created the font files, upload the web fonts to your server. Copy and paste the CSS provided, changing the paths to point to the folder where you've placed your fonts. Make sure the `font-family` name specified in the `@font-face` rule matches the one you're using in your styles, and you're good to go!

Font Failure

If your fonts are failing to display in any browser, the problem could very well be the path in your CSS. Check to make sure that the font file is actually where you expect it to be. Browser-based debugging tools—such as the Web Inspector in WebKit, Opera, and Chrome; F12 in Internet Explorer; or the Firebug Firefox extension—will indicate if the file is missing.

If you're sure that the path is correct and the file is where it's supposed to be, make sure your server is correctly configured to serve up the fonts. Windows IIS servers won't serve up files if they're unable to recognize their MIME type, so try adding WOFF to your list of MIME types (EOT and TTF should be supported out of the box):

```
.woff   application/x-font-woff
```

Finally, browsers are supposed to require that font files are served from the same domain as the page they're embedded on: if your fonts fail to work in Internet Explorer or Firefox, make sure to set CORS configurations[17] to enable fonts from different domains and CDNs.

 Developer Tools

Browsers come standard with tools to help save you time as a web developer. In most browsers you can right-click (or control-click on a Mac) and choose **Inspect Element**. A panel will open up at the bottom of your browser, highlighting the HTML of the element you've selected. You'll also see any CSS applied to that element.

While Safari comes with this tool, it needs to be manually enabled. To turn it on, go to **Safari > Preferences**, and then click the **Advanced** tab. Be sure to check the **Show Develop** menu in the menu bar checkbox.

Firefox comes with inspection tools, but Firebug—a free Firefox plugin that provides the same functionality as the other browsers' native debuggers—is more robust. You can download Firebug at http://getfirebug.com/.

Internet Explorer also has developer tools that you can access via **F12**, enabling you to inspect elements.

Other Font Considerations

Embedded fonts can improve performance and decrease maintenance time when compared to text as images. Remember, though, that font files can be big. If you need a particular font for a banner ad, it may make more sense (given the limited amount of text required) to create an image instead of including font files. At the minimum, if you're only embedding a font for your company name or logo, send just the limited character set needed for your name to your visitors. Or, better yet, save your logo as an SVG image.

When pondering whether to include multiple font files on your site, consider performance. Multiple fonts will increase your site's download time, and font overuse

---

[17] http://davidwalsh.name/cdn-fonts

can be tacky. Furthermore, the wrong font can make your content difficult to read. For body text, you should almost always stick to the usual selection of web-safe fonts.

Another point worth considering is that browsers are unable to render the `@font-face` font until it has been downloaded entirely. Browsers behave differently in how they display your content before the download is complete: some will render the text in a system font, while others won't render any text at all.

This effect is referred to as a "flash of unstyled text," or FOUT, a term coined by Paul Irish.[18] To try to prevent this from happening (or to minimize its duration), make your file sizes as small as possible, serve them gzipped, and include your `@font-face` rules in CSS files as high up as possible in your markup. If there's a script above the `@font-face` declaration in the source, some versions of IE experience a bug whereby the page will fail to render *anything* until the font has down-loaded—so be sure to declare your fonts above any scripts on your page.

Another option to mitigate `@font-face`'s impact on performance is to defer the font file download until after the page has rendered. This may be unviable for your de-signer or client, however, as it may result in a more noticeable FOUT, even if the page loads faster overall.[19]

Of course, we don't want to scare you away from using `@font-face`, but it's important that you avoid using this feature without regard for the consequences. Remember that there are trade-offs, so use web fonts where they're appropriate, and consider the available alternatives.

CSS3 Multicolumn Layouts

Nothing says "newspaper" like a row of tightly packed columns of text. There's a reason for this: newspapers break articles into multiple columns because long lines of text are too hard to read. Browser windows can be wider than printed books—even as wide as some newspapers—so it makes sense for CSS to give us the ability to flow our content into columns.

---

[18] http://www.paulirish.com/2009/fighting-the-font-face-fout/

[19] For more on `@font-face` and performance, as well as an example of how to "lazy load" your font files, see http://www.stevesouders.com/blog/2009/10/13/font-face-and-performance/.

You may be thinking that we've always been able to create column effects using the `float` property. But the behavior of floats is subtly different from what we're after. Newspaper-style columns have been close to impossible to accomplish with CSS and HTML without forcing column breaks at fixed positions. True, you could break an article into `divs`, floating each one to make it look like a set of columns. But what if your content is dynamic? Your back-end code will need to figure out where each column should begin and end in order to insert the requisite `div` tags.

With CSS3 columns, the browser determines when to end one column and begin the next without requiring any extra markup. You retain the flexibility to change the number of columns, as well as their width, without having to go back in and alter the page's markup.

For now, we're mostly limited to splitting content across a few columns while controlling their widths and the gutters between them. As support broadens, we'll be able to break columns, span elements across multiple columns, and more. Browser support for CSS3 columns is moderate: IE10 and Opera Mini are the only two browsers with full, unprefixed support. Opera mobile and desktop used to have full support, but reverted to quirky prefixed support when it switched to the Blink engine (in version 15). Firefox, Blink (Chrome) and WebKit (iOS) browsers have had support via vendor-prefixed properties for years, with some bugs still needing to be fixed.

Almost all the content on the main page of *The HTML5 Herald* is broken into columns. Let's dig deeper into the properties that make up CSS3 columns and learn how to create these effects on our site.

The `column-count` Property

The `column-count` property specifies the number of columns wanted, and the maximum number of columns allowed. The default value of `auto` means that the element has one column. Our left-most articles are broken into three columns, and the article below the ad blocks has two columns:

```
.primary article .content {
  -webkit-column-count: 3;
  -moz-column-count: 3;
  column-count: 3;
}
```

```
.tertiary article .content {
  -webkit-column-count: 2;
  -moz-column-count: 2;
  column-count: 2;
}
```

This is all we really need to create our columns. By default, the columns will have a small gap between them. The total width of the columns combined with the gaps will take up 100% of the width of the element.

Still, there are a number of other properties we can use for more granular control.

The `column-gap` Property

The `column-gap` property specifies the width of the space between columns:

```
.primary article .content,
.tertiary article .content {
  -webkit-column-gap: 10px;
  -moz-column-gap: 10px;
  column-gap: 10px;
}
```

Declare the width in length units, such as ems or pixels, or use the term `normal`. It's up to the browser to determine what `normal` means, but the spec suggests `1em`. We've declared our gaps to be `10px` wide. The resulting columns are shown in Figure 9.5.

VIDEO IS THE FINAL FRONTIER, AND NOW WE HAVE CONQUERED IT!

Aliquam erat volutpat. Mauris vel neque sit amet nunc gravida congue sed sit amet purus. Quisque lacus quam, egestas ac tincidunt a, lacinia vel velit. Morbi ac commodo nulla.

In condimentum orci id nisl volutpat bibendum. Quisque commodo hendrerit lorem quis egestas. Vivamus rutrum nunc non neque consectetur quis placerat neque lobortis. Nam vestibulum, arcu sodales feugiat consectetur, nisl orci bibendum elit, eu euismod magna sapien ut nibh. Aliquam erat

volutpat. Mauris vel neque sit amet nunc gravida congue sed sit amet purus.

Quisque lacus quam, egestas ac tincidunt a, lacinia vel velit. Morbi ac commodo nulla. In condimentum orci id nisl volutpat bibendum. Quisque commodo hendrerit lorem quis egestas. Vivamus rutrum nunc non neque consectetur quis placerat neque lobortis. Nam vestibulum, arcu sodales feugiat consectetur, nisl orci bibendum elit, eu euismod magna sapien ut nibh.

Neque sit amet nunc gravida congue sed sit amet purus. Quisque lacus quam, egestas ac tincidunt a, lacinia vel velit. Morbi ac commodo nulla. In condimentum orci id nisl volutpat bibendum. Quisque commodo hendrerit lorem quis egestas. Vivamus rutrum nunc non neque consectetur quis placerat neque lobortis. Nam vestibulum, arcu sodales feugiat consectetur, nisl orci bibendum elit, eu euismod magna sapien ut nibh.

Figure 9.5. Our left-most content area has articles split over three columns

The `column-width` Property

The `column-width` property is like having a `min-width` for your columns. The browser will include as many columns of at least the given width as it can to fill up the element, up to the value of the `column-count` property. If the columns need to be wider to fill up all the available space, they will be.

```
.parent {
    width: 400px;
    column-count: 3;
    column-width: 150px;
    column-gap: 10px;
}
```

For example, if we have a parent that is 400 pixels wide, a 10-pixel column gap, and the `column-width` is declared as 150px, the browser can fit two columns:

```
(400px width − 10px column gap) ÷ 150px width = 2.6
```

The browser rounds down to two columns, making columns that are as large as possible in the allotted space; in this case, that's 195px for each column—the total width minus the gap, divided by the number of columns. Even if the column-count were set to 3, there would still only be two columns, as there's not enough space to include three columns of the specified width. In other words, you can think of the column-width as being the *minimum* column width and column-count property as specifying the *maximum* column count.

The only situation in which columns will be narrower than the column-width is if the parent element itself is too narrow for a single column of the specified width. In this case, you'll have one column that fills the whole parent element.

It's a good idea to declare your column-width in ems, ensuring a minimum number of characters for each line in a column. Let's add a column-width of 9em to our content columns:

```
.primary article .content,
.tertiary article .content {
    ⋮
  -webkit-column-width: 9em;
  -moz-column-width: 9em;
  column-width: 9em;
}
```

Now, if you increase the font size in your browser, you'll see that the number of columns is decreased as required to maintain a minimum width. This ensures readability, as shown in Figure 9.6.

Figure 9.6. Declaring `column-width` in ems ensures a minimum number of characters on each line

The `columns` Shorthand Property

The `columns` shorthand property is a composite of the `column-width` and `column-count` properties. Declare the two parameters—the width of each column and the number of columns—as previously described:

```css
.primary article .content {
  -webkit-columns: 3 9em;
  -moz-columns: 3 9em;
  columns: 3 9em;
}
```

The math of those two declarations may not give you what you'd expect. By default, there is a gap of 1em between every two columns. If our `.content` is less than 29 ems wide (three columns of 9ems each, plus two times the `column-gap` of 1em), say 25 ems, the browser will display only two columns:

```
(25em total width — 2em column gaps) ÷ 9em column width = 2.55
```

To have three columns fit, our parent would need to be at least 29 ems wide:

```
(29em total width — 2em column gaps) ÷ 9em column width = 3 columns
```

If the `.content` is equal to or greater than 29 ems, say 38 ems, the browser will show a maximum of three columns, displaying columns that are 12 ems wide:

```
(38em total width — 2em column gaps) ÷ 3 columns = 12 ems
```

Again, think of `columns` values as the maximum number of columns and minimum width per column. The only time a column will be less than 9em in this case is if `.content` is less than 9em wide.

Columns and the `height` Property

With the aforementioned declarations—and no height specified on the element—browsers will balance the column heights automatically so that the content in each column is approximately equal in height.

But what if a height is declared? When the `height` property is set on a multicolumn block, each column is allowed to grow to that height and no further before a new column is added. Depending on the browser, the columns may start with the first column and create as many columns as necessary, or just the one if there is minimal text. This is how Opera and Chrome currently handle columns but to ensure this effect in all browsers, include `column-fill: auto;`.

If you want to declare a `height` on your element, but would also like the content to be spread evenly across your columns, you can use the `column-fill` property. When supported and set to `balance`, the browser will balance the height of the columns as though there were no height declared. This is what happens by default in Safari and Firefox.

Finally, if too little space is allocated with the `height` property, the content will overflow from the parent—or be clipped if `overflow: hidden;` is set.

 Issues with Column Height

Even with a height declared, columns may still not appear to have exactly the desired height because of the bottom margins on paragraphs. Some browsers split margins and padding between columns,[20] sometimes adding the extra spacing at the top of a column that follows. Others allow margins to go beyond the bottom of the box, rather than letting them show up at the top of the next column, which makes more sense.

As with `column-width`, you may also want to declare your height in ems instead of pixels; this way, if your user increases the font size, they are less likely to have content clipped or overflowing.

Other Column Features

Beyond the core `count`, `width`, and `gap` properties, CSS3 provides us with additional features for laying out multicolumn content.

The `column-rule` Property

Column rules are essentially borders between each column. The `column-rule` property specifies the color, style, and width of the column rule. The rule will appear in the middle of the column gap if there is content in the column to both sides of the rule. Similar to `border`, the `column-rule` property is actually shorthand for the `column-rule-color`, `column-rule-style`, and `column-rule-width` properties.

The syntax for the values is exactly the same as for borders and the related `border-width`, `border-style`, and `border-color` properties. The width can be any length unit, just like `border-width`, including the key terms of `medium`, `thick`, and `thin`. And the color can be any supported color value:

```
-webkit-column-rule: 1px solid #CCCCCC;
-moz-column-rule: 1px solid #CCCCCC;
column-rule: 1px solid #CCCCCC;
```

Column Breaks

There are three column-breaking properties that, when supported, will allow developers to define where column breaks should appear. The `break-before`, `break-after`, and `break-inside` properties take a limited number of key terms as values to define whether a column break can and should occur before, after, or inside an element respectively. Rather than being applied to the same element on which we defined our primary column properties, they're applied to other elements nested

---

[20] http://zomigi.com/blog/deal-breaker-problems-with-css3-multi-columns/

inside it. Unfortunately, only IE10+ supports these properties at the time of this writing.

The values available are the same as for `page-break-after`, `page-break-before`, and `page-break-inside`: `auto`, `always`, `avoid`, `left`, `right`, `page`, `column`, `avoid-page`, and `avoid-column`.

For example, you might want to avoid a column break occurring immediately after an `h2` element in your content. Here's how you'd do that:

```
.columns {
  column-count: 3;
  column-gap: 5px;
}

.columns h2 {
  break-after: avoid;
}
```

Until Blink and WebKit support the standard properties, we can include vendor-specific syntax that behaves similarly. Note the addition of the word `column` to the property names in the non-standard prefixed syntax:

```
-webkit-column-break-after: always;
-webkit-column-break-before: auto;
-webkit-column-break-inside: never;
```

Spanning Columns

The `column-span` property will make it possible for an element to span across several columns. If `column-span: all;` is set on an element, all content that comes *before* that element in the markup should be in columns *above* that element. All content in columns appearing in the markup *after* the element should be in columns *below* the spanned element.

The `h1`s span all the columns. The text between the two headings is divided equally across three columns, with the column rules breaking for the second heading. The rest of the text—that which follows the second heading—is again divided across the three columns, with the column rules dividing the columns but not displayed behind the spanning text:

```
article {
  columns: 3 12em;
  column-rule: 1px solid #CCCCCC;
}
h1 {
  column-span: all;
}
p {
  margin-top: 0;
}
```

We included `margin-top: 0` on the paragraphs to ensure paragraphs that start at the top of the column aren't dropped by 1em.

For cross-browser compatibility, you would add the `-webkit-` prefix for Chrome, Opera, and Safari. Firefox doesn't support `column-span` at all, and IE supports it without a prefix. Including this feature results in a very different appearance when there's no support, so you may want to develop for browsers that don't support it, and put the `column-span: all;` behind `@media` queries or `@supports` rules.

For example, for the first article on *The HTML5 Herald*, we could have applied the column properties to the `article` element rather than the `.content` div, and used `column-span: all;` to ensure that the video spanned across the full width of the article; however, this would appear badly broken in Firefox—so we instead opted to separate the video from the column content.

Other Considerations

If you've been following along with our examples, you might notice that some of your blocks of text have ugly holes in them, like the one shown in Figure 9.7.

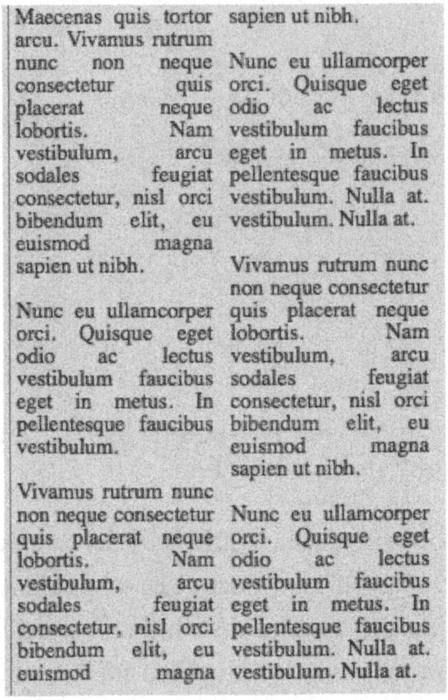

Figure 9.7. "Rivers" appear in your text when your columns are too narrow

This problem occurs when text with `text-align: justify;` is set in very narrow columns, as we're doing for *The HTML5 Herald*. Browsers are yet to know how to hyphenate words in the same way that word processors do, so they space words out awkwardly to ensure that the left and right edges stay justified.

For *The HTML5 Herald*, we've used a JavaScript library called Hyphenator[21] to hyphenate words and keep our text looking tidy. This may, however be unnecessary for your site—our columns are extremely narrow, as we're trying to replicate a newspaper style.

If you prefer to use CSS instead of JavaScript to hyphenate, there is a solution. The `&shy;` character is an invisible or "soft" hyphen you include to suggest a location within a word where it would make sense to hyphenate if necessary. The hyphen is only shown if there is a word break at that point. This differs from the regular hyphen, which is displayed whether or not there is word break at that character.

Browsers are slowly gaining the ability to hyphenate words like word processors do. The experimental `hyphens` property—with possible values of `none`, `manual`, and

---

[21] http://code.google.com/p/hyphenator/

`auto`—supports auto hyphenation in some spoken languages, as defined in the `lang` attribute in IE and Firefox with a prefix. Internet Explorer 10 and Firefox 6 both support the prefixed experimental `hyphens: auto`, if the browser has integrated the dictionary for the document's declared language. See https://developer.mozilla.org/en-US/docs/Web/CSS/hyphens.

Few real-world sites would likely need justified columns that narrow, but if you ever come across this issue, it's good to know that there are solutions available.

Progressive Enhancement

While columns still have limited browser support, there's no harm in including them in your sites unless your designer is a stickler for detail. Columns can be viewed as a progressive enhancement: making long lines easier to read. Those using browsers without support for columns will be none the wiser about what they're missing. For instance, *The HTML5 Herald* will have no columns when viewed in Internet Explorer 9, as Figure 9.8 shows. But the site certainly doesn't look broken—it's simply adapted to the capabilities of the browser.

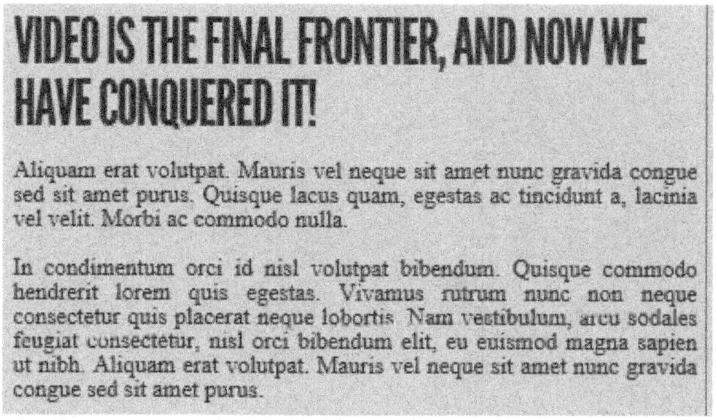

Figure 9.8. Our site has no columns when viewed in IE9—but that's okay!

If, however, columns are an important feature of your design that must be provided to all visitors, there are scripts that can help; for instance, there's Columnizer,[22] a jQuery plugin by Adam Wulf.

[22] http://welcome.totheinter.net/columnizer-jquery-plugin/

Up Next

There are many new features in CSS that progressively enhance a site, such as columns and fonts, with non-supporting browsers still rendering all the content.

When it comes to content, one size fits all. You want to send the same content to all your users no matter how they are accessing it. With browsers and devices of different sizes and resolutions, however, it's far from being "one size fits all" when it comes to presentation. You'll want to include fewer columns on a narrower screen than you would on a large screen. You may also want to include fewer fonts on a device with limited bandwidth.

Responsive websites are more than just "squishy" layouts. In the next chapter, we look at a few features that will help you send the right design to the right screen size, including flexbox, which—combined with media queries—enables on-the-fly changing of your layout.

Flexbox and Media Queries

At this point, we've added a number of CSS3 enhancements to *The HTML5 Herald*. Along the way, we've filled in some knowledge gaps by presenting aspects of CSS3 that were outside the scope of our sample site. So it's fitting that we should introduce two other CSS3 features that have received much attention among designers targeting audiences on various devices and screen sizes: flexbox and media queries.

In Chapter 1, we talked about the growth rate of mobile devices and the importance of considering the needs of mobile users. With **flexbox**, we can create layouts that easily resize to accommodate different screen widths. For example, we can provide a wide screen with a three-column layout, and provide a narrower screen with a single-column layout, all without touching the HTML. With CSS3 **media queries**, we can take that concept a step further, not only creating layouts that resize to accommodate different screen sizes, but even providing different CSS rules based on the user's screen size and resolution.

Flexbox

Flexbox, as described in CSS Flexible Box Layout Module Level 1,[1] provides for an efficient way to layout, align, and distribute space among elements within your document, even when the viewport and the size of your elements is unknown and/or dynamic. Flexbox is a flexible, float-free CSS layout method that accommodates different screen sizes and display devices. Flexbox allows the browser to alter the width or height of elements to best fill the available space on any display device: with elements expanding to fill all available free space, or shrinking to prevent overflow.

With flexbox, we can modify the appearance of the document to the user—changing the appearance of the source order—without JavaScript and without actually manipulating the DOM. Flexbox allows us to fully separate the structure of the code from how it's displayed; with CSS only we can reorder or even invert how elements are displayed, all without touching the HTML.

CSS layout has always been viewed as difficult. Flexbox makes it simple. With flexbox we can lay out elements vertically or horizontally, taking up all the space provided or the least amount of space necessary, creating elements of equal height or width with just a few lines of CSS. We can add any number of items onto one line or several lines, and even change the order of appearance of the content without touching the underlying markup.

Flex Container and Flex Item

The general idea of flexbox is that you define a **containing block** as the container of flexible items—either an inline or a block-level flex container—and then you nest flexible children into that parent container. You define whether those children are laid out vertically, horizontally, on one line, or several, in the source order or reversed, or in some other order, and what direction in which those children are laid out. The flex container can expand items to fill space or shrink items to prevent overflow:

---

[1] http://dev.w3.org/csswg/css-flexbox/

```
<ul class="container">
  <li class="flexItem">...</li>
  <li class="flexItem">...</li>
  <li class="flexItem">...</li>
</ul>
```

[2]The **flex container** is the parent element in which flex items are contained. The children of the flex container are **flex items**: when an element is turned into a flex container via the `display` property, each child of that flex container becomes a flex item. The flex container's margins collapse with the margins of its contents.

The properties applied to the parent or container include `display`, `flex-direction`, `flex-wrap`, and `flex-flow` (which is shorthand for `flex-direction` and `flex-wrap`). There are also alignment properties applied to the container, including `justify-content`, `align-items`, and `align-content`. The children, or flex items, have properties that enable the ordering and laying out of the children within the parent, including `order`, `align-self`, `flex-grow`, `flex-shrink`, `flex-basis`, and `flex` (which is shorthand for `flex-grow`, `flex-shrink`, and `flex-basis`).

Container Properties

The container can be displayed as a block or inline, but avoid using either of those as values for the container's `display` property. To make an element a flex container, we do use the well-known `display` property, but we define the block and inline presentation by using `display: flex` and `display: inline-flex` respectively, as shown in Figure 10.1. If neither value is set, the element is not a flex container and the children will not be flex items:

---

[2] In the markup above, we wouldn't need to add the `flexItem` class as we could use `.container li` instead, or even `.container > *` for less specificity: we added an unnecessary class for ease of explanation.

```
.container {
  display: flex || inline-flex;
}
```

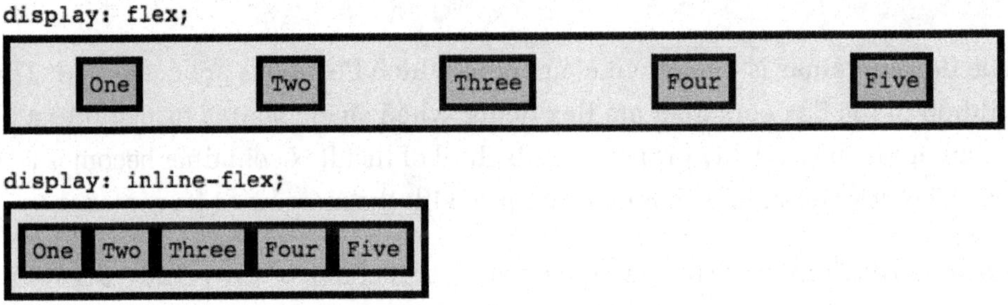

display: flex;

display: inline-flex;

Figure 10.1. The `display` property set to `flex` and `inline-flex`

The `flex-direction` property defines the axis along which the flex items follow each other. A flex container has the default `flex-direction` of row, meaning that the flex items follow each other horizontally across the main axis or `column`. The alternative is to use a `flex-direction` of `column`, in which case the flex items flow vertically. These two directions can be reversed with `row-reverse` and `column-reverse` respectively, as shown in Figure 10.2:

```
.container {
  display: flex;
  flex-direction: row || column || row-reverse || column-reverse;
}
```

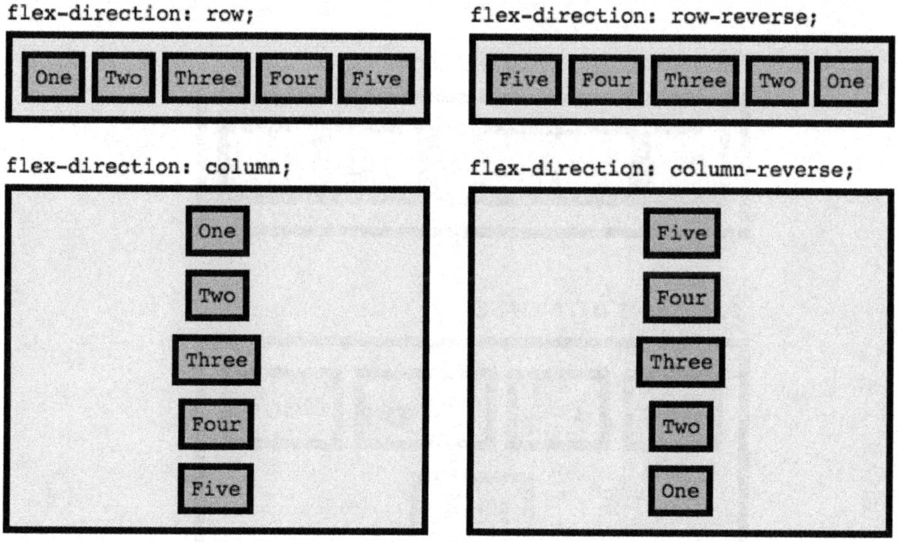

flex-direction: row;

| One | Two | Three | Four | Five |

flex-direction: row-reverse;

| Five | Four | Three | Two | One |

flex-direction: column;

One
Two
Three
Four
Five

flex-direction: column-reverse;

Five
Four
Three
Two
One

Figure 10.2. The `flex-direction` property defines the flex items' axis

The `flex-wrap` property controls whether the flex container is single-line, multi-line, or multi-lined with each new line coming visually before the previous line with the values of `nowrap`, `wrap`, and `wrap-reverse` respectively. `nowrap` is the default. You can see the effects of the different `flex-wrap` property values in Figure 10.3:

```
.container {
  display: flex;
  flex-direction: row;
  flex-wrap: nowrap || wrap || wrap-reverse;
}
```

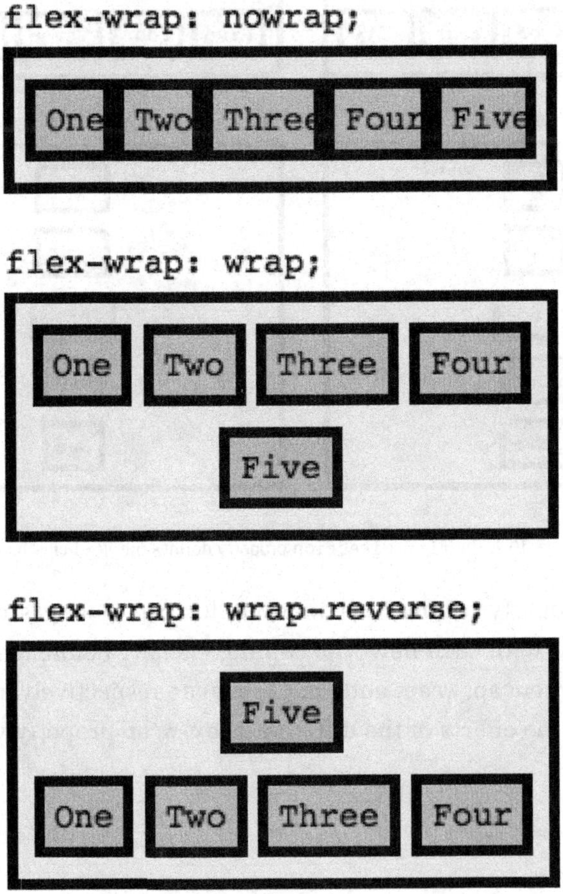

flex-wrap: nowrap;

One Two Three Four Five

flex-wrap: wrap;

One Two Three Four

Five

flex-wrap: wrap-reverse;

Five

One Two Three Four

Figure 10.3. The flex-wrap property defines whether flex items can spread across multiple lines

We're provided a shorthand of flex-flow for the flex-direction and flex-wrap properties:

```
.container {
  display: flex;
  flex-flow: row nowrap;
}
```

The `justify-content` property defines how flex items are laid out on the current line, as shown in Figure 10.4. The default is `flex-start`, which groups items to the left of the line (or the top, if `flex-direction` is set to `column`). `flex-end` groups the items to the right of the line (or bottom, if `flex-direction` is set to `column`), while `center` groups the items in the center of the line. `space-between` will push the first item to the left or top, and the last item to the right or bottom, with equal space in between all the items. The `space-around` value divides the white space equally between all the items, including around the first and last items:

```
.container {
  display: flex;
  flex-flow: row nowrap;
```

```
    justify-content: flex-start || flex-end || center || space-
➥between ||  space-around;
}
```

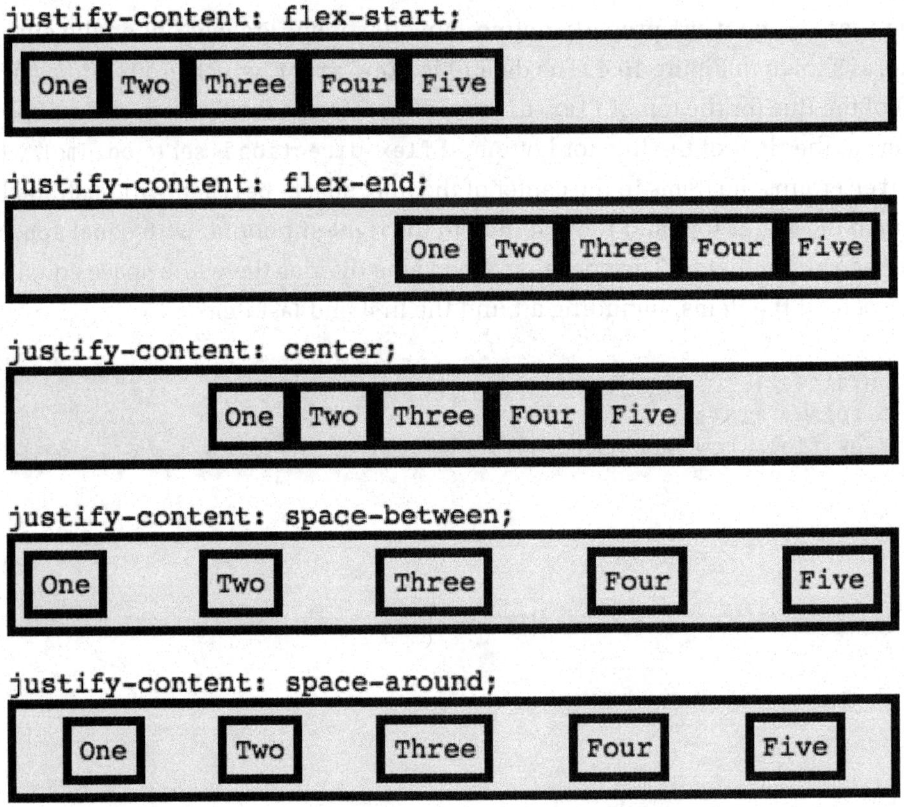

justify-content: flex-start;

| One | Two | Three | Four | Five |

justify-content: flex-end;

| One | Two | Three | Four | Five |

justify-content: center;

| One | Two | Three | Four | Five |

justify-content: space-between;

| One | Two | Three | Four | Five |

justify-content: space-around;

| One | Two | Three | Four | Five |

Figure 10.4. Examples of the justify-content property

 Mind Your Margins

Make sure the flex items, or children of the container, don't have margin set to auto. If they do, it will appear as if the justify-content were set to space-around.

While justify-content allows us to align items along the direction axis (left to right for row and top to bottom for column), the align-items property defines how flex items are laid out along the opposite axis, as shown in Figure 10.5. When flex-direction is set to row, flex-start will place the flex items flush to the top of the container, `flex-end` to the bottom, `center` will center the items vertically, while the default, `stretch`, will stretch the items so that they're all equal height—taking up 100% of the height when there's a single row. The last value, `baseline`, usually *appears* to be the same as `flex-start`, though it isn't really the case: items are aligned along their baselines:

```
.container {
  display: flex;
  flex-flow: row nowrap;
  justify-content: space-between;
```

```
   align-items: flex-start || flex-end || center || stretch ||
➥baseline;
}
```

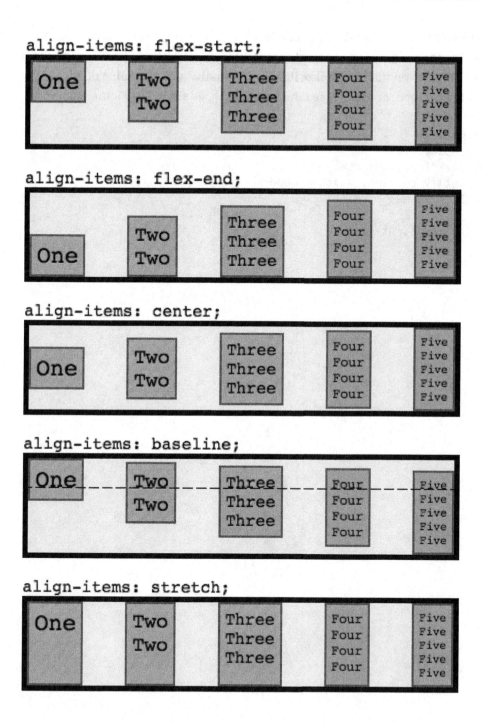

Figure 10.5. The different values of the align-items property

The flexbox layout specification also allows styling of the flex items. You can override the `align-items` property for individual flex items by setting the `align-self` property on that single flex item individually, with the value of `auto`, `flex-start`, `flex-end`, `center`, `baseline`, or `stretch`, as shown in Figure 10.6:

```css
.container {
  display: flex;
  flex-direction: row;
  justify-content: space-around;
  align-items: stretch;
}
.flexItem:first-of-type {
```

```
    align-self: auto || flex-start || flex-end || center || baseline
 ➥|| stretch;
}
```

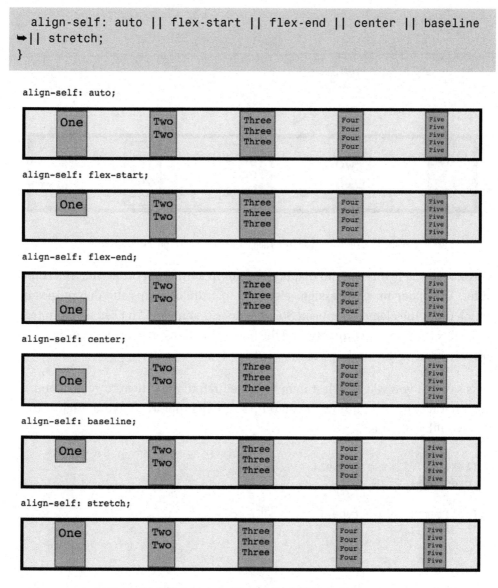

Figure 10.6. Different values of the flex item's `align-self` property

For example, to center all the flex items while stretching the first element to 100% of the height, as shown in Figure 10.7, you would use the following markup:

```
.container {
  display: flex;
  flex-direction: row;
  justify-content: space-between;
```

```
    align-items: center;
}
.flexItem:first-of-type {
    align-self: stretch;
}
```

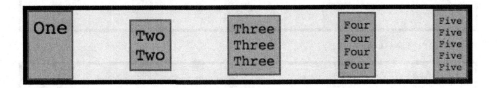

Figure 10.7. Overwriting an item's alignment with the `align-self` property

Flexbox makes it very easy to display content in a different order than the source order. The `order` property assigns elements to ordinal groups and determines in which order the elements appear. So what does that mean? You can assign integers to the flex items' `order` property, and the browser will display the items in ascending order instead of the markup's source order.

Let's say that you want the last item to come first, the first item to go last, and all the other flex items to follow the markup's source order as shown in Figure 10.8. You would write this:

```
.flexItem:first-of-type {
    order: 1;
}
.flexItem:last-of-type {
    order: -1;
}
```

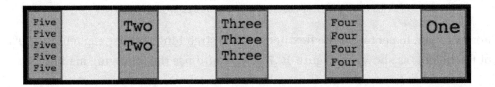

Figure 10.8. Employing the `order` property to change the order of appearance

Because the default value of order is 0, the flex item with a value less than 0 will be placed first, and the flex items with values greater than 0 will go last. If different flex items have different order values, the browser will display them in order starting with the lowest value, unless the order is reversed with a container with a flex-direction reversing value.

The order values of the multiple flex items don't need to be unique. If two or more flex items have the same order value—as flex items two, three, and four do in our case (they all have the default value of 0)—the browser will display the items with the same order value in the order in which they appear in the source markup.

 order Only Affects Visual Rendering

In using the order property, the display order is independent of the source code order for visual rendering only. Assistive technology and tabbed navigation are not impacted by the use of order, and maintain the source order.

The flex property is shorthand for flex-grow, flex-shrink, and flex-basis, in that order.

flex-grow defines how the flex item should grow if there is room. It's a unitless value for each item that defines the proportion or ratio that the particular element should occupy within the flex container.

Some examples of flex-grow are shown in Figure 10.9. If all items have flex-grow set to 1, every child will be set to an equal size inside the container. If you were to give one of the children a value of 2, that child would take up twice as much space as the others:

```
.container {
  display: flex;
}
.flexItem:first-of-type {
  flex-grow: 2;
}
```

```
.flexItem:last-of-type {
  flex-grow: 3;
}
```

```
.container {
    display: flex;
}
.items:first-of-type {
  flex-grow: 2;
}
.items:last-of-type {
  flex-grow: 3;
}
```

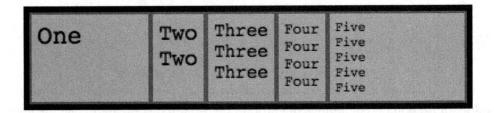

Figure 10.9. Example of the `flex-grow` property

In our scenario, if we have an item with `flex-grow` set to 2 and one set to 3, after room is made for all the items, the first item will take up 40% of the available area and the latter will take up 60% for a ratio of 2:3 of the available area (which may differ from 40% and 60% of the width of the parent).

When you use `flex-grow`, all the space is taken up, making the use of `justify-content` moot.

We can use `flex-basis` to define the default width of each item. Without it, our example is ugly. By default, flex items use the least amount of space necessary to fit their content. In our example, the flex items have been sized differently, as they are as narrow as their content with padding. We can use the `flex-basis` with a length unit value to define the default size of a flex item. The remaining space is distributed, with proportions able to be controlled by `flex-grow`. You can also set `flex-basis: content`, which automatically sizes flex items based on the item's content.

But what if there isn't enough room for all the flex items given the `flex-basis` and the size of the container? That's where `flex-shrink` comes in: it defines the ability for a flex item to shrink if necessary:

```
.container {
  display: flex;
}
.flexItem {
  flex-basis: 200px;
}
.flexItem:first-of-type {
  flex-shrink: 3;
}
.flexItem:last-of-type {
  flex-shrink: 2;
}
```

All flex items in this example will be 200px wide. If the container is more than 1000px (5x200px), any item with a `flex-grow` property will grow wider; however, if the container is less than 1000px and there isn't enough room for all the flex items, the flex items with the largest `flex-shrink` value will shrink first.

It's best to avoid setting `flex-shrink`, `flex-grow`, or `flex-basis` as individual properties. Rather, you should set all three at once with the `flex` shorthand property. Setting `flex: none` is the same as setting `flex: 0 0 auto`. The default value, if none of these properties is specified, is `flex: 0 1 auto;`.

 A Few Notes

Some properties make no sense on a flex container and are therefore ignored. The column properties, `vertical-align`, `float`, and `clear` have no effect on a flex item. On the other hand, box-model properties such as `margin`, `min-height`, and `min-width` do impact flex items.

Absolutely positioned children of a flex container are positioned so that their static position is determined in reference to the main start content-box corner of their flex container.

Flexbox's alignment property of `center` does true centering: the flex item stays centered even if it overflows the flex container. You can't currently scroll the overflowed content, but we trust this will be resolved soon:

```css
.container {
  display: flex;
  flex-direction: row;
  justify-content: space-around;
  align-items: center;
  height: 100px;
}
```

Applying Flexbox to *The HTML5 Herald*

```css
#authors {
  display: flex;
}
#authors section:nth-of-type(2) {
  order: 2;
}
```

By setting `display: flex` on the parent, the three author sections become flex items. We reorder the items with the `order` property, as shown in Figure 10.10.

Figure 10.10. Flexbox in action on *The HTML5 Herald*

By default, the three author sections will be displayed side by side. But when the page is narrow—say, on a mobile device with a a screen less than 500px wide—we want each author description to take up 100% of the width. We can use media queries to change the layout for narrow browsers.

Media Queries

Media queries are at the heart of a recent design trend called **responsive web design**. With responsive web design all page elements, including images and widgets, are designed and coded to resize and realign seamlessly and elegantly, depending on the capabilities and dimensions of the user's browser.

What are media queries?

Before CSS3, a developer could specify a media type for a stylesheet using the `media` attribute. You might have come across a link element that looked like this:

```
<link rel="stylesheet" href="print.css" media="print">
```

Notice that the `media` type is specified as `print`. Acceptable values in addition to print include `screen`, `handheld`, `projection`, `all`, and a number of others you'll see less often, if ever. The `media` attribute allows you to specify which stylesheet to load based on the type of device the site is being viewed on. This has become a fairly common method for serving a print stylesheet.

With CSS3's media queries you can, according to the W3C spec[3], "extend the functionality of media types by allowing more precise labeling of style sheets." This is done using a combination of media types and expressions that check for the presence of particular media features. So media queries let you change the presentation (the CSS) of your content for a wide variety of devices without changing the content itself (the HTML).

Syntax

Let's implement a basic media query expression:

```
<link rel="stylesheet" href="style.css" media="screen and (color)">
```

This tells the browser that the stylesheet in question should be used for all screen devices that are in color. Simple—and it should cover nearly everyone in your audience. You can do the same using `@import`:

---

[3] http://www.w3.org/TR/css3-mediaqueries/

```
@import url(styles.css) screen and (color);
```

Additionally, you can implement media queries using the `@media` at-rule, which we touched on earlier in Chapter 9 when discussing `@font-face`. `@media` is probably the most well-known usage for media queries, and is the method you'll likely use most often:

```
@media handheld and (max-width: 380px) {
  /* styles go here */
}
```

In this example, this expression will apply to all handheld devices that have a maximum display width of 380 pixels. Any styles within that block will apply only to the devices that match the expression. Note that this is likely to not be what you want: smartphones are just small-sized computers. Android and iOS happen to match `screen` and actually ignore `handheld`.

Here are a few more examples of media queries using `@media`, so that you can see how flexible and varied the expressions can be. This style will apply only to screen-based devices that have a minimum device width (or screen width) of 320px and a maximum device width of 480px:

```
@media only screen and (min-device-width: 320px) and
➥(max-device-width: 480px) {
  /* styles go here */
}
```

Here's a slightly more complex example:

```
@media only screen and (-webkit-min-device-pixel-ratio: 1.5),
➥only screen and (min-device-pixel-ratio: 1.5) {
  /* styles go here */
}
```

In this example, we use the `only` keyword, along with the `and` keyword in addition to a comma—which behaves like an `or` keyword. This code will specifically target the iPhone 4's higher resolution display, which could come in handy if you want that device to display a different set of images. Prefixing media queries with `only` causes CSS3 non-compliant browsers to ignore the rule.

The Flexibility of Media Queries

Using the aforementioned syntax, media queries allow you to change the layout of your site or application based on a wide array of circumstances. For example, if your site uses a two-column layout, you can specify that the sidebar column drop to the bottom and/or become horizontally oriented, or you can remove it completely on smaller resolutions. On small devices such as smartphones, you can serve a completely different stylesheet that eliminates everything except the bare necessities.

Additionally, you can change the size of images and other elements that aren't normally fluid to conform to the user's device or screen resolution. This flexibility allows you to customize the user experience for virtually any type of device while keeping the most important information and your site's branding accessible to all users.

In *The HTML5 Herald*, we want to change the layout for narrow screens. Our newspaper is 758px wide. On devices under 500px wide, the scrolling required to view the page gives a bad user experience. With media queries, we can narrow the entire layout of the page, providing a better user experience for those using narrow browsers:

```
@media screen and (max-width: 500px) {
  body {
    width: 100%;
    min-width: 320px;
  }
  body main > div:nth-of-type(n),
  aside,
  aside article {
    width: 100%;
    padding: 0 1em;
    box-sizing: border-box;
  }
  body > header h1 {
    font-size: 7vw;
  }
}
```

The above CSS targets browsers that are 500px wide or narrower, making the width of the document 100% but not less than 320px wide, and making the aside, advertisements, and different sections as wide as the device. In addition, we make the main heading font size responsive at 7vw, or 7% of the viewport width. This way the heading is never too small, and never wider than the newspaper itself.

Returning to the layout of the site's author listing, to make the author listing appear at 100% width instead of appearing in three columns, we can also use media queries; we change the `flex-direction` when the browser or viewport width is 500px wide or smaller:

```
@media screen and (max-width: 500px) {
  ...
  #authors {
    flex-direction: column;
  }
}
```

ALEXIS GOLDSTEIN

Maecenas quis tortor arcu. Vivamus rutrum nunc non neque consectetur quis placerat neque lobortis. Nam vestibulum, arcu sodales feugiat consectetur, nisl orci bibendum elit, eu euismod magna sapien ut nibh.

ESTELLE WEYL

Maecenas quis tortor arcu. Vivamus rutrum nunc non neque consectetur quis placerat neque lobortis. Nam vestibulum, arcu sodales feugiat consectetur, nisl orci bibendum elit, eu euismod magna sapien ut nibh.

LOUIS LAZARIS

Maecenas quis tortor arcu. Vivamus rutrum nunc non neque consectetur quis placerat neque lobortis. Nam vestibulum, arcu sodales feugiat consectetur, nisl orci bibendum elit, eu euismod magna sapien ut nibh.

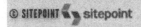

Figure 10.11. Using media queries on *The HTML5 Herald to list our authors*

Now in narrow browsers, we've changed the `flex-direction` from the default of `row` to `column`, so that the authors appear top to bottom instead of side by side, as shown in Figure 10.11.

Browser Support

Support for media queries is very good:

- IE9+
- Firefox 3.5+
- Safari 3.2+
- Chrome 8+
- Opera 10.6+
- iOS 3.2+
- Opera Mini 5+
- Opera Mobile 10+
- Android 2.1+

The only area of concern is previous versions of Internet Explorer. There are two options for dealing with this: you can supply these versions of IE with a "default" stylesheet that's served without using media queries, providing a layout suitable for the majority of screen sizes, or you can use a JavaScript-based polyfill. One such ready-made solution can be found at http://code.google.com/p/css3-mediaqueries-js/.

So by taking advantage of CSS3 media queries, you can easily create a powerful way to target nearly every device and platform conceivable.

Further Reading

In a book such as this, it's impossible to describe every aspect of media queries. That could be another book in itself—and an important one at that. But if you'd like to look into media queries a little further, be sure to check out the following articles:

- "Responsive Web Design" on *A List Apart*[4]

- "How to Use CSS3 Media Queries to Create a Mobile Version of Your Site" on *Smashing Magazine*[5]

---

[4] http://www.alistapart.com/articles/responsive-web-design/
[5] http://www.smashingmagazine.com/2010/07/19/how-to-use-css3-media-queries-to-create-a-mobile-version-of-your-website/

Living in Style

We've now covered all the new features in CSS that went into making *The HTML5 Herald*—and quite a few that didn't. While we haven't covered *everything* CSS3 has to offer, we've mastered several techniques that you can use today, and a few that should be usable in the very near future. Remember to check the specifications—as these features are all subject to change—and keep up to date with the state of browser support. Things are moving quickly for a change, which is both a great boon and an additional responsibility for web developers.

Up next, we'll switch gears to cover some of the new JavaScript APIs. As we've mentioned, these aren't strictly speaking part of HTML5 or CSS3, but they're often bundled together when people speak of these new technologies. Plus, they're a lot of fun, so why not get our feet wet?

11

Geolocation, Offline Web Apps, and Web Storage

Much of what is loosely considered to be a part of HTML5 isn't, strictly speaking, HTML at all—it's a set of additional APIs that provide a wide variety of tools to make our websites even better. We introduced the concept of an API way back in Chapter 1, but here's a quick refresher: an API is an interface for programs. So, rather than a visual interface where a user clicks on a button to make something happen, an API gives your code a virtual "button" to press in the form of a method it calls, giving it access to a set of functionality.

In this chapter, we'll be covering three APIs: Geolocation, Offline Web Applications, and Web Storage. With these APIs, we can find a visitor's current location, make our website available offline as well as perform faster online, and store information about the state of our web application so that when a user returns to our site, they can pick up where they left off.

In addition, we'll also provide an overview of other APIs. To learn about the APIs we won't be covering, you may want to check out HTML5 API demos,[1] a repository where you can find information about many JavaScript and HTML5 APIs.

JavaScript Ahead!

A word of warning: as you know, the P in API stands for Programming—so there'll be some JavaScript code in the next two chapters. If you're fairly new to JavaScript, don't worry! We'll do our best to walk you through how to use these new features employing simple examples with thorough explanations. We'll be assuming you have a sense of the basics, but JavaScript *is* an enormous topic. To learn more, SitePoint's *JavaScript: Novice to Ninja* by Darren Jones is an excellent resource for beginners.[2] You may also find the Mozilla Developer Network's JavaScript Guide useful.[3]

Geolocation

The first API we'll cover is geolocation. Geolocation allows your visitors to share their current location. With that location information, you can display it on a map using a maps library such as Google Maps or the MapQuest API.

Depending on how your visitors are accessing your site, their location may be determined by any, or a combination, of the following:

- IP address
- wireless network connection
- cell tower
- GPS hardware on the device

Which of the above methods are used will depend on the browser, as well as the device's capabilities. Most browsers attempt to combine methods in order to be more accurate. The browser then determines the location and passes it back to the Geolocation API. One point to note, as the W3C Geolocation spec states: "No guarantee is given that the API returns the device's actual location."[4]

---

[1] https://github.com/AurelioDeRosa/HTML5-API-demos
[2] Melbourne: SitePoint, 2014
[3] https://developer.mozilla.org/en/JavaScript/Guide
[4] http://dev.w3.org/geo/api/spec-source.html#introduction

Geolocation is supported in:

- Safari 5+
- Chrome 5+
- Firefox 3.5+
- Internet Explorer 9+
- iOS (Mobile Safari) 3.2+
- Android 2.1+
- Opera 10.6—12, then 16+ (Opera began supporting gelocation in version 10.6. When Opera switched to the Blink layout engine in version 15, geolocation was temporarily dropped. It returned in version 16 and later)

Privacy Concerns

Some users will decline sharing their location with you, as there are privacy concerns inherent to this information. Thus, your visitors must opt in to share their location; nothing will be passed along to your site or web application unless the user agrees.

The decision is made via a prompt. Figure 11.1 shows what the prompt looks like in Chrome.

Figure 11.1. Geolocation user prompt

Chrome May Block This Prompt

Be aware that Chrome may block your site from showing this prompt entirely if you're viewing your page locally, rather than from an internet server. If this happens, you'll see an icon in the address bar alerting you to it.

There's no way around this at present, but you can either test your functionality in other browsers, or deploy your code to a testing server (this can be a local server on your machine, a virtual machine, or an actual internet server).

Geolocation Methods

With geolocation, you can determine the current position of your users. You can also be notified of changes to their position, which could be employed, for example, in a web application that provided real-time driving directions.

These different tasks are controlled through the three methods currently available in the Geolocation API:

- getCurrentPosition

- watchPosition

- clearPosition

We'll be focusing on the first method, getCurrentPosition.

Checking for Support with Modernizr

Before we attempt to use geolocation, we should ensure that our visitor's browser supports it. We can do that with Modernizr.

We'll start by creating a function called determineLocation. We've put it in its own JavaScript file, **geolocation.js**, and included that file in our page.

Inside the function, we'll first use Modernizr to check if geolocation is supported:

```
function determineLocation() {
  if (Modernizr.geolocation) {
    navigator.geolocation.getCurrentPosition(displayOnMap);
  } else {
    // geolocation is not supported in this browser
  }
}
```

Let's examine this line by line:

We declare a function called determineLocation to contain our location-checking code.

We check the Modernizr object's geolocation property to see whether geolocation is supported in the current browser. For more information on how the Modernizr object works, consult Appendix A. If geolocation is supported, we continue on to line three, which is inside the if statement. If geolocation is unsupported, we move on to the code inside the else statement.

Let's assume that geolocation is supported.

Retrieving the Current Position

The `getCurrentPosition` method takes one, two, or three arguments. Here's a summary of the method's definition from the W3C's Geolocation API specification:[5]

```
void getCurrentPosition(successCallback, errorCallback, options);
```

Only the first argument, `successCallback`, is required. `successCallback` is the name of the function you want to call once the position is determined.

In our example, if the location is successfully found, the `displayOnMap` function will be called with a new `Position` object. This `Position` object will contain the current location of the device.

What's a callback?

A **callback** is a function that is passed as an argument to another function. A callback is executed after the parent function is finished. In the case of `getCurrentPosition`, the `successCallback` will only run once `getCurrentPosition` is completed and the location has been determined.

For more information on callbacks, see this post by Mike Vollmer at recurial.com.[6]

Geolocation's `Position` Object

Let's take a closer look at the `Position` object, as defined in the Geolocation API. The `Position` object has two attributes: one that contains the coordinates of the position (`coords`), and another that contains the Geolocation API timestamp of when the position was determined (`timestamp`):

---

[5] http://dev.w3.org/geo/api/spec-source.html
[6] http://recurial.com/programming/understanding-callback-functions-in-javascript/

```
interface Position {
  readonly attribute Coordinates coords;
  readonly attribute DOMTimeStamp timestamp;
};
```

 Specification Interfaces

The HTML5, CSS3, and related specifications contain plenty of "interfaces" like the above. These can seem scary at first, but never fear. They're just summarized descriptions of everything that can go into a certain property, method, or object. Most of the time the meaning will be clear—and if not, they're always accompanied by textual descriptions of the attributes.

But where are the latitude and longitude stored? They're inside the coords object. The coords object is also defined in the W3C Geolocation spec. It implements an interface called Coordinates, and these are its attributes:

```
interface Coordinates {
  readonly attribute double latitude;
  readonly attribute double longitude;
  readonly attribute double? altitude;
  readonly attribute double accuracy;
  readonly attribute double? altitudeAccuracy;
  readonly attribute double? heading;
  readonly attribute double? speed;
};
```

The question mark after double in some of those attributes simply means that there's no guarantee that the attribute will be there. If the browser is unable to obtain these attributes, their value will be null. For example, very few computers or mobile devices contain an altimeter—so most of the time there will be no altitude value from a geolocation call. The only three attributes that are guaranteed to be there are latitude, longitude, and accuracy.

latitude and longitude are self-explanatory, and give you exactly what you would expect: the user's latitude and longitude. The accuracy attribute tells you, in meters, how accurate is the latitude and longitude information.

The altitude attribute is the altitude in meters, and the altitudeAccuracy attribute is the altitude's accuracy, also in meters.

The `heading` and `speed` attributes are only relevant if we're tracking the user across multiple positions. These attributes would be important if we were providing real-time cycling or driving directions, for example. If present, `heading` tells us the direction the user is moving (in degrees) in relation to true north. And `speed`, if present, tells us how quickly the user is moving in meters per second.

Grabbing the Latitude and Longitude

Our `successCallback` is set to the function `displayOnMap`. Here's what this function looks like:

```
function displayOnMap(position) {
  var latitude = position.coords.latitude;
  var longitude = position.coords.longitude;
  // Let's use Google Maps to display the location
}
```

The first line of our function grabs the `Coordinates` object from the `Position` object that was passed to our callback by the API. Inside the object is the property `latitude`, which we store inside a variable called `latitude`. We do the same for longitude, storing it in the variable `longitude`.

Using Google Maps API

In order to display the user's location on a map, we'll leverage the Google Maps JavaScript API. Before we can use this, though, we need to add a reference to it in our HTML page. Instead of downloading the Google Maps JavaScript library and storing it on our server, we can point to Google's publicly available version of the API:

```
    :
<!-- google maps API-->
<script type="text/javascript"
```

```
            src="https://maps.googleapis.com/maps/api/js?key=API_KEY">
</body>
</html>
```

 Where to Get the API Key

You may have noticed in the code the link to the Google Maps API has the parameter `key=API_KEY`.

While the Google Maps API will work without an API key, it's a good idea to obtain one. Directions for obtaining an API key can be found in the Google Maps documentation.[7]

Loading a Map

Now that we've included the Google Maps JavaScript file, we need to, first, add an element to the page to hold the map, and, second, provide a way for the user to call our `determineLocation` method by clicking a button.

To take care of the first step, let's create a fourth box in the sidebar of *The HTML5 Herald* below the three advertisement boxes. We'll wrap it inside an `article` element, as we did for all the other ads. Inside it, we'll create a div called `mapDiv`, and a form with a button for users to click to display their location. Let's also add a heading to tell the user what we're trying to find out:

```
<article class="ad-ad4">
  <div id="mapDiv">
    <h1>Where in the world are you?</h1>
    <form id="geoForm">
      <input type="button" id="geobutton" value="Tell us!">
    </form>
  </div>
</article>
```

We'll also add a bit of styling to this new HTML:

---

[7] https://developers.google.com/maps/documentation/javascript/tutorial#api_key

```
.ad4 {
  position: relative;
}

.no-geolocation .ad4 {
  display: none;
}

.ad4 h1 {
  font-size: 20px;
  font-family: AcknowledgementMedium;
  text-align: center;
}
```

Figure 11.2 reveals what our new sidebar box looks like.

Figure 11.2. The new widget that enables users to tell us their location

The second step is to call `determineLocation` when we hit the button. First, we grab the button itself. Then, we attach our function to the button's `click` event:

```
var geobutton = document.getElementById('geobutton');
geobutton.addEventListener('click', determineLocation);
```

With this code in place, `determineLocation` will be called whenever the button is clicked.

Displaying Our Location in Google Maps

Now, let's return to our `displayOnMap` function and deal with the nitty-gritty of actually displaying the map. First, we'll create a `myOptions` variable to store some of the options that we'll pass to Google Maps:

```
function displayOnMap(position) {
  var latitude = position.coords.latitude;
  var longitude = position.coords.longitude;

  // Let's use Google Maps to display the location
  var myOptions = {
    zoom: 14,
    mapTypeId: google.maps.MapTypeId.ROADMAP
  };
```

The first option that we'll set is the zoom level. For a complete map of the Earth, use zoom level 0. The higher the zoom level, the closer you'll be to the location, and the smaller your frame (or viewport) will be. We'll use zoom level 14 to zoom in to street level.

The second option that we'll set is the kind of map we want to display. We can choose from the following:

- `google.maps.MapTypeId.ROADMAP`

- `google.maps.MapTypeId.SATELLITE`

- `google.maps.MapTypeId.HYBRID`

- `google.maps.MapTypeId.TERRAIN`

If you've used the Google Maps website before, you'll be familiar with these map types. ROADMAP is the default, while SATELLITE shows you photographic tiles. HYBRID is a combination of ROADMAP and SATELLITE, and TERRAIN will display elements such as elevation and water. We'll use the default, ROADMAP.

Google Maps Options

To learn more about Google Maps options, see the Map Options section of the Google Maps tutorial.[8]

Now that we've set our options, it's time to create our map! We do this by creating a new Google Maps object with new `google.maps.Map()`.

---

[8] http://code.google.com/apis/maps/documentation/javascript/tutorial.html#MapOptions

The first parameter we pass is the result of the DOM method `getElementById`, which we use to grab the form that houses the button triggering our geolocation call. Passing the results of this method into the new Google Map means that the map created will be placed inside that element, replacing the form with the Google Map.

The second parameter we pass is the collection of options we just set. We store the resulting Google Maps object in a variable called `map`:

```
function displayOnMap(position) {
  var latitude = position.coords.latitude;
  var longitude = position.coords.longitude;

  // Let's use Google Maps to display the location
  var myOptions = {
    zoom: 14,
    mapTypeId: google.maps.MapTypeId.ROADMAP
  };

  var map = new google.maps.Map(document.getElementById("geoForm"),
➥myOptions);
```

Now that we have a map, let's add a marker with the location we found for the user. A marker is the little red drop we see on Google Maps that marks our location.

In order to create a new Google Maps marker object, we need to pass it another kind of object: a `google.maps.LatLng` object—which is just a container for a latitude and longitude. The first new line creates this by calling new `google.maps.LatLng` and passing it the `latitude` and `longitude` variables as parameters.

Now that we have a `google.maps.LatLng` object, we can create a marker. We call new `google.maps.Marker`, and then between two curly braces ({}) we set position to the `LatLng` object, map to the map object, and title to `"Hello World!"`. The title is what will display when we hover our mouse over the marker:

```
function displayOnMap(position) {
  var latitude = position.coords.latitude;
  var longitude = position.coords.longitude;

  // Let's use Google Maps to display the location
  var myOptions = {
    zoom: 14,
```

```
    mapTypeId: google.maps.MapTypeId.ROADMAP
};

var map = new google.maps.Map(document.getElementById("geoForm"),
➥myOptions);

var initialLocation = new google.maps.LatLng(latitude, longitude);

var marker = new google.maps.Marker({
  position: initialLocation,
  map: map,
  title: "Hello World!"
});
}
```

The final step is to center our map at the initial point, and we do this by calling
`map.setCenter` with the `LatLng` object:

```
map.setCenter(initialLocation);
```

You can find a plethora of documentation about Google Maps' JavaScript API, version
3 in the online documentation.[9]

A Final Word on Older Mobile Devices

While the W3C Geolocation API is well supported in current mobile device browsers,
you may need to allow for older mobile devices and support all the Geolocation
APIs available. If this is the case, you should take a look at the open-source library
geo-location-javascript.[10]

Offline Web Applications

The visitors to our websites are increasingly on the go. With many using mobile
devices all the time, it's unwise to assume that our visitors will always have a live
internet connection. Wouldn't it be nice for our visitors to browse our site or use
our web application even if they're offline? Thankfully, we can cater for this with
Offline Web Applications.

---

[9] http://code.google.com/apis/maps/documentation/javascript/
[10] http://code.google.com/p/geo-location-javascript/

HTML5's Offline Web Applications allows us to interact with websites offline. This might sound like a contradiction: a web application exists online by definition. But there are an increasing number of web-based applications that could benefit from being usable offline. You probably use a web-based email client, such as Gmail; wouldn't it be useful to be able to compose drafts in the app while you were on the subway traveling to work? What about online to-do lists, contact managers, or office applications? These are all examples of applications that benefit from being online, but which we'd like to continue using if our internet connection cuts out in a tunnel.

The Offline Web Applications spec is supported in:

- Safari 4+
- Chrome 5+
- Firefox 3.5+
- Opera 10.6+
- iOS (Mobile Safari) 2.1+
- Android 2.0+

It is currently unsupported in all versions of IE.

How It Works: the HTML5 Application Cache

Offline Web Applications works by leveraging what is known as the application cache. The application cache can store your entire website offline: all the JavaScript, HTML, and CSS, as well as your images and resources.

This sounds great, but you may be wondering what happens when there's a change? That's the beauty of the application cache: your application is automatically updated every time the user visits your page while online. If even one byte of data has changed in one of your files, the application cache will reload that file.

 Application Cache versus Browser Cache

Browsers maintain their own caches in order to speed up the loading of websites; however, these caches are only used to avoid having to reload a given file—and not in the absence of an internet connection. That's even if all the files for a page are cached by the browser. If you try to click on a link while your internet connection is down, you'll receive an error message.

> With Offline Web Applications, we have the power to tell the browser which files should be cached or fetched from the network, and what we should fall back to in the event that caching fails. It gives us far more control about how our websites are cached.

Setting Up Your Site to Work Offline

There are three steps to making an Offline Web Application:

1. Create a **cache.appcache** manifest file.
2. Ensure that the manifest file is served with the correct content type.
3. Point all your HTML files to `cache.appcache` in the `manifest` attribute.

The HTML5 Herald isn't really an application at all, so there's no real need to provide offline functionality. Yet it's simple enough to do, and there's no real downside, so we'll go through the steps of making it available offline to illustrate how it's done.

The cache.appcache File

Despite its fancy name, the **cache.appcache** file is really nothing more than a text file that adheres to a certain format. You can name the file whatever you like (**cache.appcache**, **mysite.appcache**, **herald.appcache** etc), so long as the extension is **.appcache**.

Here's an example of a simple `cache.appcache` file:

```
CACHE MANIFEST

CACHE:
index.html
photo.jpg
main.js

NETWORK:
*
```

The first line of the `cache.appcache` file must read `CACHE MANIFEST`. After this line, we enter `CACHE:`, and then list all the files we'd like to store on our visitor's hard drive. This `CACHE:` section is also known as the **explicit section** (since we're explicitly telling the browser to cache these files).

Upon first visiting the page, the visitor's browser makes a local copy of all files defined in the section. On subsequent visits, the browser will load the local copies of the files.

After listing all the files we'd like stored offline, we can specify an online whitelist. This will define any files that should never be stored offline—usually because they require internet access for their content to be meaningful. For example, you may have a PHP script, **lastTenTweets.php**, that grabs your last ten updates from Twitter and displays them on an HTML page. The script would only be able to pull your last ten tweets while online, so it makes no sense to store the page offline.

The first line of this section is the word NETWORK. Any files specified in the NETWORK section will always be reloaded when the user is online, and will never be available offline.

Here's what that example online whitelist section would look like:

```
NETWORK:
lastTenTweets.php
```

Unlike the explicit section, where we had to painstakingly list every file we wanted to store offline, in the online whitelist section we can use a shortcut: the wildcard *. This asterisk tells the browser that any files or URLs not mentioned in the explicit section (and therefore not stored in the application cache) should be fetched from the server.

Here's an example of an online whitelist section that uses the wildcard:

```
NETWORK:
*
```

All Files Must Be Included

Every URL in your website must be accounted for in the **.appcache** file, even URLs that you link to. If it's unaccounted for in the manifest file, that resource or URL will fail to load, even if you're online. To avoid this problem, you should use the * (asterisk) in the NETWORK section.

You can also add comments to your **.appcache** file by beginning a line with # (hash). Everything after the # will be ignored. Be careful to avoid having a comment as the first line of your **.appcache** file; as we mentioned earlier, the first line must be CACHE MANIFEST. You can, however, add comments to any other line.

It's good practice to have a comment with the version number of your **.appcache** file (we'll see why a bit later on):

```
CACHE MANIFEST
# version 0.1

CACHE:
index.html
photo.jpg
main.js

NETWORK:
*
```

Setting the Content Type on Your Server

The next step in making your site available offline is to ensure that your server is configured to serve the manifest files correctly. This is done by setting the content type provided by your server, along with the **.appcache** file (we discussed content type in Chapter 5, so you can skip back there now if you need a refresher).

Assuming you're using the Apache web server, add the following to your **.htaccess** file:

```
AddType text/cache-manifest .manifest
```

Pointing Your HTML to the Manifest File

The final step to making your website available offline is to point your HTML pages to the manifest file. We do that by setting the manifest attribute on the html element in each of our pages:

```
<!DOCTYPE html>
<html manifest="cache.appcache">
```

Once we've done that, we're finished! Our web page will now be available offline. Better still, since any content that hasn't changed since the page has been viewed will be stored locally, our page will now load much faster—even when our visitors are online.

 Set the `manifest` Attribute on Every Page

Each HTML page on your website must set the `manifest` attribute on the `html` element. Ensure that you do this, or your application might not be stored in the application cache! While it's true that you should only have one **.appcache** file for the entire application, every HTML page of your web application needs `<html manifest="cache.appcache">`.

Seeking Permission to Store the Site Offline

As with geolocation, browsers provide a permission prompt when a website is using a **cache.appcache** file. Unlike geolocation, though, not all browsers are required to do this. When present, the prompt asks users to confirm that they'd like the website to be available offline. Figure 11.3 shows the prompt's appearance in Firefox.

Figure 11.3. Prompt to allow offline web application storage

Going Offline to Test

Once we have completed the three steps to make an offline website, we can test out our page by going offline. Firefox and Opera provide a menu option that lets you work offline, so there's no need to cut your internet connection. (Note that you do need to have the menu bar enabled in these browsers, otherwise it will fail to work). To do this in Firefox, go to **File > Work Offline** as shown in Figure 11.4.

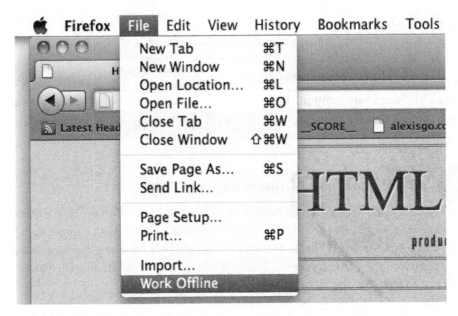

Figure 11.4. Testing offline web applications with Firefox's Work Offline mode

However, while it's convenient to go offline from the browser menu, it's most ideal to turn off your network connection altogether when testing Offline Web Applications.

Testing if the Application Cache Is Storing Your Site

Going offline is a good way to spot-check if our application cache is working, but for more in-depth debugging we'll need a finer instrument. Fortunately, Chrome's Web Inspector tool has some great features for examining the application cache.

To check whether our **cache.appcache** file has the correct content type, here are the steps to follow in Chrome (http://html5laboratory.com/s/offline-application-cache.html has a sample you can use to follow along):

1. Navigate to the URL of your home page in Chrome.

2. Open up the Web Inspector (click the wrench icon, then choose **Tools > Developer Tools**).

3. Click on the **Console** tab, and look for any errors that may be relevant to the **cache.appcache** file. If everything is working well, you should see a line that starts

with "Document loaded from Application Cache with manifest" and ends with the path to your **cache.appcache** file. If you have any errors, they will show up in the console, so be on the lookout for errors or warnings here.

4. Click on the **Resources** tab.

5. Expand the application cache section. Your domain (www.html5laboratory.com in our example) should be listed.

6. Click on your domain. Listed on the right should be all the resources stored in Chrome's application cache, as shown in Figure 11.5.

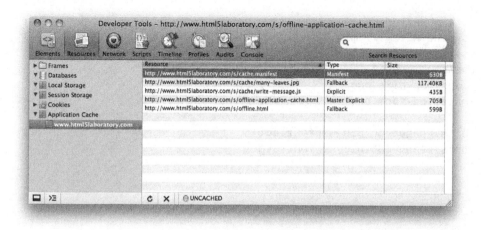

Figure 11.5. Viewing what is stored in Chrome's application cache

Making *The HTML5 Herald* Available Offline

Now that we understand the ingredients required to make a website available offline, let's practice what we've learned on *The HTML5 Herald*. The first step is to create our **herald.appcache** file. You can use a program such as TextEdit on a Mac or Notepad on Windows to create it, but you have to make sure the file is formatted as plain text. If you're using Windows, you're in luck! As long as you use Notepad to create this file, it will already be formatted as plain text. To format a file as plain text in TextEdit on a Mac, choose **Format > Make Plain Text**. Start off your file by including the line CACHE MANIFEST at the top.

Next, we add all the resources we'd like available offline in the explicit section, which starts with the word CACHE:. We must list all our files in this section. Since there's nothing on the site that requires network access (well, there is *one* thing, but we'll get to that shortly), we'll just add an asterisk to the NETWORK section to catch any files we may have missed in the explicit section.

Here's an excerpt from our **herald.appcache** file:

```
CACHE MANIFEST
#v1

CACHE:
index.html
register.html

js/hyphenator.js
js/modernizr-1.7.min.js
css/screen.css
css/styles.css
images/bg-bike.png
images/bg-form.png
⋮
fonts/League_Gothic-webfont.eot
fonts/League_Gothic-webfont.svg
⋮

NETWORK:
*
```

Once you've added all of your resources to the file, save it as **herald.appcache**. Be sure that the extension is set to **.appcache** rather than **.txt** or something else.

Then, if you're yet to do so already, configure your server to deliver your manifest file with the appropriate content type.

The final step is to add the manifest attribute to the html element in our two HTML pages.

We add the manifest attribute to both **index.html** and **register.html**, like this:

```
<!DOCTYPE html>
<html lang="en" manifest="herald.appcache">
```

And we're set! We can now browse *The HTML5 Herald* at our leisure, whether or not we have an internet connection.

Limits to Offline Web Application Storage

While no specific storage limit is defined for the application cache in the Offline Web Applications spec, it does state that browsers should create and enforce a storage limit. As a general rule, assume that you've no more than 5MB of space with which to work.

Several of the files we specified to be stored offline are video files. Depending on how large your video files are, it might make little sense to have them available offline, as they could exceed the browser's storage limit.

What can we do in that case? We could place large video files in the NETWORK section, but then our users will simply see an unpleasant error when the browser tries to pull the video while offline.

A better alternative is to use an optional section of the appcache file: the fallback section.

The Fallback Section

The **fallback section** allows us to define what the user will see should a resource fail to load. In the case of *The HTML5 Herald*, rather than storing our video file offline and placing it in the explicit section, it makes more sense to leverage the fallback section.

Each line in the fallback section requires two entries. The first is the file for which you want to provide fallback content. You can specify either a specific file, or a partial path such as media/, which would refer to any file located in the **media** folder. The second entry is what you'd like to display should the file specified fail to load.

If the files are unable to be loaded, we can provide a still image of the film's first frame instead. We'll use the partial path **media/** to define the fallback for both video files at once:

```
FALLBACK:
media/ images/ford-plane-still.png
/ /offline.html
```

Of course, this is redundant since, as you know from Chapter 5, the HTML5 video element already includes a fallback image to be displayed in the event the video doesn't load.

For some more practice with this concept, let's add another fallback. In the event that none of our pages load, it would be nice to define a fallback file that tells you the site is offline. We can create a simple **offline.html** file:

```
<!DOCTYPE html>
<html lang="en" manifest="/herald.appcache">
  <head>
    <meta charset="utf-8">
    <title>You are offline!</title>
    <link rel="stylesheet" href="css/styles.css?v=1.0"/>
  </head>
  <body>
    <h1>Sorry, we are now offline!</h1>
  </body>
</html>
```

In the fallback section of our cache manifest, we can now specify /, which will match any page on the site. If any page fails to load or is not in the application cache, it will fall back to the **offline.html** page:

```
FALLBACK:
media/ images/video-fallback.jpg
/ /offline.html
```

 Safari 5

> There is a bug in Safari 5 where media files such as **.mp3** and **.mp4** won't load from the offline application cache.

Refreshing the Cache

The files that you've specified in the explicit section of the manifest will be cached until further notice. This can cause headaches while developing: you might change a file and be left scratching your head when you're unable to see your changes reflected on the page.

Even more importantly, once your files are sitting on a live website, you'll want a way to tell browsers that they need to update their application caches. This can be done by modifying the **herald.appcache** file. When a browser loads a site for which it already has an **.appcache** file, it will check to see if the manifest file has changed. If there are no changes, it will assume that its existing application cache is all it needs to run the application, so it won't download anything else. If the **.appcache** file has changed, the browser will rebuild the application cache by re-downloading all the specified files.

This is why we specified a version number in a comment in our **herald.appcache**. This way, even if the list of files remains exactly the same, we have a way of indicating to browsers that they should update their application cache; all we need to do is increment the version number.

Caching the Cache

This might sound absurd, but your offline site access **herald.appcache** file may itself be cached by the browser. Why, you may ask? Because of the way HTTP handles caching.

In order to speed up the performance of web pages overall, caching is performed by browsers according to rules set out via the HTTP specification.[11] What do you need to know about these rules? That the browser receives certain HTTP headers, including Expire headers. These Expire headers tell the browser when a file should be expired from the cache and when it needs updating from the server.

If your server is providing the manifest file with instructions to cache it (as is often the default for static files), the browser will happily use its cached version of the file instead for fetching your updated version from the server. As a result, it will

---

[11] http://www.w3.org/Protocols/rfc2616/rfc2616-sec13.html

skip re-downloading any of your application files because it thinks the manifest has not changed!

If you find that you're unable to force the browser to refresh its application cache, try clearing the regular browser cache. You could also change your server settings to send explicit instructions not to cache the **herald.appcache** file.

If your site's web server is running Apache, you can tell Apache not to cache the **herald.appcache** file by adding the following to your **.htaccess** file:

```
<Files herald.appcache>
  ExpiresActive On
  ExpiresDefault "access"
</Files>
```

The `<Files herald.appcache>` entry tells Apache to only apply the rules that follow to the **herald.appcache** file. The combination of `ExpiresActive On` and `ExpiresDefault "access"` forces the web server to always expire the `herald.appcache` file from the cache. The effect is that the **herald.appcache** file will never be cached by the browser.

Are we online?

Sometimes you'll need to know if your user is viewing the page offline or online. For example, in a web mail app saving a draft while online involves sending it to the server to be saved in a database; but while offline, you would want to save that information locally instead, and wait until the user is back online to send it to your server.

The Offline Web Applications API provides a few handy methods and events for managing this. For *The HTML5 Herald*, you may have noticed that the page works well enough while offline: you can navigate from the home page to the sign-up form, play the video, and generally mess around without any difficulty. However, when you try to use the geolocation widget we built earlier in this chapter, things don't go so well. This makes sense—without an internet connection, there's no way for our page to figure out your location (unless your device has a GPS), much less communicate with Google Maps to retrieve the map.

Let's look at how we can fix this. We'd like to provide a message to users indicating that this functionality is unavailable while offline. It's actually very easy—browsers that support Offline Web Applications give you access to the `navigator.onLine` property, which will be `true` if the browser is online and `false` if it's not. Here's how we'd use it in our `determineLocation` method:

```
function determineLocation() {
  if (navigator.onLine) {
    // find location and call displayOnMap
  } else {
    alert("You must be online to use this feature.");
  }
}
```

Give it a spin. Using Firefox or Opera, navigate to the page and click the button to load the map. Once you're satisfied that it works, choose Work Offline and reload the page; now try clicking the button again. This time you'll receive a helpful message telling you that you need to be online to access the map.

Some other features that might be of use to you include events that fire when the browser goes online or offline. These events fire on the `window` element, and are simply called `window.online` and `window.offline`. These can, for example, allow your scripts to respond to a change in state by either synchronizing information up to the server when you go online, or saving data locally when you drop offline.

There are a few other events and methods for dealing with the application cache, but the ones we've covered here are the most important. They'll suffice to have most websites and applications working offline without a hitch.

Further Reading

If you'd like to learn more about Offline Web Applications, here are a few good resources:

- WHATWG Offline Web Applications spec[12]
- HTML5 Laboratory's "Using the cache manifest to work offline"[13]

---

[12] http://www.whatwg.org/specs/web-apps/current-work/multipage/offline.html#offline
[13] http://www.html5laboratory.com/working-offline.php

- Opera's Offline Application Developer's Guide[14]
- Peter Lubbers' SlideShare presentation on Offline Web Applications[15]
- Mark Pilgrim's walk-through of Offline Web Applications[16]
- Safari's Offline Applications Programming Guide[17]

Web Storage

The Web Storage API defines a standard for how we can save data locally on a user's computer or device. Before the emergence of the Web Storage standard, web developers often stored user information in cookies, or by using plugins. With Web Storage, we now have a standardized definition for how to store up to 5MB of data created by our websites or web applications. Better still, Web Storage already works in Internet Explorer 8.0!

Web Storage is a great complement to Offline Web Applications, because you'll need somewhere to store all that user data while you're working offline and Web Storage provides it.

Web Storage is supported in these browsers:

- Safari 4+
- Chrome 5+
- Firefox 3.6+
- Internet Explorer 8+
- Opera 10.5+
- iOS (Mobile Safari) 3.2+
- Android 2.1+

Two Kinds of Storage

There are two kinds of HTML5 Web Storage: session storage and local storage.

---

[14] http://dev.opera.com/articles/view/offline-applications-html5-appcache/

[15] http://www.slideshare.net/robinzimmermann/html5-offline-web-applications-silicon-valley-user-group

[16] http://diveintohtml5.org/offline.html

[17] http://developer.apple.com/library/safari/#documentation/iPhone/Conceptual/SafariJSDatabaseGuide/OfflineApplicationCache/OfflineApplicationCache.html

Session Storage

Session storage lets us keep track of data specific to one window or tab. It allows us to isolate information in each window or tab. Even if the user is visiting the same site in two windows (or two tabs), each window (or tab) will have its own individual session storage object and thus separate, distinct data.

Session storage is not persistent—it only lasts for the duration of a user's session on a specific site (in other words, for the time that a browser window or tab is open and viewing that site).

Local Storage

Unlike session storage, **local storage** allows us to save persistent data to the user's computer via the browser. When a user revisits a site at a later date, any data saved to local storage can be retrieved.

Consider shopping online: it's not unusual for users to have the same site open in multiple windows or tabs. Let's say that you're shopping for shoes, and you want to compare the prices and reviews of two brands. You may have one window open for each brand, but regardless of what brand or style of shoe you're looking for, you're always going to be searching for the same shoe size. It's cumbersome to have to repeat this part of your search in every new window.

Local storage can help. Rather than require the user to specify the shoe size they're browsing for every time they launch a new window, we could store this information in local storage. That way, when the user opens a new window to browse for another brand or style, the results would just present items available in that shoe size. Furthermore, because we're storing the information to the user's computer, we'll be able to access this information when they visit the site at a later date.

 Each Browser's Web Storage is Unique

One important point to remember when working with Web Storage is that if the user visits your site in Safari, any data will be stored to Safari's Web Storage store. If the user then revisits your site in Chrome, the data that was saved via Safari will be unavailable. Where the Web Storage data is stored depends on the browser, and each browser's storage is separate and independent.

Local Storage versus Cookies

Local storage can at first glance seem to play a similar role to HTTP cookies, but there are a few key differences. First of all, cookies are intended to be read on the server side, whereas local storage is only available on the client side. If you need your server-side code to react differently based on some saved values, cookies are the way to go. Yet, cookies are sent along with each HTTP request to your server—and this can result in significant overhead in terms of bandwidth. Local storage, on the other hand, just sits on the user's hard drive waiting to be read, so it costs nothing to use. (But you can send what's stored in local storage to a server as well using an Ajax request, if you wish.)

In addition, we have significantly more space to store data using local storage. With cookies, we can only store 4KB of information in total. With local storage, the maximum is much greater, though it varies a bit across desktop and mobile. On the desktop, the maximum for Chrome, Opera, Firefox, and IE is 10MB, and 5MB for Safari. On mobile, the maximum is 2MB for Android, 5MB for mobile Safari and iOS, and 10MB for Chrome and Firefox on mobile.

What Web Storage Data Looks Like

Data saved in Web Storage is stored as key/value pairs. Here are a few examples of simple key/value pairs:

- key: *name*, value: *Alexis*
- key: *painter*, value: *Picasso*
- key: *email*, value: *info@me.com*

Getting and Setting Our Data

The methods most relevant to Web Storage are defined in an object called Storage. Here is the complete definition of Storage:[18]

```
interface Storage {
  readonly attribute unsigned long length;
  DOMString key(in unsigned long index);
  getter any getItem(in DOMString key);
  setter creator void setItem(in DOMString key, in any value);
```

---

[18] http://dev.w3.org/html5/webstorage/#the-storage-interface

```
    deleter void removeItem(in DOMString key);
    void clear();
};
```

The first methods we'll discuss are getItem and setItem. We store a key/value pair in either local or session storage by calling setItem, and we retrieve the value from a key by calling getItem.

If we want to store the data in or retrieve it from session storage, we simply call setItem or getItem on the sessionStorage global object. If we want to use local storage instead, we'd call setItem or getItem on the localStorage global object. In the examples to follow, we'll be saving items to local storage.

When we use the setItem method, we must specify both the key we want to save the value under, and the value itself. For example, if we'd like to save the value "6" under the key "size", we'd call setItem like this:

```
localStorage.setItem("size", "6");
```

To retrieve the value we stored to the "size" key, we'd use the getItem method specifying only the key:

```
var size = localStorage.getItem("size");
```

Converting Stored Data

Web Storage stores all values as strings, so if you need to use them as anything else, such as a number or even an object, you'll have to convert them. To convert from a string to a numeric value, we can use JavaScript's parseInt method.

For our shoe size example, the value returned and stored in the size variable will actually be the string "6", rather than the number 6. To convert it to a number, we use parseInt:

```
var size = parseInt(localStorage.getItem("size"));
```

The Shortcut Way

We can quite happily continue to use getItem(key) and setItem(key, value); however, there's a shortcut we can use to save and retrieve data.

Instead of localStorage.getItem(key), we can simply say localStorage[key]. For example, we could rewrite our retrieval of the shoe size:

```
var size = localStorage["size"];
```

And instead of localStorage.setItem(key, value), we can say localStorage[key] = value:

```
localStorage["size"] = 6;
```

 Out of Key

What happens if you request getItem on a key that was never saved? In this case, getItem will return null.

Removing Items and Clearing Data

To remove a specific item from Web Storage, we can use the removeItem method. We pass it the key we want to remove, and it removes both the key and its value.

To remove *all* data stored by our site on a user's computer, we can utilize the clear method. This will delete all keys and all values stored for our domain.

Storage Limits

Internet Explorer "allows web applications to store nearly 10MB of user data."[19] Chrome, Safari, Firefox, and Opera all allow for up to 5MB of user data, which is the amount suggested in the W3C spec. This number may evolve over time, as the spec itself states: "A mostly arbitrary limit of five megabytes per origin is recommended. Implementation feedback is welcome and will be used to update this suggestion

---

[19] https://msdn.microsoft.com/en-us/library/bg142799(v=vs.85).aspx

in the future." In addition, Opera allows users to configure how much disk space is allocated to Web Storage.

Rather than worrying about how much storage each browser has, a better approach is to test to see if the quota is exceeded before saving important data. The way you test for this is by catching the QUOTA_EXCEEDED_ERR exception. Here's one example of how we can do this:

```
try {
  sessionStorage["name"] = "Susan";
} catch (exception) {
  if (exception === QUOTA_EXCEEDED_ERR) {
    // we should tell users that their quota has been exceeded.
  }
}
```

 Trying to Catch Exceptions

Sometimes problems happen in our code. Designers of APIs know this, and in order to mitigate the effects of these problems, they rely on exceptions. An exception occurs when something unexpected happens. The authors of APIs can define specific exceptions to be thrown when particular problems occur. Then developers using those APIs can decide how they'd like to respond to a given type of exception.

In order to respond to exceptions, we can wrap any code we think may throw an exception in a **try/catch** block. This works the way you might expect: first, you *try* to do something. If it fails with an exception, you can *catch* that exception and attempt to recover gracefully.

To read more about **try/catch** blocks, see the "try...catch" article at the Mozilla Developer Networks' JavaScript Reference.[20]

Security Considerations

Web Storage has what's known as **origin-based security**, which means that data stored via Web Storage from a given domain is only accessible to pages from that domain. It's impossible to access any Web Storage data stored by a different domain. For example, assume that we control the domain html5isgreat.com, and we store

---

[20] https://developer.mozilla.org/en/JavaScript/Reference/Statements/try...catch

data created on that site using local storage. Another domain (say, google.com), does not have access to any of the data stored by html5isgreat.com. Likewise, html5is-great.com has no access to any of the local storage data saved by google.com.

Adding Web Storage to *The HTML5 Herald*

We can use Web Storage to add a **Remember me on this computer** checkbox to our registration page. This way, once the user has registered, future forms that may need filling out on the site would already have this information.

Let's define a function that grabs the value of the form's input elements for name and email address:

```
function saveData() {
  var name = document.getElementById("name").value;
  var email = document.getElementById("email").value;
}
```

Here we're storing the value of the email and name form fields in variables called email and name respectively.

Once we have retrieved the values in the two input elements, our next step is to actually save these values to localStorage:

```
function saveData() {
  var name = document.getElementById("name").value;
  var email = document.getElementById("email").value;

  localStorage.setItem("name", name);
  localStorage.setItem("email", email);
}
```

Let's also store the fact that the "Remember me" checkbox was checked, saving this information to local storage:

```
function saveData() {
  var name = document.getElementById("name").value;
  var email = document.getElementById("email").value;

  localStorage.setItem("name", name);
```

```
    localStorage.setItem("email", email);
    localStorage.setItem("remember", true);
}
```

Now that we have a function that saves the visitor's name and email address, let's call it if they check the **Remember me on this computer** checkbox. We'll do this by watching for the change event on the checkbox; this event will fire whenever the checkbox's state changes, whether it's due to a click on the checkbox itself, a click on its label, or a keyboard press:

```
var rememberMe = document.getElementById("rememberme");
rememberMe.addEventListener("change", saveData, false);
```

 IE8 Support

> For simplicity, we are using addEventListener in this chapter. This function is supported in all major modern browsers except IE8. If you look at the code for the book, you'll see that we use a simple helper function called addEvent that employs addEventListener if it's supported, or an old method called at-tachEvent if not—a method that IE8 supports.

Next, let's make sure that the checkbox is actually checked, since the change event will fire when the checkbox is unchecked as well:

```
function saveData() {
  if (document.getElementById("rememberme").checked === true) {
  var name - document.getElementById("name").value;
  var email = document.getElementById("email").value;

  localStorage["name"] = name;
  localStorage["email"] = email;
  localStorage["remember"] = true;
  }
}
```

Finally, let's ensure that Web Storage is present in our visitor's browser:

```
function saveData() {
  if (document.getElementById("rememberme").checked === true) {
  var name = document.getElementById("name").value;
```

```
   var email = document.getElementById("email").value;

   localStorage["name"] = name;
   localStorage["email"] = email;
   localStorage["remember"] = true;
   }
 }
```

Now we're saving our visitor's name and email whenever the checkbox is checked, so long as local storage is supported. The problem is that we have yet to actually do anything with the data!

Let's add another function to check and see whether the name and email have been saved and, if so, fill in the appropriate input elements with that information. Let's also precheck the "Remember me" checkbox if we've set the key remember to true in local storage:

```
function loadStoredDetails() {
  var name = localStorage["name"];
  var email = localStorage["email"];
  var remember = localStorage["remember"];

  if (name) {
    document.getElementById("name").value = name;
  }
  if (email) {
    document.getElementById("email").value = email;
  }
  if (remember === "true") {
    document.getElementById("rememberme").setAttribute("checked",
➥"checked");
  }
}
```

Again, we want to check to ensure that Web Storage is supported by the browser before taking these actions:

```
function loadStoredDetails() {
  if (Modernizr.localstorage) {
    var name = localStorage["name"];
    var email = localStorage["email"];
    var remember = localStorage["remember"];
```

```
    if (name) {
      document.getElementById("name").value = name;
    }
    if (email) {
      document.getElementById("email").value = email;
    }
    if (remember === true) {
      document.getElementById("rememberme").setAttribute("checked",
➥"checked");
    }
  } else {
    // no support for Web Storage
  }
}
```

At the beginning of **rememberMe.js**, we call the `loadStoredDetails` function once the page loads:

```
loadStoredDetails();
```

Now if the user has previously visited the page and checked **Remember me on this computer**, their name and email will already be populated on subsequent visits to the page.

As a final step, we should clear out any values saved previously if the user **unchecks** the "Remember me" checkbox:

```
if (document.getElementById("rememberme").checked === true) {
    var name = document.getElementById("name").value;
    var email = document.getElementById("email").value;

    localStorage.setItem("name", name);
    localStorage.setItem("email", email);
    localStorage.setItem("remember", "true");
}
// if they uncheck the "Remember me" checkbox, clear out
// all the values
```

```
else {
    localStorage.clear();
}
```

Viewing Our Web Storage Values with Web Inspector

We can use the Safari or Chrome Web Inspector to look at or even change the values of our local storage. In Safari, we view the stored data under the **Storage** tab, as shown in Figure 11.6.

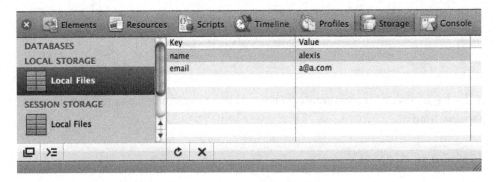

Figure 11.6. Viewing the values stored in local and session storage

In Chrome, the data can be viewed through the **Resources** tab.

Since users own any data saved to their hard drive, they can actually modify the data in Web Storage should they choose to do so.

Let's try this ourselves. If you double-click on the **email** value in Web Inspector's **Storage** tab while viewing the **register.html** page, you can actually modify the value stored there, as Figure 11.7 shows.

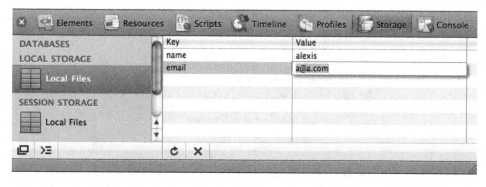

Figure 11.7. Modifying the values stored in Web Storage

There's nothing we as developers can do to prevent this, since our users own the data on their computers. We can and should, however, bear in mind that savvy users have the ability to change their local storage data. In addition, the Web Storage spec states that any dialogs shown in browsers asking users to clear their cookies should now also allow them to clear their local storage. The message is we can't be 100% sure that the data we store is accurate, nor that it will always be there. Thus, sensitive data should never be kept in local storage.

If you'd like to learn more about Web Storage, here are a few resources you can consult:

- W3C's Web Storage specification[21]
- Mozilla Developer Network's Web Storage documentation[22]
- Web Storage tutorial from IBM's developerWorks[23]

Additional HTML5 APIs

We'd like to mention some other APIs briefly, to give you an overview of what they are, and provide resources should you want to learn more.

Web Workers

The new Web Workers API allows us to run large scripts in the background without interrupting our main page or web app. Prior to Web Workers, it was impossible to

---

[21] http://dev.w3.org/html5/webstorage/#the-storage-interface
[22] https://developer.mozilla.org/en/DOM/Storage
[23] http://www.ibm.com/developerworks/xml/library/x-html5mobile2/

run multiple JavaScript scripts concurrently. Have you ever come across a dialog like the one shown in Figure 11.8?

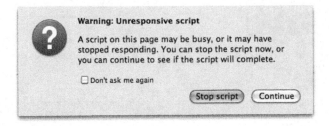

Figure 11.8. A script that runs for too long freezes the whole page

With Web Workers, we should see less of these types of warnings. The new API allows us to capture scripts that take a long time to run and require no user interaction, and run them behind the scenes concurrently with any other scripts that *do* handle user interaction. This concept is known as **threading** in programming, and Web Workers brings us thread-like features. Each "worker" handles its own chunk of script without interfering with other workers or the rest of the page. To ensure the workers stay in sync with each other, the API defines ways to pass messages from one worker to another.

Web Workers are supported in:

- Safari 4+
- Chrome 4+
- Firefox 3.5+
- IE10+
- Opera 11.5+
- Android 4.4+

To learn more about Web Workers, see:

- HTML5 Rocks article "The Basics of Web Workers"[24]
- Mozilla Developer Network tutorial "Using Web Workers"[25]
- W3C Web Workers' specification[26]

---

[24] http://www.html5rocks.com/tutorials/workers/basics/
[25] https://developer.mozilla.org/En/Using_web_workers
[26] http://dev.w3.org/html5/workers/

Web Sockets

Web Sockets defines a "protocol for two-way communication with a remote host."[27] We'll avoid going into this topic for a couple of reasons. First, this API is of great use to server-side developers, but is less relevant to front-end developers and designers. Second, Web Sockets are still in development and have actually run into some security issues. Firefox 4 and Opera 11 have disabled Web Sockets by default due to these issues.[28]

Web Sockets are supported in:

- Safari 7.1+
- Chrome 31+
- Firefox 34+
- Opera 26+
- iOS (Mobile Safari) 7.1+
- IE 10+
- Android 4.4+

Web Sockets are currently unsupported in all versions of IE and on Android.

To learn more about Web Sockets, see the specification at the W3C.[29]

IndexedDB

There are going to be times when the 5MB of storage and simplistic key/value pairs offered by the Web Storage API falls short of your needs. If you require the ability to store substantial amounts of data and have more complex relationships between your data, you'll likely need a fully fledged database to take care of your storage requirements.

Usually databases are unique to the server side, but there is a database solution that's been proposed to fill the need on the client side: Indexed Database API, or IndexedDB for short.

---

[27] http://www.w3.org/TR/websockets/

[28] See http://hacks.mozilla.org/2010/12/websockets-disabled-in-firefox-4/ and http://dev.opera.com/articles/view/introducing-web-sockets/.

[29] http://www.w3.org/TR/2009/WD-websockets-20091222/

What about Web SQL?

There was an additional database proposal previously called Web SQL, but its specification is no longer being updated. Web SQL was at one point seen as a viable option, but it's since been abandoned in favor of IndexedDB.

IndexedDB is supported in:

- Partial support in Safari 7.1+
- Firefox 10+
- Chrome 23+
- Opera 15+
- Partial support in iOS 8
- Android 4.4+
- Partial support in IE 10+

If you would like to learn more, here are a few good resources:

- Mark Pilgrim's summary of local storage in HTML5[30]
- W3C's IndexedDB specification[31]

Back to the Future

In this chapter, we've had a glimpse into the new JavaScript APIs available in the latest generation of browsers. While these might lack full browser support for some time, tools such as Modernizr can help us gradually incorporate them into our real-world projects, bringing an extra dimension to our sites and applications.

In the next—and final—chapter, we'll look at one more API, as well as two techniques for creating complex graphics in the browser. These open up a lot of potential avenues for creating web apps that leap off the page.

---

[30] http://diveintohtml5.org/storage.html#future
[31] http://dev.w3.org/2006/webapi/IndexedDB/

12

Canvas, SVG, and Drag and Drop

The HTML5 Herald is becoming quite dynamic for an "ol' timey" newspaper! We've added a video with the new `video` element, made our site available offline, added support to remember the user's name and email address, and used geolocation to detect where our user is.

But there's still much we can do to make it even more fun. First, the video is a little at odds with the rest of the paper, since it's in color. Second, the geolocation feature, while fairly speedy, could use a progress indicator to let the user know we haven't left them stranded. And finally, it would be nice to add one more dynamic piece to our page. We'll take care of all three of these items using the APIs we'll discuss in this chapter: Canvas, SVG, and Drag and Drop.

Canvas

With HTML5's Canvas API, we can draw anything we can imagine, all through JavaScript. This can improve the performance of our websites by avoiding the need to download images off the network. With canvas, we can draw shapes and lines, arcs and text, gradients and patterns. In addition, canvas gives us the power to manipulate pixels in images and even video. We'll start by introducing some of the basic drawing features of canvas, but then move on to using its power to transform our video—taking our modern-looking color video and converting it into conventional black and white to match the overall look and feel of *The HTML5 Herald*.

The Canvas API is supported in:

- Chrome 4+
- Firefox 2+
- Opera 9.6+
- Safari 3.1+
- iOS 3.2+
- Internet Explorer 9.0+
- Android 3.0+

A Bit of Canvas History

Canvas was first developed by Apple. Since they already had a framework—Quartz 2D—for drawing in two-dimensional space, they went ahead and based many of the concepts of what woud come to be known as HTML5's canvas on that framework. It was then adopted by Mozilla and Opera, and then standardized by the WHATWG (and subsequently picked up by the W3C, along with the rest of HTML5).

There's some good news here. If you aspire to do development for the iPhone or iPad (referred to jointly as iOS), or for the Mac, what you learn in canvas should help you understand some of the basic concepts of Quartz 2D. If you already develop for the Mac or iOS and have worked with Quartz 2D, many canvas concepts will look very familiar to you.

Creating a canvas Element

The first step to using canvas is to add a canvas element to the page:

```
<canvas>
  Sorry! Your browser doesn't support Canvas.
</canvas>
```

The text in between the canvas tags will only be shown if the canvas element is not supported by the visitor's browser.

Since drawing on the canvas is done using JavaScript, we'll need a way to grab the element from the DOM. We'll do so by giving our canvas an ID:

```
<canvas id="myCanvas" class="myCanvas">
  Sorry! Your browser doesn't support Canvas.
</canvas>
```

The `canvas` element takes both a `width` and `height` attribute, which must also be set.

Why not set width and height using CSS?

You may be asking yourself, why not set the width and height via CSS? It's because the `width` and `height` attributes determine how large the canvas's coordinate system is. If we don't specify `width` and `height`, the `canvas` element will default to a width of 300 and a height of 150. If we set the width and height for a canvas only in CSS, the `canvas` element will be 300 by 150, and the CSS properties will simply determine how large the box is that displays the image.

Let's add a `width` and `height` attribute to the `canvas` element:

```
<canvas id="myCanvas" class="myCanvas" width="200" height="200">
  Sorry! Your browser doesn't support Canvas.
</canvas>
```

Finally, let's add a border to our canvas using some CSS to visually distinguish it on the page. Canvas has no default styling, so it's difficult to see where it is on the page unless you give it some kind of border:

```
.myCanvas {
  border: dotted 2px black;
}
```

Now that we've styled it, we can actually view the canvas container on our page; Figure 12.1 shows what it looks like.

Figure 12.1. An empty canvas with a dotted border

Drawing on the Canvas

All drawing on the canvas happens via the Canvas JavaScript API. In this chapter, we'll walk you through several different things you can draw onto the `canvas` element. Each example will have a new function, and all of these different functions live in a file called **canvas.js**.

A Canvas Playground

We have created a separate file at *The HTML5 Herald*, **canvas.html**, for you to see the examples outlined in this chapter. At **canvas.html** there are seven different `canvas` elements, each demonstrating a different technique shown in this chapter.

But first, let's start with the basics. Before we can draw onto a canvas, we need to grab hold of the `canvas` element on our page:

```
var canvas = document.getElementById("myCanvas");
```

Getting the Context

Once we've stored our `canvas` element in a variable, we then set up the canvas's **context**. The context is the place where your drawing is rendered. Currently, there's only wide support for drawing to a two-dimensional context. The W3C Canvas spec defines the context in the `CanvasRenderingContext2D` interface. Most methods we'll be using to draw onto the canvas are defined in this interface.

We obtain our drawing context by calling the `getContext` method and passing it the string `"2d"`, since we'll be drawing in two dimensions:

```
var canvas = document.getElementById("myCanvas");
var context = canvas.getContext("2d");
```

The object that's returned by `getContext` is an instance of `CanvasRenderingContext2D`. In this chapter, we'll refer to it as simply "the context object" for brevity.

 What about 3D?

WebGL is a new API for 3D graphics being managed by the Khronos Group, with a WebGL working group that includes Apple, Mozilla, Google, and Opera.

By combining WebGL with HTML5 Canvas, you can draw in three dimensions. WebGL is currently fully supported in Chrome 18+, Internet Explorer 11+, and iOS 8+, and partially supported in Firefox 4+, Safari 5.1, Opera 12+, and Chrome 37+ for Android. To learn more, see http://www.khronos.org/webgl/.

Filling Our Brush with Color

On a real-life painting canvas, you must first saturate your brush with paint before you can begin. In the HTML5 canvas, you must do the same, and we do so with the `strokeStyle` or `fillStyle` properties. Both `strokeStyle` and `fillStyle` are set on a context object, and both take one of three values: a string representing a color, a `CanvasGradient` object, or a `CanvasPattern` object.

Let's start by using a color string to style the **stroke**. You can think of the stroke as the border of the shape you're going to draw. To draw a rectangle with a red border, we first define the stroke color:

```
var canvas = document.getElementById("myCanvas");
var context = canvas.getContext("2d");
context.strokeStyle = "red";
```

To draw a rectangle with a red border and blue fill, we must also define the fill color:

```
var canvas = document.getElementById("myCanvas");
var context = canvas.getContext("2d");
context.strokeStyle = "red";
context.fillStyle = "blue";
```

We can use any CSS color value to set the stroke or fill color, as long as we specify it as a string: a hexadecimal value such as #00FFFF, a color name such as red or blue, or an RGB value such as rgb(0, 0, 255). We can even use the property rgba to set a semitransparent stroke or fill color.

Let's change our blue fill to blue with a 50% opacity:

```
var canvas = document.getElementById("myCanvas");
var context = canvas.getContext("2d");
context.strokeStyle = "red";
context.fillStyle = "rgba(0, 0, 255, 0.5)";
```

Drawing a Rectangle to the Canvas

Once we've defined the color of the stroke and the fill, we're ready to start drawing! Let's begin by drawing a rectangle. We can repeat the steps we just took: grabbing the canvas and the context, and setting a fill and stroke style. But now, we'll draw a rectangle. We can do this by calling the fillRect and strokeRect methods. Both of these methods take the X and Y coordinates where you want to begin drawing the fill or the stroke, and the width and height of the rectangle. We'll add the stroke and fill 10 pixels from the top and 10 pixels from the left of the canvas's top-left corner:

```
var canvas = document.getElementById("myCanvas");
var context = canvas.getContext("2d");
context.strokeStyle = "red";
context.fillStyle = "rgba(0, 0, 255, 0.5)";
context.fillRect(10, 10, 100, 100);
context.strokeRect(10, 10, 100, 100);
```

This will create a semitransparent blue rectangle with a red border, such as the one in Figure 12.2.

Figure 12.2. A simple rectangle—not bad for our first canvas drawing!

The Canvas Coordinate System

As you may have gathered, the coordinate system in the canvas element is different from the Cartesian coordinate system you learned in math class. In the canvas coordinate system, the top-left corner is (0,0). If the canvas is 200 pixels by 200 pixels, then the bottom-right corner is (200,200), as Figure 12.3 illustrates.

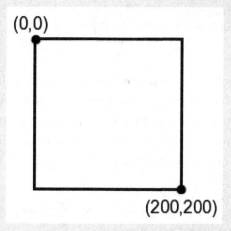

Figure 12.3. The canvas coordinate system goes top-to-bottom and left-to-right

Variations on `fillStyle`

Instead of a color as our `fillStyle`, we could have used a `CanvasGradient` or a `CanvasPattern` object. Let's create a pattern on the second `canvas` element (whose ID is `demo2`) on the `canvas.html` page.

We create a `CanvasPattern` by calling the `createPattern` method. `createPattern` takes two parameters: the image to create the pattern with, and how that image should be repeated. The repeat value is a string, and the valid values are the same as those in CSS: `repeat`, `repeat-x`, `repeat-y`, and `no-repeat`.

Instead of using a semitransparent blue `fillStyle`, let's create a pattern using our bicycle image. We'll do this in a new function called `drawPattern`. After doing the basics (grabbing the canvas and the context and setting a stroke), we must create an `Image` object and set its `src` property to our image:

```
function drawPattern() {
  var canvas = document.getElementById("demo2");
  var context = canvas.getContext("2d");
  context.strokeStyle = "red";

  var img = new Image();
  img.src = "../images/bg-bike.png";
}
```

Setting the `src` attribute will tell the browser to start downloading the image; however, if we try to use it immediately to create our gradient, we might run into some problems, because the image may still be loading (depending on whether it is in the browser cache). To be on the safe side, we'll use the image's `onload` property to create our pattern once the image has been fully loaded by the browser:

```
function drawPattern() {
  var canvas = document.getElementById("demo2");
  var context = canvas.getContext("2d");
  context.strokeStyle = "red";

  var img = new Image();
  img.src = "../images/bg-bike.png";
```

```
    img.onload = function() {
    };
}
```

In our `onload` event handler, we call `createPattern`, passing it the `Image` object and the string `repeat` so that our image repeats along both the X and Y axes. We store the results of `createPattern` in the variable `pattern`, and set the `fillStyle` to that variable:

```
function drawPattern() {
    ⋮
  var img = new Image();
  img.src = "../images/bg-bike.png";
  img.onload = function() {
    var pattern = context.createPattern(img, "repeat");
    context.fillStyle = pattern;
    context.fillRect(10, 10, 100, 100);
    context.strokeRect(10, 10, 100, 100);
  };
}
```

 Anonymous Functions

You may be asking yourself, "what is that `function` statement that comes right before the call to `img.onload`?" It's an **anonymous function**. Anonymous functions are much like regular functions except, as you might guess, they are without names.

When you see an anonymous function defined as an event listener, it means that the anonymous function is being bound to that event. In other words, the code inside that anonymous function will be run when the load event is fired.

Now, our rectangle's fill is a pattern made up of our bicycle image, as Figure 12.4 shows.

Figure 12.4. A pattern fill on a canvas

We can also create a `CanvasGradient` object to use as our `fillStyle`. To create a CanvasGradient, we call one of two methods: `createLinearGradient()` or `createeRadialGradient()`; then we add one or more color stops to the gradient.

`createLinearGradient`'s x0 and y0 represent the starting location of the gradient. x1 and y1 represent the ending location.

Let's try creating a gradient in the third `canvas` element. To create a gradient that begins at the top of the canvas and blends the color down to the bottom, we'd define our starting point at the origin (0,0), and our ending point 200 pixels down from there (0,200):

```
function drawGradient() {
  var canvas = document.getElementById("demo3");
  var context = canvas.getContext("2d");
  context.strokeStyle = "red";
  var gradient = context.createLinearGradient(0, 0, 0, 200);
}
```

Next, we specify our color stops. The color stop method is simply `addColorStop()`.

The `offset` is a value between 0 and 1. An `offset` of 0 is at the start of the gradient, and an `offset` of 1 is at the end of the gradient. The `color` is a string value that, as with the `fillStyle`, can be a color name, a hexadecimal color value, an `rgb()` value, or an `rgba()` value.

and begins to blend into white halfway down
olor stop with an `offset` of 0 and a purple

```
eLinearGradient(0, 0, 0, 200);
ue");
ite");
;
), 100);
00, 100);
```

r CanvasGradient to be the `fillStyle` of our

Figure 12.5. Creating a linear gradient with canvas

Drawing Other Shapes by Creating Paths

We're not limited to drawing rectangles—we can draw any shape we can imagine!
Unlike rectangles and squares, however, there's no built-in method for drawing
circles or other shapes. To draw more interesting shapes, we must first lay out the
path of the shape.

Paths create a blueprint for your lines, arcs, and shapes, but paths are invisible
until you give them a stroke! When we drew rectangles, we first set the `strokeStyle`
and then called `fillRect`. With more complex shapes, we need to take three steps:

layout the path, stroke the path, and fill the path. As with drawing rectangles, we can just stroke the path, or fill the path—or we can do both.

Let's draw a circle on the fourth canvas element at **canvas.html**. We'll write a generic function that draws a circle that we can pass the canvas element we want to draw onto—that way, we can reuse this function in a later example. The first step is to begin the path of the circle. We do that with the method beginPath(), which resets the default path for you to begin drawing a new shape:

```
function drawCircle(canvas) {
  var context = canvas.getContext("2d");
  context.beginPath();
}
```

Now we need to create an arc. An **arc** is a segment of a circle, but as there's no method for creating a circle, we can draw a 360° arc. We create it using the arc method:

```
function drawCircle(canvas) {
  var canvas = document.getElementById("myCanvas");
  var context = canvas.getContext("2d");
  context.beginPath();
  context.arc(50, 50, 30, 0, Math.PI*2, true);
}
```

The signature for the arc method is: arc(x, y, radius, startAngle, endAngle, anticlockwise).

x and y represent where on the canvas you want the arc's path to begin. Imagine this as the center of the circle that you'll be drawing. radius is, of course, the distance from the center to the edge of the circle.

startAngle and endAngle represent the start and end angles along the circle's circumference that you want to draw. The units for the angles are in radians, and a circle is 2π radians. We want to draw a complete circle, so we'll use 2π for the endAngle. In JavaScript, we can obtain this value by multiplying Math.PI by 2.

Radians Explained

Radians are a unit used to measure angles, and the symbol π denotes a measurement in radians. One radian is equal to 180 degrees. Two radians, or 2π, are equal to 360 degrees. For a review of radians, see the "Intuitive Guide to Angles, Degrees and Radians" at betterexplained.com.[1]

`anticlockwise` is an optional argument. If you wanted the arc to be drawn counterclockwise instead of clockwise, you would set this value to `true`. Since we are drawing a full circle, it's of no consequence which direction we draw it in, so we omit this argument.

Our next step is to close the path, as we've now finished drawing our circle. We do that with the `closePath` method:

```
function drawCircle(canvas) {
  var context = canvas.getContext("2d");
  context.beginPath();
  context.arc(100, 100, 50, 0, Math.PI*2, true);
  context.closePath();
}
```

Now we have a path—but unless we stroke it or fill it, we'll be unable to see it. Thus, we must set a `strokeStyle` if we'd like to give it a border, and we must set a `fillStyle` if we'd like our circle to have a fill color. By default, the width of the stroke is one pixel, which is stored in the `lineWidth` property of the `context` object. Let's make our border a bit bigger by setting the `lineWidth` to 3:

```
function drawCircle(canvas) {
  var context = canvas.getContext("2d");
  context.beginPath();
  context.arc(50, 50, 30, 0, Math.PI*2, true);
  context.closePath();
  context.strokeStyle = "red";
```

---

[1] http://betterexplained.com/articles/intuitive-guide-to-angles-degrees-and-radians/

```
    context.fillStyle = "blue";
    context.lineWidth = 3;
}
```

Lastly, we fill and stroke the path. Note that this time, the method names are different from those we used with our rectangle. To fill a path you simply call `fill`, and to stroke it you call `stroke`:

```
function drawCircle(canvas) {
  var context = canvas.getContext("2d");
  context.beginPath();
  context.arc(100, 100, 50, 0, Math.PI*2, true);
  context.closePath();
  context.strokeStyle = "red";
  context.fillStyle = "blue";
  context.lineWidth = 3;
  context.fill();
  context.stroke();
}
```

Figure 12.6 shows the finished circle.

Figure 12.6. Our shiny new circle

To learn more about drawing shapes, the Mozilla Developer Network has an excellent tutorial.[2]

---

[2] https://developer.mozilla.org/en/Canvas_tutorial/Drawing_shapes

Saving Canvas Drawings

If we create an image programmatically using the Canvas API, but decide we'd like to have a local copy of our drawing, we can use the API's `toDataURL` method to save our drawing. `toDataURL` creates a URL with the image in it, (either a png or jpg, whichever is specified). You can then right-click the image at this URL, and save it as a PNG or JPEG.

In the fifth demo on the **canvas.html** page, let's redraw a circle, but add a button called `saveButton` that allows us to save this circle drawn onto the canvas:

```
<h2>Demo 5: Saving canvas drawings</h2>
<canvas width="200" height="200" id="demo5" class="myCanvas">
  Sorry! Your browser doesn't support Canvas.
</canvas>

<button name="saveButton" id="saveButton">Save Drawing</button>
```

When the button is clicked, we want to open the canvas drawing as an image in a new tab. To do that, we'll define a new JavaScript function called `saveDrawing`:

```
function saveDrawing() {
  var canvas5 = document.getElementById("demo5");
  window.open(canvas5.toDataURL("image/png"));
}
```

Next, let's add code to **canvas.js** to call our `saveDrawing` function when the **Save** button is clicked:

```
var button = document.getElementById("saveButton");
button.addEventListener("click", saveDrawing, false);
```

 Adding IE8 Support

For simplicity, we are using `addEventListener` in this chapter. This function is supported in all major, modern browsers, but not IE8, which we want support for in our code examples. You'll see in the book's code that we use a simple helper function called `addEvent` that uses `addEventListener` if it's supported; In the case where there's no support, it uses an old method called `attachEvent`, the method IE8 supports.

When the button is clicked, a new tab opens with a PNG file loaded into it, as shown in Figure 12.7.

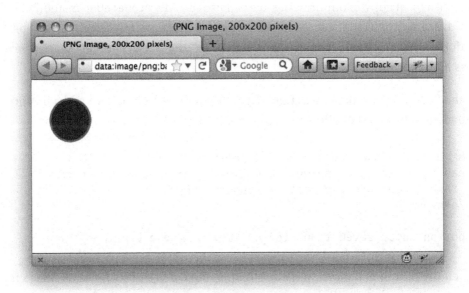

Figure 12.7. Our image loads in a new window

To learn more about saving our canvas drawings as files, see the W3C Canvas spec[3] and the "Saving a canvas image to file" section of Mozilla's Canvas code snippets.[4]

Drawing an Image to the Canvas

We can also draw images onto the canvas element. In this example, we'll be redrawing onto the canvas an image that already exists on the page.

For the sake of illustration, we'll use the HTML5 logo[5] as our image for the next few examples. Let's start by adding it to our page in an img element:

```
<h2>Demo 6: Drawing an image to the canvas</h2>
<canvas width="200" height="200" id="demo6" class="myCanvas">
  Sorry! Your browser doesn't support Canvas.
```

---

[3] http://www.w3.org/TR/2011/WD-html5-20110525/the-canvas-element.html

[4] https://developer.mozilla.org/en/Code_snippets/Canvas

[5] http://www.w3.org/html/logo/

```
</canvas>

<img src="images/html5-logo.png" id="myImageElem">
```

Then, in our **canvas.js** file, we'll create a new function called `drawImageToCanvas` in order to redraw the HTML `img` element onto the canvas.

Before we attempt to redraw an HTML `img` element on the page, we must ensure that the element has loaded. In order to do that, we'll add an event listener that will run our code only once the window's `load` event has fired:

```
window.addEventListener("load", drawImageToCanvas, false);
```

Next, after grabbing the `canvas` element and setting up the canvas's context, we can grab an image from our page via `document.getElementById`:

```
function drawImageToCanvas() {
  var canvas = document.getElementById("demo6");
  var context = canvas.getContext("2d");
  var image = document.getElementById("myImageElem");
}
```

We'll use the same CSS that we used before to make the area of the `canvas` element visible:

```
.myCanvas {
  border: dotted 2px black;
}
```

Let's modify it slightly to space out our canvas and our image:

```
.myCanvas {
  border: dotted 2px black;
  margin: 0 20px;
}
```

Figure 12.8 shows our empty canvas next to our image.

Figure 12.8. An image and a canvas sitting on a page, doing very little

We can use canvas's `drawImage` method to redraw the image from our page into the canvas:

```
function drawImageToCanvas() {
  var canvas = document.getElementById("demo6");
  var context = canvas.getContext("2d");
  var image = document.getElementById("myImageElem");
  context.drawImage(image, 0, 0);
}
```

Because we've drawn the image to the (0,0) coordinate, the image appears in the top-left of the canvas, as you can see in Figure 12.9.

Figure 12.9. Redrawing an image inside a canvas

We could instead draw the image at the center of the canvas by changing the X and Y coordinates that we pass to `drawImage`. Since the image is 64 by 64 pixels and the canvas is 200 by 200 pixels, if we draw the image to (68, 68),[6] the image will be in the center of the canvas, as in Figure 12.9.

Figure 12.10. Displaying the image in the center of the canvas

Manipulating Images

Redrawing an image element from the page onto a `canvas` is fairly unexciting. It's really no different from using an `img` element. Where it does become interesting is how we can manipulate an image after we've drawn it into the `canvas`.

Once we've drawn an image on the `canvas`, we can use the `getImageData` method from the Canvas API to manipulate the pixels of that image. For example, if we wanted to convert our logo from color to black and white, we can do so using methods in the Canvas API.

`getImageData` will return an `ImageData` object, which contains three properties: `width`, `height`, and `data`. The first two are self-explanatory; it's the last one, `data`, that interests us.

`data` contains information about the pixels in the `ImageData` object in the form of an array. Each pixel on the `canvas` will have four values in the data array, which correspond to that pixel's R, G, B, and A values. A stands for Alpha, a measure of

---

[6] Half of the canvas's dimensions minus half of the image's dimensions: (200/2) - (64/2) = 68.

the element's transparency, with 0 meaning the element is totally transparent, 1 meaning it's totally opaque, and 0.5 meaning it's 50% transparent.

The getImageData method allows us to examine a small section of a canvas, so let's use this feature to become more familiar with the data array. getImageData takes four parameters, corresponding to the four corners of a rectangular piece of the canvas we'd like to inspect. If we call getImageData on a very small section of the canvas, say context.getImageData(0, 0, 1, 1), we'd be examining just one pixel (the rectangle from 0,0 to 1,1). The array that's returned is four items long, as it contains a red, green, blue, and alpha value for this lone pixel:

```
var canvas = document.getElementById("myCanvas");
var context = canvas.getContext("2d");
var image = document.getElementById("myImageElem");
// draw the image at x=0 and y=0 on the canvas
context.drawImage(image, 68, 68);
var imageData = context.getImageData(0, 0, 1, 1);
var pixelData = imageData.data;
console.log(pixelData.length);
```

We log the length of the pixelData array to the console, and the output confirms that the data array for a one-pixel section of the canvas will have four values.

Security Errors with getImageData

If you tried out this code by double-clicking the file in Chrome or Firefox (in other words, you're not using a web server to view the file), you may have noticed that it failed to work—the image on the canvas is in color. That's because when you're running the code locally on your computer, you'll be using the file:// protocol to open local files. And files loaded with the file:// protocol are considered to come from different domains, which is deemed a security error.

What you'll see specifically is an error in getImageData. The error is a security error, though in our case it's an unnecessary one.

The true security issue that Chrome and Firefox are attempting to prohibit is a user on one domain manipulating images on another domain. For example, stopping me from loading an official logo from http://google.com/ and then manipulating the pixel data.

The W3C Canvas spec describes it this way:[7]

> Information leakage can occur if scripts from one domain can access
> information (e.g. read pixels) from images from another domain
> (this is called a cross-origin request). To mitigate this, canvas ele-
> ments are defined with a flag indicating whether they are origin-
> clean.

This origin-clean flag will be set to `false` if the image you want to manipulate is on a different domain from the JavaScript doing the manipulating. Unfortunately, in Chrome and Firefox, this origin-clean flag is also set to `false` while you're testing from files on your hard drive, as they're seen as being files that live on different domains.

If you want to test pixel manipulation using canvas in Firefox or Chrome, you'll need to either test it on a web server running on your computer (http://localhost/), or test it online.

Converting an Image from Color to Black and White

Let's look at how we'd go about using `getImageData` to convert a full color image into black and white on a canvas. We'll create a new function in the **canvas.js** file called `manipulateImage` to do so.

Assuming that we've already placed an image onto the canvas, as we did above, we can use a `for` loop to iterate through each pixel in the image and change it to gray-scale.

First, we'll call `getImageData(0, 0, 200, 200)` to retrieve the entire canvas. Then, we'll grab the red, green, and blue values of each pixel, which appear in the array in that order:

```
function manipulateImage() {
  var canvas = document.getElementById("demo7");
  var context = canvas.getContext("2d");
  var image = document.getElementById("secondImage");
  context.drawImage(image, 68, 68);
```

---

[7] http://dev.w3.org/html5/2dcontext/

```
  var imageData = context.getImageData(0, 0, 200, 200);

  var red, green, blue, greyscale;

  for (var i = 0; i < imageData.data.length; i += 4) {
    red = imageData.data[i];
    green = imageData.data[i + 1];
    blue = imageData.data[i + 2];
  }
}
```

Notice that our `for` loop is incrementing `i` by 4 instead of the usual 1. This is because each pixel takes up four values in the `imageData` array—one number each for the R, G, B, and A values.

Next, we must determine the grayscale value for the current pixel. It turns out that there's a mathematical formula for converting RGB to grayscale; you simply need to multiply each of the red, green, and blue values by some specific numbers, seen in this code block:

```
function manipulateImage() {
  ⋮
  for (var i = 0; i < imageData.data.length; i += 4) {
    red = imageData.data[i];
    green = imageData.data[i + 1];
    blue = imageData.data[i + 2];

    grayscale = red * 0.3 + green * 0.59 + blue * 0.11;
}
```

Now that we have the proper grayscale value, we're going to store it back into the red, green, and blue values in the `data` array:

```
function manipulateImage() {

  ⋮

  for (var i = 0; i < imageData.data.length; i += 4) {
    var red = imageData.data[i];
    var green = imageData.data[i + 1];
    var blue = imageData.data[i + 2];

    var grayscale = red * 0.3 + green * 0.59 + blue * 0.11;
```

```
    imageData.data[i] = grayscale;
    imageData.data[i + 1] = grayscale;
    imageData.data[i + 2] = grayscale;
  }
}
```

So now we've modified our pixel data by individually converting each pixel to grayscale. The final step? Putting the image data we've modified back into the canvas via a method called putImageData. This method does exactly what you'd expect: it takes an image's data and writes it onto the canvas. Here's the method in action:

```
function manipulateImage() {
  var canvas = document.getElementById("demo7");
  var context = canvas.getContext("2d");
  var image = document.getElementById("secondImage");
  context.drawImage(image, 60, 60);

  var imageData = context.getImageData(0, 0, 200, 200);

  for (var i = 0; i < imageData.data.length; i += 4) {
    var red = imageData.data[i];
    var green = imageData.data[i + 1];
    var blue = imageData.data[i + 2];

    var grayscale = red * 0.3 + green * 0.59 + blue * 0.11;

    imageData.data[i] = grayscale;
    imageData.data[i + 1] = grayscale;
    imageData.data[i + 2] = grayscale;
  }
  context.putImageData(imageData, 0, 0);
}
```

With that, we've drawn a black-and-white version of the validation image into the canvas.

Manipulating Video with Canvas

We can take the code we've already written to convert a color image to black and white and enhance it to make our color video black and white, matching the old-timey feel of *The HTML5 Herald* page. We'll do this in a new separate JavaScript file called **videoToBW.js**, so that we can include it on the site's home page.

The file begins, as always, by setting up the canvas and the context:

```
function makeVideoOldTimey() {
  var video = document.getElementById("video");
  var canvas = document.getElementById("canvasOverlay");
  var context = canvas.getContext("2d");
}
```

Next, we'll add a new event listener to react to the play event firing on the video element.

We want to call a custom function called draw when the video begins playing (we'll review what happens in this custom function right after this code block). To do so, we'll add an event listener to our video element that responds to the play event:

```
function makeVideoOldTimey() {
  var video = document.getElementById("video");
  var canvas = document.getElementById("canvasOverlay");
  var context = canvas.getContext("2d");

  video.addEventListener("play", function() {
    draw(video,context,canvas);
  }, false);

}
```

The draw function, which is a custom function that we'll define, will be called when the play event fires. It will be passed the video, context, and canvas objects. We're using an anonymous function here instead of a normal named function because we're unable to actually pass parameters to named functions when declaring them as event handlers without wrapping them in an another function.

Since we want to pass several parameters to the draw function—video, context, and canvas—we must call it from inside an anonymous function.

Let's look at the custom draw function:

```
function draw(video, context, canvas) {
  if (video.paused || video.ended) return false;

  drawOneFrame(video, context, canvas);
}
```

Before doing anything else, we check to see if the video is paused or has ended, in which case we'll just cut the function short by returning `false`. Otherwise, we continue on to the `drawOneFrame` function. The `drawOneFrame` function is nearly identical to the code we had earlier for converting an image from color to black and white, except that we're drawing the `video` element onto the `canvas` instead of a static image:

```
function drawOneFrame(video, context, canvas){
  // draw the video onto the canvas
  context.drawImage(video, 0, 0, canvas.width, canvas.height);

  var imageData = context.getImageData(0, 0, canvas.width,
➥canvas.height);
  var pixelData = imageData.data;
  // Loop through the red, green and blue pixels,
  // turning them grayscale

  var red, green, blue, greyscale;
  for (var i = 0; i < pixelData.length; i += 4) {
    red = pixelData[i];
    green = pixelData[i + 1];
    blue = pixelData[i + 2];
    //we'll ignore the alpha value, which is in position i+3

    grayscale = red * 0.3 + green * 0.59 + blue * 0.11;

    pixelData[i] = grayscale;
    pixelData[i + 1] = grayscale;
    pixelData[i + 2] = grayscale;
  }
```

```
    context.putImageData(imageData, 0, 0);
}
```

 Getting Better Performance

You may notice a difference between the code sample used in converting an image to black and white, and the code sample for converting a video. In the video conversion, we've created another variable, `pixelData`, which stores the array of pixels in it. You may be wondering why we bother doing this, instead of just accessing `imageData.data`. The reason is performance. Creating the `pixelData` variable, which is then used several times in the `for` loop, saves us several property lookups. There would be no issue if we were just doing one color conversion, but since we're performing this action over and over again as the video plays, tiny delays matter.

After we've drawn one frame, what's the next step? We need to draw another frame! The `setTimeout` method allows us to keep calling the `draw` function over and over again, without pause. The final parameter is the value for delay, which tells the browser how long, in milliseconds, to wait before calling the function. Because it's set to 0, we are essentially running `draw` continuously. This goes on until the video has either ended, or been paused:

```
function draw(video, context, canvas) {
  if (video.paused || video.ended) return false;

  drawOneFrame(video, context, canvas);

  // Start over!
  setTimeout(function(){ draw(video, context, canvas); }, 0);
}
```

What's the final result of this code? Our color video of a plane taking off now plays in black and white!

Displaying Text on the Canvas

If we were to view *The HTML5 Herald* from a file on a computer, we'd encounter security errors in Firefox and Chrome when trying to manipulate an entire video, as we did with a simple image. We can add a bit of error-checking in order to make our video work anyway, whether or not we view it from our local machine in Chrome or Firefox.

The first step is to add an error handling `try`/`catch` block to catch the error:

```
function drawOneFrame(video, context, canvas){
  context.drawImage(video, 0, 0, canvas.width, canvas.height);

  try {
    var imageData = context.getImageData(0, 0, canvas.width,
➥canvas.height);
    var pixelData = imageData.data;
    for (var i = 0; i < pixelData.length; i += 4) {
      var red = pixelData[i];
      var green = pixelData[i + 1];
      var blue = pixelData[i + 2];
      var grayscale = red * 0.3 + green * 0.59 + blue * 0.11;
      pixelData[i] = grayscale;
      pixelData[i + 1] = grayscale;
      pixelData[i + 2] = grayscale;
    }

    imageData.data = pixelData;
    context.putImageData(imageData, 0, 0);
  } catch (err) {
    // error handling code will go here
  }
}
```

If an error occurs when trying to call `getImageData`, it would be nice to let the user know what is going wrong. We'll do just that, using the `fillText` method of the Canvas API.

Before we write any text to the `canvas`, we should clear what's already there. We've already drawn the first frame of the video into the `canvas` using the call to `drawImage`. How can we clear it?

It turns out that if we reset the width or height of the canvas, the canvas will be cleared. So, let's reset the width:

```
function drawOneFrame(video, context, canvas){
  context.drawImage(video, 0, 0, canvas.width, canvas.height);

  try {
    ⋮
  } catch (err) {
    canvas.width = canvas.width;
  }
}
```

Next, let's change the background color from black to transparent, since the canvas element is positioned on top of the video:

```
function drawOneFrame(video, context, canvas){
  context.drawImage(video, 0, 0, canvas.width, canvas.height);

  try {
    ⋮
  } catch (err) {
    // clear the canvas
    context.clearRect(0,0,canvas.width,canvas.height);
    canvas.style.backgroundColor = "transparent";
    context.fillStyle = "white";
  }
}
```

Before we can draw any text to the now transparent canvas, we first must set up the style of our text—similar to what we did with paths earlier. We do that with the fillStyle and textAlign methods:

videoToBW.js (excerpt)

```
function drawOneFrame(video, context, canvas){
  context.drawImage(video, 0, 0, canvas.width, canvas.height);

  try {(review code style)
    ⋮
  } catch (err) {
    // clear the canvas
    context.clearRect(0,0,canvas.width,canvas.height);
    canvas.style.backgroundColor = "transparent";
    context.fillStyle = "white";
```

```
      context.textAlign = "left";
   }
}
```

We can also set a specific font and font style we'd like to use. The `font` property of the context object works the same way the CSS `font` property does. We'll specify a font size of 18px and a comma-separated list of font families:

```
function drawOneFrame(video, context, canvas){
  context.drawImage(video, 0, 0, canvas.width, canvas.height);

  try {
    ⋮
  } catch (err) {
    // clear the canvas
    context.clearRect(0,0,canvas.width,canvas.height);
    canvas.style.backgroundColor = "transparent";
    context.fillStyle = "white";
    context.textAlign = "left";

    context.font = "18px LeagueGothic, Tahoma, Geneva, sans-serif";
  }
}
```

Notice that we're using League Gothic; any fonts you've included with `@font-face` are also available for use on the canvas. Finally, we draw the text. We use a method of the context object called `fillText`, which takes the text to be drawn and the x,y coordinates where it should be placed. Since we want to write out a fairly long message, we'll split it up into several sections, placing each one on the canvas separately:

```
function drawOneFrame(video, context, canvas){
  context.drawImage(video, 0, 0, canvas.width, canvas.height);

  try {
    ⋮
  } catch (err) {
    // clear the canvas
    context.clearRect(0,0,canvas.width,canvas.height);
    canvas.style.backgroundColor = "transparent";
    context.fillStyle = "white";
    context.textAlign = "left";
```

```
    context.font = "18px LeagueGothic, Tahoma, Geneva, sans-serif";
    context.fillText("There was an error rendering ", 10, 20);
    context.fillText("the video to the canvas.", 10, 40);
    context.fillText("Perhaps you are viewing this page from", 10,
➥70);
    context.fillText("a file on your computer?", 10, 90);
    context.fillText("Try viewing this page online instead.", 10,
➥130);

    return false;
  }
}
```

As a last step, we return `false`. This lets us check in the `draw` function whether an exception was thrown. If it was, we want to stop calling `drawOneFrame` for each video frame, so we exit the `draw` function:

```
function draw(video, context, canvas) {
  if (video.paused || video.ended) return false;

  drawOneFrame(video, context, canvas);

  // Start over!
  setTimeout(function(){ draw(video, context, canvas); }, 0);
}
```

Accessibility Concerns

A major downside of canvas in its current form is its lack of accessibility. The canvas doesn't create a DOM node, is not a text-based format, and is thus essentially invisible to tools such as screen readers. For example, even though we wrote text to the canvas in our last example, that text is essentially no more than a bunch of pixels and is therefore inaccessible—it's just like an image that contains text.

The HTML5 community is aware of these failings, and while no solution has been finalized, debates on how canvas could be changed to make it accessible are underway. You can read a compilation of the arguments and currently proposed solutions on the W3C's wiki page.[8]

---

[8] http://www.w3.org/html/wg/wiki/AddedElementCanvas

Further Reading

To read more about canvas and the Canvas API, here are a couple of good resources:

- "HTML5 Canvas—the Basics" at Dev.Opera[9]

- Safari's HTML5 Canvas Guide[10]

SVG

We mentioned SVG previously in Chapter 7. In this chapter, we'll dive into SVG in more detail and learn how to use it in other ways.

First, a quick refresher: SVG stands for **Scalable Vector Graphics**, a specific file format that allows you to describe vector graphics using XML. A major selling point of vector graphics in general is that, unlike bitmap images (such as GIF, JPEG, PNG, and TIFF), vector images preserve their quality even as you blow them up or shrink them down. We can use SVG to do many of the same tasks we can do with canvas, including drawing paths, shapes, text, gradients, and patterns. There are also very useful open-source tools relevant to SVG, some of which we'll leverage in order to add a spinning progress indicator to *The HTML5 Herald*'s geolocation widget.

 What's XML?

XML stands for eXtensible Markup Language. Like HTML, it's a markup metalanguage. In plain English, it's a system meant to annotate text. Just as we can use HTML tags to wrap our content and give it meaning, so can XML tags be used to describe data, such as the content of a file.

Basic SVG, including using SVG in an HTML `img` element, is supported in:

- Chrome 4+
- Safari 3.2+
- Firefox 3+
- Opera 9.6+
- iOS 3.2+

---

[9] http://dev.opera.com/articles/view/html-5-canvas-the-basics/
[10] http://developer.apple.com/library/safari/#documentation/AudioVideo/Conceptual/HTML-canvas-guide/Introduction/Introduction.html

- Internet Explorer 9.0+
- Android browser 4.4+

Unlike canvas, images created with SVG are available via the DOM. This enables technologies such as screen readers to see what's present in an SVG object through its DOM node, as well as allowing you to inspect SVG using your browser's developer tools. Since SVG is an XML file format, it's also more accessible to search engines than canvas.

Drawing in SVG

Drawing a circle in SVG is arguably easier than drawing a circle with canvas. Here's how we do it:

```
<svg xmlns="http://www.w3.org/2000/svg" viewBox="0 0 400 400">
  <circle cx="50" cy="50" r="25" fill="red"/>
</svg>
```

The `viewBox` attribute defines the starting location, width, and height of the SVG image.

The `circle` element defines a circle, with `cx` and `cy` the X and Y coordinates of the center of the circle. The radius is represented by `r`, while `fill` defines the fill style.

To view an SVG file, you simply open it via the **File** menu in any browser that supports SVG. Figure 12.11 shows what our circle looks like.

Figure 12.11. A circle drawn using SVG

We can also draw rectangles in SVG, and add a stroke to them as we did with canvas.

This time, let's take advantage of SVG being an XML—and thus text-based—file format, and utilize the `<desc>` tag, which allows us to provide a description for the image we're going to draw:

```
<svg xmlns="http://www.w3.org/2000/svg" viewbox="0 0 400 400">
  <desc>Drawing a rectangle</desc>
</svg>
```

Next, we populate the `<rect>` tag with a number of attributes that describe the rectangle. This includes the X and Y coordinate where the rectangle should be drawn, the width and height of the rectangle, the fill, the stroke, and the width of the stroke:

```
<svg xmlns="http://www.w3.org/2000/svg" viewbox="0 0 400 400">
  <desc>Drawing a rectangle</desc>
      <rect x="10" y="10" width="100" height="100"
           fill="blue" stroke="red" stroke-width="3"  />

</svg>
```

Figure 12.12 shows what our rectangle looks like.

Figure 12.12. A rectangle drawn with SVG

Unfortunately, it's not always this easy. If you want to create complex shapes, the code begins to look a little scary. As an example of what SVG looks like, let's examine the first few lines of a more complex image in SVG:

```
<svg xmlns="http://www.w3.org/2000/svg"
  width="122.88545" height="114.88568">
<g
```

```
inkscape:label="Calque 1"
inkscape:groupmode="layer"
id="layer1"
transform="translate(-242.42282,-449.03699)">
<g
   transform="matrix(0.72428496,0,0,0.72428496,119.87078,183.8127)"
   id="g7153">
<path
   style="fill:#ffffff;fill-opacity:1;stroke:#000000;stroke-width
:2.761343;stroke-linecap:round;stroke-linejoin:round;stroke-miterl
imit:4;stroke-opacity:1;stroke-dasharray:none;stroke-dashoffset:0"
   d="m 249.28667,389.00422 -9.7738,30.15957 -31.91999,7.5995 c -
2.74681,1.46591 -5.51239,2.92436 -1.69852,6.99979 l 30.15935,12.57
796 -11.80876,32.07362 c -1.56949,4.62283 -0.21957,6.36158 4.24212
,3.35419 l 26.59198,-24.55691 30.9576,17.75909 c 3.83318,2.65893 6
.12086,0.80055 5.36349,-3.57143 l -12.10702,-34.11764 22.72561,-13
.7066 c 2.32805,-1.03398 5.8555,-6.16054 -0.46651,-6.46042 l -33.5
0135,-0.66887 -11.69597,-27.26175 c -2.04282,-3.50583 -4.06602,-7.
22748 -7.06823,-0.1801 z"
   id="path7155"
   inkscape:connector-curvature="0"
   sodipodi:nodetypes="ccccccccccccccc" />
```

Eek!

To save ourselves some work (and sanity), instead of creating SVG images by hand, we can use an image editor to help. One open source tool that you can use to make SVG images is Inkscape, which is available for download at http://inkscape.org/.

As we mentioned at the start of the chapter, it would be nice to add a progress indicator to our geolocation example from Chapter 11, one that lets the user know we're still waiting for the map to load and haven't left them stranded.

Instead of starting from scratch, we've searched the public domain to find a good progress-indicating spinner image from which to begin. A good resource to know about for public domain images is http://openclipart.org/, where you can find images that are free to use and free of copyright. The images have been donated by their creators for use in the public domain, even for commercial purposes, without the need for permission.

We will be using an image of three arrows as the basis of our progress spinner, shown in Figure 12.13. The original can be found at openclipart.org.[11]

Figure 12.13. The image we'll be using for our progress indicator

SVG Filters

To make our progress spinner match our page a bit better, we can use a filter in Inkscape to make it black and white. Start by opening the file in Inkscape, then choose **Filters > Color > Moonarize**.

You may notice that if you test out *The HTML5 Herald* in an older version of IE or Safari that our black-and-white spinner is still … in color. That's because SVG filters are only supported in IE10 and later, and Safari 6 and later. Here's a complete list of SVG filter support:

- all recent versions of Chrome, Firefox, and Opera
- iOS 6.1+
- Android browser 4.4+

A safer approach would be to avoid using filters, and instead modify the color of the original image.

We can do this in Inkscape by selecting the three arrows in the **spinner.svg** image, and then selecting **Object > Fill and Stroke**. The **Fill and Stroke** menu will appear on the right-hand side of the screen, as seen in Figure 12.14.

---

[11] http://www.openclipart.org/people/JoBrad/arrows_3_circular_interlocking.svg

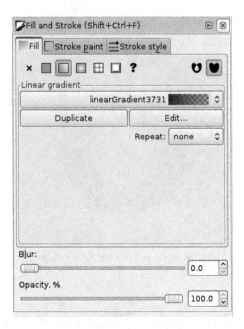

Figure 12.14. Modifying color using Fill and Stroke

From this menu, we can choose to edit the existing linear gradient by clicking the **Edit** button. We can then change the red, green, and blue values to 0 to make our image black and white.

We've saved the resulting SVG as **spinnerBW.svg**.

Using the Raphaël Library

Raphaël[12] is an open-source JavaScript library that makes drawing and animating with SVG much easier.

Drawing an Image to Raphaël's Container

Much as with canvas, you can draw images into a container that you create using Raphaël.

Let's add a div to our main index file. We'll use this as the container for the SVG elements that we'll create using Raphaël. We've given this div the ID of spinner:

---

[12] http://raphaeljs.com/

```
<article class="ad-ad4">
  <div id="mapDiv">
    <h1 id="geoHeading">Where in the world are you?</h1>
    <form id="geoForm">
      <input type="button" id="geobutton" value="Tell us!">
    </form>
    <div class="spin" id="spinner"></div>
  </div>
</article>
```

We have styled this div to be placed in the center of the parent mapDiv using the following CSS (note that without this, the element won't be centered):

```
.spin {
  position: absolute;
  top: 8px;
  left: 55px;
}
```

Now in our geolocation JavaScript file, **geolocation.js**, let's put the spinner in place while we're fetching the map. The first step is to turn our div into a Raphaël container. This is as simple as calling the Raphael method, and passing in the element we'd like to use along with a width and height:

```
function determineLocation() {
  if (navigator.onLine) {
    if (Modernizr.geolocation) {
      navigator.geolocation.getCurrentPosition(displayOnMap);

      var container = Raphael(document.getElementById("spinner"),
➡125, 125);
```

Next, we draw the spinner SVG image into the newly created container with the Raphaël method image, which is called on a Raphaël container object. This method takes the path to the image, the starting coordinates where the image should be drawn, and the width and height of the image:

```
var container = Raphael(document.getElementById("spinner"), 125,
➥125);
var spinner = container.image("images/spinnerBW.svg", 0, 0, 125,
➥125);
```

With this code our spinner image will appear once the geolocation code begins to run, and will spin until the map is displayed.

Rotating a Spinner with Raphaël

Now that we have our container and the spinner SVG image drawn into it, we want to animate the image to make it spin. Raphaël has animation features built in with the `animate` method. Before we can use this method, though, we first need to tell it which attribute to animate. Since we want to rotate our image, we'll create an object that specifies how many degrees of rotation we want.

We create a new object `attrsToAnimate` specifying that we want to animate the rotation, and we want to rotate by 720 degrees (two full turns). The way we do that is to set the value of the `transform` property to `"r720"`, with the `"r"` indicating the transform is a rotation:

```
var container = Raphael(document.getElementById("spinner"),125,125);
var spinner = container.image("images/spinnerBW.png",0,0,125,125);
var attrsToAnimate = { transform: "r720" };
```

The final step is to call the `animate` method, and specify how long the animation should last. In our case, we'll let it run for a maximum of 60 seconds. Since animate takes its values in milliseconds, we'll pass it `60000`:

```
var container = Raphael(document.getElementById("spinner"),125,125);
var spinner = container.image("images/spinnerBW.png",0,0,125,125);
var attrsToAnimate = { transform: "r720" };
spinner.animate(attrsToAnimate, 60000);
```

That's great! We now have a spinning progress indicator to keep our visitors in the know while our map is loading. There's still one problem, though: it remains after the map has loaded. We can fix this by adding one line to the beginning of the existing `displayOnMap` function:

```
function displayOnMap(position) {
  document.getElementById("spinner").style.display = "none";
}
```

This line sets the `display` property of the spinner element to `none`, effectively hiding the spinner div and the SVG image we've loaded into it.

Canvas versus SVG

Now that we've learned about canvas and SVG, you may be asking yourself which is the right one to use? The answer is: it depends on what you're doing.

Both canvas and SVG allow you to draw custom shapes, paths, and fonts. But what's unique about each?

Canvas allows for pixel manipulation, as we saw when we turned our video from color to black and white. One downside of canvas is that it operates in what's known as **immediate mode**. This means that if you ever want to add more to the canvas, you're unable to simply add to what's already there. Every time you finish drawing a shape, the canvas no longer has access to that shape, because it won't persist as an object that you can modify. So if you want to add to what you've already drawn on the canvas, you must redraw the new shape from scratch. Still, canvas does allow you to save the images you create to a PNG or JPEG file.

There's also no access to what's drawn on the canvas via the DOM. Because of this, canvas is much faster than SVG (here's one speed comparison[13]), and canvas is generally the better choice if you're looking to design a game requiring lots of animations.

By contrast, what you draw to SVG is accessible via the DOM, because its mode is **retained mode**, meaning that the structure of the image is preserved in the XML document that describes it. SVG also has, at this time, a more complete set of tools to help you work with it, such as the Raphaël library and Inkscape. However, since SVG is a file format—rather than a set of methods that allows you to dynamically draw on a surface—you can't manipulate SVG images the way you can manipulate pixels on canvas. It would have been impossible, for example, to use SVG to convert our color video to black and white as we did with canvas.

---

[13] http://codepen.io/chris-creditdesign/details/BIADJ

In summary, if you need to paint pixels to the screen and have no concerns about the ability to retrieve and modify your shapes, canvas is probably the better choice. If, on the other hand, you need to be able to access and change specific aspects of your graphics, SVG might be more appropriate.

Drag and Drop

We've spent quite a bit of time this chapter focusing on drawing with code. Let's shift gears a little now and look at an API we can use to add some fun user interaction to our website, the Drag and Drop API. This API allows us to specify that certain elements are draggable, and then specify what should happen when these draggable elements are dragged over or dropped onto other elements on the page.

Drag and Drop is supported in:

- All recent versions of Chrome, Firefox, and Safari

- Partial support in Internet Explorer 7.0+ (IE10 doesn't allow setting the drag image, but supports all other features)

- Opera 12+

The API is unsupported by Android. It is also unsupported by design in iOS, as Apple directs you to use the DOM Touch API instead.[14]

There are two major kinds of functionality you can implement with Drag and Drop: dragging files from your computer into a web page—in combination with the File API—or dragging elements into other elements on the same page. In this chapter, we'll focus on the latter.

Using Drag and Drop with the File API

If you'd like to learn more about how to combine Drag and Drop with the File API in order to let users drag files from their desktop onto your websites, an excellent

---

[14] http://developer.apple.com/library/safari/#documentation/AppleApplications/Reference/SafariWeb-Content/HandlingEvents/HandlingEvents.html

guide can be found at the Mozilla Developer Network.[15] All modern browsers support the File API.[16]

There are several steps to adding drag and drop to your page:

1. Set the `draggable` attribute on any HTML elements you'd like to be draggable.

2. Add an event listener for the `dragstart` event on any draggable HTML elements.

3. Add an event listener for the `dragover` and `drop` events on any elements that you want to have accept dropped items.

Feeding the WAI-ARIA Cat

In order to add a bit of fun and frivolity to our page, let's add a few images of mice so that we can drag them onto our cat image and watch the cat react and devour them. Before you start worrying (or call the Society for the Prevention of Cruelty to Animals), rest assured that we mean computer mice, of course. We'll use another image from OpenClipArt for our mice.[17]

The first step is to add these new images to our **index.html** file. We'll give each mouse image an ID as well:

```
<article id="ac3">
  <h1>Wai-Aria? HAHA!</h1>
  <h2>Form Accessibility</h2>

  <img src="images/cat.png" alt="WAI-ARIA Cat">

  <div class="content">
    <p id="mouseContainer" class="mc">
      <img src="images/computer-mouse-pic.svg"
➥alt="mouse treat" id="mouse1" draggable="true">
      <img src="images/computer-mouse-pic.svg"
➥alt="mouse treat" id="mouse2" draggable="true">
      <img src="images/computer-mouse-pic.svg"
```

---

[15] https://developer.mozilla.org/en/Using_files_from_web_applications
[16] http://caniuse.com/#feat=fileapi
[17] http://www.openclipart.org/detail/111289

```
➥alt="mouse treat" id="mouse3" draggable="true">
    </p>
⋮
```

We style the "mouseContainer" div to have its text center aligned (assuming drag and drop is supported, which is what the .draganddrop class is checking for):

```
.draganddrop .mc {
  text-align: center;
}
```

Figure 12.15 shows our images in their initial state.

Figure 12.15. Three little mice, ready to be fed to the WAI-ARIA cat

Making Elements Draggable

The next step is to make our images draggable. In order to do that, we add the draggable attribute to them, and set the value to true:

```
<img src="images/computer-mouse-pic.svg" width="30"
➥alt="mouse treat" id="mouse1" draggable="true">
<img src="images/computer-mouse-pic.svg" width="30"
```

```
↪alt="mouse treat" id="mouse2" draggable="true">
<img src="images/computer-mouse-pic.svg" width="30"
↪alt="mouse treat" id="mouse3" draggable="true">
```

draggable is not Boolean!

Note that draggable is *not* a Boolean attribute, so you have to explicitly set it to true.

Now that we have set draggable to true, we have to set an event listener for the dragstart event on each image. We'll have to do this for all three of our img elements that contain the computer mouse images. So we begin by using querySelectorAll to grab all the img elements whose parent element has the ID set to mouseContainer:

```
var mice = document.querySelectorAll("#mouseContainer img");
```

Next, we'll loop through all the img elements contained in the mice variable, and add an event listener for the dragstart event on each computer mouse:

```
var mouse = null;
for (var i=0; i < mice.length; i++) {
  mouse = mice[i];
  mouse.addEventListener('dragstart', function (event) {
    // handle the dragstart event
  });
}
```

The DataTransfer Object

DataTransfer objects are one type of object outlined in the Drag and Drop API. These objects allow us to set and get data about the elements that are being dragged. Specifically, DataTransfer lets us define two pieces of information:

- the type of data we're saving of the draggable element
- the value of the data itself

In the case of our draggable mouse images, we want to be able to store the ID of these images so that we know which image is being dragged around.

To do this, we first tell DataTransfer that we want to save some plain text by passing in the string text/plain. Then we give it the ID of our mouse image:

```
mouse.addEventListener("dragstart", function (event) {
  event.dataTransfer.setData("text/plain", this.id);
});
```

When an element is dragged, we save the ID of the element in the DataTransfer object, to be used again once the element is dropped.

Accepting Dropped Elements

Now our mouse images are set up to be dragged. Yet, when we try to drag them around, we're unable to drop them anywhere—which is no fun.

The reason is that by default, elements on the page aren't set up to receive dragged items. In order to override the default behavior on a specific element, we must stop it from happening. We can do that by creating two more event listeners.

The two events we need to monitor for are dragover and drop. As you'd expect, dragover fires when you drag an item over an element, and drop fires when you drop an item on it.

We'll need to prevent the default behavior for both these events, since the default prohibits you from dropping an element.

Let's start by adding an ID to our cat image so that we can bind event handlers to it:

```
<article id="ac3">
  <h1>Wai-Aria? HAHA!</h1>
  <h2 id="catHeading">Form Accessibility</h2>

  <img src="images/cat.png" id="cat" alt="WAI-ARIA Cat">
```

You may have noticed that we also gave an ID to the h2 element. This is so we can change this text once we've dropped a mouse onto the cat.

Now let's handle the dragover event:

```
var cat = document.getElementById("cat");
cat.addEventListener("dragover", function(event) {
  event.preventDefault();
});
```

That was easy! In this case, we merely ensured that the mouse picture can actually be dragged over the cat picture. We simply need to prevent the default behavior, and JavaScript's preventDefault method serves this purpose exactly.

The code for the drop handler is a bit more complex, so let us review it piece by piece. Our first task is to figure out what the cat should say when a mouse is dropped on it. In order to demonstrate that we can retrieve the ID of the dropped mouse from the DataTransfer object, we'll use a different phrase for each mouse, regardless of the order in which they're dropped. We've given three cat-appropriate options: "MEOW!", "Purrr ...", and "NOMNOMNOM."

We'll store these options inside an object called mouseHash, where the first step is to declare our object:

```
cat.addEventListener("drop", function(event) {
  var mouseHash = {};
```

Next, we're going to take advantage of JavaScript's objects allowing us to store key/value pairs inside them, as well as storing each response in the mouseHash object, associating each response with the ID of one of the mouse images:

```
cat.addEventListener("drop", function(event) {
  var mouseHash = {
    mouse1: 'NOMNOMNOM',
    mouse2: 'Meow',
    mouse3: 'Purrrrrr ...'
  };
}
```

Our next step is to grab the h2 element that we'll change to reflect the cat's response:

```
var catHeading = document.getElementById('catHeading');
```

Remember when we saved the ID of the dragged element to the DataTransfer object using `setData`? Well, now we want to retrieve that ID. If you guessed that we'll need a method called `getData` for this, you guessed right:

```
var mouseID = event.originalEvent.dataTransfer.getData("text/plain");
```

Note that we've stored the mouse's ID in a variable called `mouseID`. Now that we know which mouse was dropped, and we have our heading, we just need to change the text to the appropriate response:

```
catHeading.innerHTML = mouseHash[mouseID];
```

We use the information stored in the `item` variable (the dragged mouse's ID) to retrieve the correct message for the `h2` element. For example, if the dragged mouse is `mouse1`, calling `mouseHash[item]` will retrieve "NOMNOMNOM" and set that as the `h2` element's text.

Given that the mouse has now been "eaten," it makes sense to remove it from the page:

```
var mousey = document.getElementById(item);
mousey.parentNode.removeChild(mousey);
```

Last but not least, we must also prevent the default behavior of not allowing elements to be dropped on our cat image, as we did before:

```
event.preventDefault();
```

Figure 12.16 shows our happy cat, with one mouse to go.

Figure 12.16. This cat's already consumed two mice

Further Reading

We've only touched on the basics of the Drag and Drop API, in order to give you a taste of what's available. We've shown you how you can use DataTransfer to pass data from your dragged items to their drop targets. What you do with this power is up to you.

To learn more about the Drag and Drop API, here are a couple of good resources

- Mozilla Developer Network's Drag and Drop documentation[18]

- W3C's Drag and Drop specification[19]

That's All, Folks!

With these final bits of interactivity, our work on *The HTML5 Herald* has come to an end, and your journey into the world of HTML5 and CSS3 is well on its way! We've tried to provide a solid foundation of knowledge about as many of the cool new features available in today's browsers as possible, but how you build on that is up to you.

We hope we've given you a clear picture of how most of these features can be used today on real projects. Many are already well supported, and browser development is once again progressing at a rapid clip. And when it comes to those elements for which support is still lacking, you have the aid of an online army of ingenious developers. These community-minded individuals are constantly working at creating

---

[18] https://developer.mozilla.org/En/DragDrop/Drag_and_Drop
[19] http://dev.w3.org/html5/spec/dnd.html

fallbacks and polyfills to help us push forward and build the next generation of websites and applications.

Get to it!

Appendix A: Modernizr

Modernizr is an open-source JavaScript library that enables us to test for individual features of HTML5, CSS3, and some APIs in our users' browsers. Instead of testing solely for a particular browser and trying to make decisions based on that, Modernizr allows us to ask specific questions such as "does this browser support geolocation?" and receive a clear "yes" or "no" answer. Modernizr does this by **feature detection**: checking whether the browser that our user is currently utilizing supports a given feature.

The first step to using Modernizr is to download it from the website,[1] where it's recommended that you begin with the Development version—we agree! This version will test for every single feature of HTML5, CSS3, and the new APIs. This is a good idea when you're starting your project, as chances are you'll be a little unsure about all the different features you'll be using.

Once you're ready to move your project into production, you can return to Modernizr's download page and create a custom build, checking off the particular features you'd like to detect. Why be so specific? Because it takes time for Modernizr to test for the presence of a given feature, it's best for performance reasons to only check the HTML5 features that you'll use, as shown in Figure A.1. A custom build of Modernizr will also be minified (which isn't true of the Development version), so the size of the library will be much smaller.

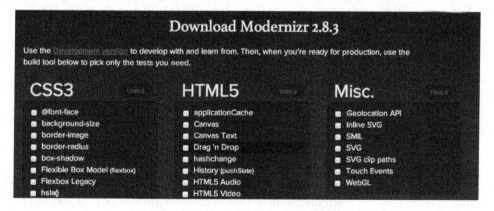

Figure A.1. Modernizr's download page prompt

[1] http://modernizr.com/download/

Once you have a copy of the library, you'll need to include the file in your pages. We'll add it to the head in this example:

```
<!DOCTYPE html>
<html>
<head>
  <meta charset="utf-8">
  <title>My Beautiful Sample Page</title>
  <script src="modernizr-2.8.3.min.js"></script>
</head>
```

You can use Modernizr in two ways: with CSS, and with JavaScript. Let's discover more.

Using Modernizr with CSS

When Modernizr runs, it will add a new class name to the html tag for every feature you have asked it to detect. It will prefix the feature with no- if the browser offers no support for it.

For example, if you're using Safari 6.2—which supports almost everything in HTML5 and CSS3—and you use the development version of Modernizr—which checks for all available HTML5 features—your opening html tag will look a little like this after Modernizr runs (we're only showing a snippet of it to save space in this book):

```
<html class="js no-blobworkers no-adownload applicationcache
audiodata webaudio audio no-lowbattery no-batteryapi no-battery-api
blobconstructor blob-constructor canvas todataurljpeg todataurlpng
no-todataurlwebp canvastext contenteditable no-contentsecuritypolicy
no-contextmenu cookies cors cssanimations backgroundcliptext
bgpositionshorthand bgpositionxy bgrepeatround bgrepeatspace
backgroundsize bgsizecover borderimage borderradius boxshadow
boxsizing csscalc checked csscolumns cubicbezierrange
⋮
testobjfntrue testchainone testchaintwo testchainthree">
```

As you can see, the complete list of all the features Modernizr tests for is comprehensive! Again, as has been mentioned, this is great while you're still testing. But once you're ready for your website to move into production, you should create a custom build of Modernizr and test only for the features you intend to use in the project, ensuring you have the smallest amount of Modernizr code necessary for your project.

Once we've downloaded Modernizr and included it in our project, we then add the class `no-js` to our `html` element in our HTML source:

```
<html class="no-js">
```

Why do we do this? If JavaScript is disabled, Modernizr won't run at all—but if JavaScript *is* enabled, Modernizr's first job will be to change `no-js` to `js`. This way, you'll have hooks to base your styles on the presence or absence of JavaScript.

You might be thinking, "That sounds pretty cool, but what am I actually supposed to do with this information?" What we can do is use these classes to provide two flavors of CSS: styles for browsers that support certain features, and different styles for browsers that don't.

Because the classes are set on the `html` element, we can use descendant selectors to target any element on the page based on support for a given feature.

Here's an example. Any element with a class of `.ad2` that lives inside an element with a class of `.cssgradients` (in other words, the `html` element when Modernizr has detected support for gradients) will receive whichever style we specify:

```
.cssgradients .ad2 {
  /* gradients are supported! Let's use some! */
  background-image: linear-gradient(#FFF 0%, #000 100%);
}
```

But what if CSS gradients *aren't* supported? We could change the styling to use a simple PNG background image that recreates the same gradient look. Here's how we might do that:

```
.no-cssgradients .ad2 {
  background-image: url(../images/put_a_replacement_img_here.png);
}
```

Another way we could use the classes Modernizr adds to the `html` element is with Drag and Drop. We discussed Drag and Drop in Chapter 12, where we added several images of computer mice that can be dragged onto our cat picture to be eaten. These images are all stored in a div with an ID of mouseContainer.

In some mobile browsers, drag and drop will fail to work, so why show the mouse images at all? We can use Modernizr to hide the div if Drag and Drop is unsupported:

```
.no-draganddrop .mc { // mc is short for "mouse container"
  visibility: hidden;
  height: 0;
}
```

If Drag and Drop *is* supported, we simply align all the content in the div horizontally:

```
.draganddrop .mc {
  text-align: center;
}
```

Using Modernizr with JavaScript

We can also use Modernizr in our JavaScript to provide some fallback if the visitor's browser has no support for any of the HTML5 elements, CSS3 properties, or (some of) the APIs you use.

When Modernizr runs, as well as adding all those classes to your html element, it will also create a global JavaScript object that you can use to test for support of a given feature. Appropriately enough, the object is called Modernizr. It contains a property for every HTML5, CSS3, and API feature it can test.

Here are a few examples:

```
Modernizr.draganddrop;
Modernizr.geolocation;
Modernizr.textshadow;
```

Each property will be either true or false, depending on whether or not the feature is available in the visitor's browser. This is useful, because we can ask questions such as "Is geolocation supported in my visitor's browser?" and then take actions depending on the answer.

Here's an example of using an `if`/`else` block to test for drag and drop support using Modernizr:

```
if (Modernizr.draganddrop) {
  // go ahead and use the drag and drop API,
  // it's supported!
}
else {
  // There is no support for drag and drop.
  // We can use jQuery UI Draggable(http://jqueryui.com/)
  // or the dropfile polyfill https://github.com/MrSwitch/dropfile
  // instead
}
```

Further Reading

To learn more about Modernizr, see:

- the Modernizr documentation[2]

- a fairly comprehensive and up-to-date list of polyfills for HTML5 and CSS3 properties that can be used in conjunction with Modernizr, maintained at the Modernizr wiki[3]

- "Taking Advantage of HTML5 and CSS3 with Modernizr,[4]" an A List Apart article

---

[2] http://modernizr.com/docs/

[3] https://github.com/Modernizr/Modernizr/wiki/HTML5-Cross-browser-Polyfills

[4] http://www.alistapart.com/articles/taking-advantage-of-html5-and-css3-with-modernizr/

Appendix B: WAI-ARIA

In Chapter 2 and Chapter 3, we covered considerable ground explaining how our pages can become more semantic and potentially more accessible using HTML5's new semantic elements. Improved semantics alone, however, is often insufficient to make a sophisticated web application fully accessible.

In order to have the content and functionality of our pages as accessible as possible for our users, we need the boost that WAI-ARIA provides, extending what HTML5 already does. We'll avoid going into an extensive discussion on WAI-ARIA here—that's a topic that could fill many chapters—but we felt it was important to mention it here so that you're aware of your options.

WAI-ARIA stands for Web Accessibility Initiative-Accessible Rich Internet Applications. The overview of WAI-ARIA on the W3C site[1] explains it as:

> [...] a way to make Web content and Web applications more access-
> ible to people with disabilities. It especially helps with dynamic
> content and advanced JavaScript-heavy user interface controls de-
> veloped with Ajax, HTML, JavaScript, and related technologies.

Users who rely on screen reader technology, or who are unable to use a mouse, are often excluded from using certain website and web application functionality—for example, sliders, progress bars, and tabbed interfaces. With WAI-ARIA, you're able to deal with these shortcomings in your pages—even if the content and functionality is trapped in complex application architecture. Thus, parts of a website that would normally be inaccessible can be made available to users who are reliant on assistive technology.

How WAI-ARIA Complements Semantics

WAI-ARIA assigns **roles** to elements, and gives those roles **properties** and **states**. Here's a simple example:

---

[1] http://www.w3.org/WAI/intro/aria.php

```
<li role="menuitemcheckbox" aria-checked="true">Sort by Date</li>
```

The application might be using the list item as a linked element to sort content; yet without the role and aria-checked attributes, a screen reader would have no way to determine what this element is for. Semantics alone (in this case, a list item) tells it nothing. By adding these attributes, the assistive device is better able to understand what this function is for.

For semantic elements—for example header, h1, and nav—WAI-ARIA attributes in most cases are unnecessary, as those elements already express what they are. Instead, they should be used for elements whose functionality and purpose cannot be immediately discerned from the elements themselves (or for elements that have little or no accessibility support in one or more of the major browsers).

The Current State of WAI-ARIA

The WAI-ARIA specification is still improving, as is HTML5, so these technologies are yet to provide all the benefits we would like. Although we've described the way that WAI-ARIA can extend the semantics of our page elements, it may be necessary to include WAI-ARIA roles on elements that *already* express their meaning in their names, because assistive technology doesn't support all the new HTML5 semantics yet. In other words, WAI-ARIA can serve as a sort of stopgap, to provide accessibility for HTML5 pages while screen readers are catching up.

Let's look at a site navigation, for example:

```
<nav role="navigation">
  <ul>
    ⋮
  </ul>
</nav>
```

It would seem that we're doubling up here: the nav element implies that the list of links contained within it make up a navigation control, but we've still added the WAI-ARIA role navigation to it. In many cases, this sort of doubling up will often be necessary. In the case of the nav element, Internet Explorer is the only browser that doesn't correctly expose a role of "navigation" by default, so for now, adding this attribute is necessary.

Does this mean that WAI-ARIA will become redundant once HTML5 semantics and accessibility are fully supported? No. There are roles in WAI-ARIA without corresponding HTML5 elements; for example, the timer[2] role. While you might represent a timer using the HTML5 `time` element and then update it with JavaScript, you'd have no way of indicating to a screen reader that it was a timer, rather than just an indication of a static time.

For a screen reader to access WAI-ARIA roles, the browser must expose them through an accessibility API. This allows the screen reader to interact with the elements similarly to how it would access native desktop controls.

Browser support for ARIA features has been growing and is currently very good. All the latest versions of browsers support WAI-ARIA at least partially. A fairly up to date guide for support of accessibility features like WAI-ARIA in browsers on certain OSes can be found on the Paciello Group's website[3].

Finally, it's worth noting that not all users who could benefit from WAI-ARIA roles are utilizing them. In Janaury 2014, WebAIM (Web Accessibility In Mind) conducted their fifth screen reader user survey,[4] which revealed that about 28% of participants either seldom or never navigated web pages by means of ARIA landmarks. The good news is, the number of users utilizing ARIA landmarks is increasing. In 2010, in a similar survey[5], more than 50% either didn't use or didn't know ARIA roles existed.

In short, there is pretty good support for WAI-ARIA and you won't hurt your HTML5 documents by including these attributes. They pass markup validation in HTML5 and even though the full benefits are yet to be seen, they'll only increase over time.

Further Reading

As mentioned, a full primer on all of the WAI-ARIA roles is beyond the scope of this book, but if you're interested in learning more, we recommend the official

---

[2] http://www.w3.org/TR/wai-aria/roles#timer

[3] http://www.paciellogroup.com/blog/2014/10/rough-guide-browsers-operating-systems-and-screen-reader-support-updated/

[4] http://webaim.org/projects/screenreadersurvey5/

[5] http://webaim.org/projects/screenreadersurvey3/#landmarks

specification[6] first and foremost. The W3C has also put together a shorter Primer[7] and an Authoring Practices guide[8].

You can also check out Stephan Max's Introduction to WAI-ARIA[9] on SitePoint. Finally, you might find it useful to review HTML5 Accessibility[10] a website maintained by accessibility expert Steve Faulkner that summarizes in chart form how different browsers handle HTML5's semantic elements from an accessibility standpoint.

---

[6] http://www.w3.org/TR/wai-aria/

[7] http://www.w3.org/TR/wai-aria-primer/

[8] http://www.w3.org/TR/wai-aria-practices/

[9] http://www.sitepoint.com/introduction-wai-aria/

[10] http://www.html5accessibility.com/

Appendix C: Microdata

Microdata is another technology that's rapidly gaining adoption and support, but, unlike WAI-ARIA, it's technically part of HTML5. Although still early in development, it's worth mentioning the Microdata specification here,[1] because the technology provides a peek into what may be the future of document readability and semantics.

In the spec, **Microdata** is defined as a mechanism that "allows machine-readable data to be embedded in HTML documents in an easy-to-write manner, with an unambiguous parsing model."

With Microdata, page authors can add specific labels to HTML elements, annotating them so that they can be read by machines or bots. This is done by means of a customized vocabulary. For example, you might want a script or other third-party service to be able to access your pages and interact with specific elements on the page in a certain manner. With Microdata, you can extend existing semantic elements (such as `article` and `figure`) to allow those services to have specialized access to the annotated content.

This can appear confusing, so let's think about a real-world example. Let's say your site includes reviews of movies. You might have each review in an `article` element, with a number of stars or a percentage score for your review. But when a machine comes along, such as Google's search spider, it has no way of knowing which part of your content is the actual review—all it sees is a bunch of text on the page.

Why would a machine want to know what you thought of a movie? It's worth considering that Google has recently started displaying richer information in its search results pages, in order to provide searchers with more than just textual matches for their queries. It does this by reading the review information encoded into those sites' pages using Microdata or other similar technologies. An example of movie review information is shown in Figure C.1.

---

[1] http://www.w3.org/TR/microdata/

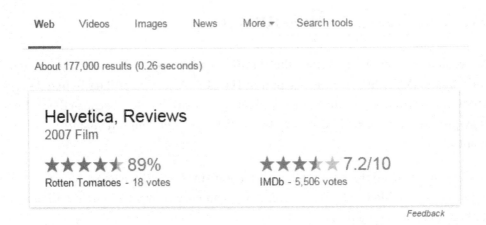

Figure C.1. Google leverages Microdata to show additional information in search results

By using Microdata, you can specify exactly which parts of your page correspond to reviews, people, events, and more—all in a consistent vocabulary that software applications can understand and make use of.

Aren't HTML5's semantics enough?

The HTML5 spec now includes a number of new elements to allow for more expressive markup. But it would be counterproductive to add elements to HTML that would only be used by a handful of people. This would bloat the language, making its features unmaintainable from all perspectives—whether that's specification authors, browser vendors, or standards bodies.

Microdata, on the other hand, allows developers to use custom vocabularies (either existing ones or their own) for specific situations—ones that aren't possible using HTML5's semantic elements. Thus existing HTML elements and new elements added in HTML5 are kept as a sort of semantic baseline, while specific annotations can be created by developers to target their own needs.

The Microdata Syntax

Microdata works with existing, well-formed HTML content, and is added to a document by means of name-value pairs (also called **properties**). Microdata prohibits you from creating new elements; instead it gives you the option to add customized attributes that expand on the semantics of existing elements.

Here's a simple example:

```
<aside itemscope>
  <h1 itemprop="name">John Doe</h1>
  <p><img src="http://www.sitepoint.com/bio-photo.jpg" alt="John
➥Doe" itemprop="photo"></p>
  <p><a href="http://www.sitepoint.com" itemprop="url">Author's
➥website</a></p>
</aside>
```

In the example above, we have a run-of-the-mill author bio placed inside an `aside` element. The first oddity you'll notice is the Boolean `itemscope` attribute. This identifies the `aside` element as the container that defines the scope of our Microdata vocabulary. The presence of the `itemscope` attribute defines what the spec refers to as an **item**. Each item is characterized by a group of name-value pairs.

The ability to define the scope of our vocabularies allows us to define multiple vocabularies on a single page. In this example, all name-value pairs inside the `aside` element are part of a single Microdata vocabulary.

After the `itemscope` attribute, the next item of interest is the `itemprop` attribute, which has a value of `"name"`. At this point, it's probably a good idea to explain how a script would obtain information from these attributes, as well as what we mean by "name-value pairs."

Understanding Name–Value Pairs

A name is a property defined with the help of the `itemprop` attribute. In our example, the first property name happens to be one called `name`. There are two additional property names in this scope: `photo` and `url`.

The values for a given property are defined differently, depending on the element the property is declared on. For most elements, the value is taken from its text content; for instance, the `name` property in our example would obtain its value from the text content between the opening and closing `h1` tags. Other elements are treated differently.

The `photo` property takes its value from the `src` attribute of the image, so the value consists of a URL pointing to the author's photo. The `url` property, although defined on an element that has text content (namely, the phrase "Author's website"), doesn't use this text content to determine its value; instead, it obtains its value from the `href` attribute.

Other elements that don't use their associated text content to define Microdata values include `meta`, `iframe`, `object`, `audio`, `link`, and `time`. For a comprehensive list of elements that obtain their values from somewhere other than the text content, see the Values section of the Microdata specification.[2]

Microdata Namespaces

What we've described so far is acceptable for Microdata that's not intended to be reused—but that's a little impractical. The real power of Microdata is unleashed when, as we discussed, third-party scripts and page authors can access our name-value pairs and find beneficial uses for them.

In order for this to happen, each item must define a type by means of the `itemtype` attribute. Remember that an item in the context of Microdata is the element that has the `itemscope` attribute set. Every element and name-value pair inside that element is part of that item. The value of the `itemtype` attribute, therefore, defines the namespace for that item's vocabulary. Let's add an `itemtype` to our example:

```
<aside itemscope itemtype="http://schema.org/Person">
  <h1 itemprop="name">John Doe</h1>
  <p><img src="http://www.sitepoint.com/bio-photo.jpg" alt="John Doe
➥" itemprop="photo"></p>
```

---

[2] http://www.w3.org/TR/microdata/#values

```
  <p><a href="http://www.sitepoint.com" itemprop="url">Author's
➥website</a></p>
</aside>
```

In our item, we're using the "http://schema.org/Person" URL, which is from Schema.org,[3] a collaborative project supported by several major search engines. This website houses a number of Microdata vocabularies, including Organization, Person, Review, Event, and more.

Further Reading

This brief introduction to Microdata barely does the topic justice, but we hope it will provide you with a taste of what's possible when extending the semantics of your documents with this technology.

It's a very broad topic that requires reading and research outside of this source. With that in mind, here are a few links to check out if you want to delve deeper into the possibilities offered by Microdata:

- "Extending HTML5—Microdata"[4] on HTML5 Doctor

- the W3C Microdata specification[5]

- Mark Pilgrim's excellent overview of Microdata[6]

- Google's Rich Snippets Help[7]

- "Using Schemas to Improve Content Visibility in Search Results"[8] on SitePoint

---

[3] http://schema.org/

[4] http://html5doctor.com/microdata/

[5] http://www.w3.org/TR/microdata/

[6] http://diveintohtml5.info/extensibility.html

[7] http://www.google.com/support/webmasters/bin/answer.py?hl=en&answer=99170

[8] http://www.sitepoint.com/using-schemas-improve-content-visibility-search-results/

CPSIA information can be obtained
at www.ICGtesting.com
Printed in the USA
LVOW03s1948011215

464890LV00032B/276/P